ADVISE AND DISSENT

ADVISE & DISSENT

Memoirs of South Dakota and the U.S. Senate

JAMES G. ABOUREZK

LAWRENCE
HILL
BOOKS

Library of Congress Cataloging-in-Publication Data

Abourezk, James.
    Advise and dissent : memoirs of South Dakota and the U.S. Senate /
James G. Abourezk. — 1st ed.
        p.   cm.
    ISBN 1-55652-066-2
    1. Abourezk, James. 2. Legislators—United States—Biography.
3. United States. Congress. Senate—Biography. 4. South Dakota—
Politics and government. I. Title.
    E840.8.A19A3   1989
328.73'092—dc20   89-15354
                                                                CIP

Printed in the United States of America
First edition
First printing
Published by Lawrence Hill Books
An imprint of Chicago Review Press, Inc.
814 North Franklin Street
Chicago, Illinois 60610
ISBN 1-55652-066-2

For my father and mother
Charles and Lena Abourezk

and for my brothers and sisters and their families
Helen and Fayez, Chick and Elda, Tom and Twila,
Virginia and Dick

and for Mary and our children and their children
Charlie and Dell, Darcie, Denise, Corinne, Richard,
Lena and Jamil

Nikki and Little Paul

Big Paul and Kathy

and for Margaret and Chesley

Contents

Foreword

I'm quoting former Oklahoma Senator Fred Harris here:

> "If I'm reincarnated I'd like to come back as Jim Abourezk. There I was, up there on that Hill, trying to be nice to everyone for five years, and the sixth year I realized it didn't make a damn bit of difference. All you do is become a member of the establishment and you **still** don't get all that much accomplished. Abourezk figured that out the first two weeks he was up there."

I should quit right there, not knowing any way to improve on Fred's description of Abourezk, a U.S. senator who got things done the old fashioned way: he did what he thought was right. Who is this Lebanese-American, Sioux Indian reservation–born, civil engineer–lawyer populist? Maybe we can learn something if we read the personal story of a politician who has always been dedicated to the high principle that this country belongs to its people, and not just to the rich and powerful. What shapes such a person? For Abourezk, it could have been one of any number of influences: his Lebanese immigrant parents, his early life on the Rosebud Sioux Indian Reservation, his tutorship by an intensely political medical doctor who practiced both medicine and politics on the prairie. But millions of Americans come from immigrant roots, and thousands more have lived on Indian reservations. Perhaps it was the combination of all the influences that produced a U.S. senator who held the concept of principle above all else.

Abourezk is not always right, Lord knows, but everyone knows exactly where he stands. He doesn't hide his true feelings behind meaningless words. He doesn't try to finesse either issues or people. It was that honesty that won him four elections in a state that perhaps didn't totally agree with his position on a lot of issues. How else can you explain an officeholder from South Dakota being the champion of a minority controversial within his own state— the American Indians? Or his willingness to take on the multinational oil companies who have ways of getting even with their political opponents?

His standing up for small farmers was to be expected, because he represented them, but he went beyond mere support, trying hard to change the insidious structure that keeps them hanging by their economic thumbnails. It was his incisiveness, his innate ability to detect and pierce the sanctimonious and self-serving charades of the powerful, that made him such a formidable advocate in the Senate.

The country benefited immeasurably from the combination of intelligence and bluntness, seriousness and fun that such populist leaders as Fred Harris, George McGovern, and Jim Abourezk brought to high office, and they are living models for some of us who are following the populist paths that they have blazed. One of the most endearing qualities of Senator Abourezk was that he never took himself too seriously, an attitude that was best expressed when he was asked on election night in 1970 what he would do if he won: "Ask for a recount," he said. Instead of adopting the "imperial demeanor" that tempts some members of this elite body of lawmakers, Abourezk just considered himself a guy trying to do a job for the workaday people he cared about.

Maybe that's because he was no one's "protégé," the darling of no special interest group. There was no part of his way that was greased. He was someone of the people, which is why populist is the best label one can put on him. He made his way with the strength of his convictions. It was those convictions that brought him respect, then followers, and eventually campaign victories that took him right to the halls of Congress.

We have a saying in Texas: The only thing you'll find in the middle of the road are yellow stripes and dead armadillos. Abourezk is one creature you'll never find there. The memoirs of his early life in South Dakota and of his later political life in Washington demonstrate that. They also show that you don't have to abandon your beliefs and your principles to get elected. You just have to show the voters that you stand for something, that you're on their side, and that you've not fallen in with the wrong crowd.

Anyway, that's the way Abourezk is. It's too bad his Lebanese immigrant parents did not live to see him serve his country in the Senate and beyond. They would have been proud of him.

Jim Hightower
Texas Commissioner
of Agriculture
September 1989

Introduction

Had someone told me ten years earlier, I never would have believed that a U.S. president would be begging me to do something for him. I was on the Senate floor when a page told me that President Carter wanted me on the phone. I was very cool. "Not again?" I said, with just a touch of exasperation in my voice.

It was Jimmy Carter's umpteenth effort to convince me to vote for the Panama Canal Treaty. Returning the Panama Canal to Panamanian sovereignty was a major centerpiece of Carter's Administration. He had invested heavy political capital in negotiating the treaty, as well as in selling it to the Senate and to the American public. It had come down to my vote, the 67th, the one he needed to ratify it. Carter had tried everything to get my vote in favor of the treaty, including calling everyone of my known friends both in and out of Washington. As though to prove that politics is more a marketplace than a method of governing, at one point he invited me to the Oval Office for a private meeting where, in return for my vote, he offered, of all things, to invite the president of Lebanon to Washington for an official visit. I assume he thought that because I was of Lebanese descent this would be all the leverage he needed. However, in 1978, I had nothing more than a passing interest in the president of Lebanon, but I had, a number of times before the cloakroom call, insisted that the president of the United States and James Schlesinger, the buccaneer who he had appointed as secretary of energy, stop trying by every devious means they knew to deregulate natural gas prices, an act that would, without question, sharply drive up the price of natural gas for the consumer. It was, to me, an example of the kind of highway robbery that business monopolies carry out whenever they can, and I was dead set against the government helping them do it.

Although bills to deregulate natural gas finally passed both the Senate and the House in 1977, the two versions were not exactly alike and had to be brought into alignment by the Energy Conference Committee, a committee of both House and Senate members from their respective Energy Committees. The Conference Committee—I was one of the members—was unable to agree on anything and the negotiations broke down. That was when Carter and Schlesinger began holding secret sessions in the White House with selected Conference Committee members, trying to get agreement from them before bringing the bill back to the full committee to ram it through. Their behavior was not only unusual; it was highly improper, if not illegal. When I found out about it I was determined to stop it, and the only weapon I had was my vote on the Panama Canal Treaty. President Carter and I both knew that he needed my vote to put it over the top, which was why I announced that I would vote against it unless he and Schlesinger stopped trying to improperly influence the Energy Conference Committee.

I went into the cloakroom phone booth to hear the most obsequious plea to date from the president. "Jim, I'm begging you, I'm pleading with you to vote yes on the treaty."

I couldn't believe what I was hearing. "This is embarrassing, Mr. President," I told him, truly embarrassed. "You're the president of the United States. You don't have to plead with anybody, especially not with me."

As he began sweet-talking me again, I smelled smoke—real smoke—from a fire. I spun around to look out the glass door of the phone booth. Senator John Culver of Iowa had carefully inserted a folded paper towel into the crack between the door of the phone booth and the door jamb and had lit a match to it. It was burning toward me, like a fuse. "Good God!" I shouted.

"What's wrong?" asked Carter, now concerned he had said the wrong thing during his pitch.

"I'm sorry, Mr. President," I said, "it's just John Culver trying to burn me out of the phone booth."

If this makes the U.S. Senate sound like a fraternity—exciting and fun—do not be misled. For most of my adult life I had thought, as do most people, that being a U.S. senator was probably the best job in the world. But viewing the position from the outside is totally different from being on the inside. I had no objection to serving for one term, but I had no desire to offer myself for another. There are men and women who would kill to be reelected, term after term. I was not one of them. I served one term in the U.S. House of Representatives from 1971 to 1973. Then I ran for the U.S. Senate where I served one six-year term from 1973 to 1979. At the end of that term I voluntarily stepped down, refusing to run again.

In answer to the many people who asked why I had left office, I said at the time that I wanted to spend more time with my family. I had deprived my family of my presence for much too long. I discovered, too late, that my kids took my absence personally. It was only a few years ago that they began speaking to me again. Then came the ultimate irony. When I left the Senate and started spending more time with my first wife, Mary, both of us discovered she didn't much like me. We separated in 1980, ultimately divorcing in 1981. But I did not leave the Senate only because of my family. I learned that senators necessarily spend more of their time preparing the groundwork for the next election than running the government. It is the officeholder, not the public, who benefits from this system.

My days in the Senate were usually spent running back and forth to the floor for votes, sitting in boring committee hearings, and, in between the dozens of phone calls each day, receiving lobbyists, constituents, fund-raisers, and staff members. My nights were usually taken up sitting on the Senate floor waiting for some egomaniacal, long-winded senator to grind out a boring speech that he had neither written nor read before he came to the floor, so that I could vote on the bill that was the subject of his speech. Those giving the speeches did so, I believed, not to convince anyone, but to make certain of their day in the sun. Few votes were ever changed by virtue of floor debate. They were certainly not changed by any so-called floor debate on routine legislation, which involved no emotional commitment on the part of anyone, either proponent or opponent. I sometimes thought that the boredom was enforced, that those who spoke at great length did so to see how many senators would simply give up and go home. While most ordinary Americans were at home eating dinner with their families, I was eating the skin on the inside of my cheeks at the utter folly of it all.

For most people, weekends are the time to unwind from stress caused by the frustration of their occupations. But this is not the case in politics. Weekends are when politicians must travel to some place in the United States to raise money, or to please someone who has already raised money, or to hold a town meeting in the home state—the latter being the only really necessary and productive thing that senators do. The drive to raise money becomes so pervasive that on more than one occasion I caught myself feeling resentful that my job as a member of Congress intruded on my job as a candidate. But that's the story of congressional politics in today's world.

The U.S. Senate is, however, one place in the world that allows a poor boy to live as though he were a millionaire. Where else are your doors opened for you, is your travel all over the world provided free of charge, can you meet with world leaders who would otherwise never let you into their countries, have your bad jokes laughed at, and your boring speeches applauded? It's the ultimate place to have one's ego massaged, over and over. Perhaps that's why politicians will put up with guff that would otherwise be unendurable, so that they can stay in office forever. There is one more advantage. As Maine Senator Bill Hathaway once said, the job requires no heavy lifting.

After having my own ego massaged for two years in the House and one year in the Senate, I decided that I had had enough. I stopped to look at myself and my life and finally said, "This is ridiculous." I saw no benefit in prolonging the agony. I made a decision, within a year after being sworn in, that there were better ways to spend my time, that I wouldn't run again when my term was over. I didn't need it anymore and promised myself that I would get out at the end of my term, no matter what the pressures were to run again, and they were heavy. I was glad to be gone, but I have to say that I wouldn't have missed the time I spent there for the world, mostly because of all the things I learned about politics, about the people who slosh around in it, and about myself.

The most frequent question I'm asked is, "Do you ever regret leaving the Senate?" Only once, during the summer of 1987, when the Iran-contra Committee was quavering with fright before Oliver

North on national television. I wanted, as they say, "a piece of him." Beyond that, I have no regrets, with perhaps one other exception. I wish that I still had the WATS line that I was furnished in the Senate. One can practice law, as I've been doing since 1979, without a WATS line, but it would be much sweeter with one.

Mark Raskin is a founder and senior fellow of the Institute for Policy Studies, a Washington think tank. When I told him in 1977 that I intended not to run again for the Senate, he began putting heavy pressure on me to change my mind, citing all the reasons why I should stay. "It's important to the country," he said emphatically, "that people with your kind of public spirit stay in office, if nothing more than to keep the charlatans and conmen out of it."

Since I had no intention of changing my mind, I finally asked Mark why, if he thought it was that important, didn't he run for the Senate.

"Well, to me, serving in the Senate is just like mucking out the barnyard," Mark responded. "Somebody's got to do it. I just don't want it to be me."

1

"Rosebud"

The Abourezk dynasty, as it were, had its American beginnings in Wood, South Dakota, seventeen miles southeast of White River, the Mellette County seat. Wood, which today has a population of no more than one hundred people, was the ultimate destination of my father, Beshara Abu Rizk, (who later Anglicized his name to Charles Thomas Abourezk), when he emigrated here from Lebanon in 1898. Mellette County was still part of the Rosebud Sioux Indian Reservation in those days, before the federal government, in another act of largesse and accommodation to whites, opened it up for white settlement in 1911. Today, Mellette, Todd, Gregory, and Tripp Counties are collectively known as the "Rosebud."

When I had a little free time after I came to Washington, I went to the National Archives to locate Charlie's immigration card in the microfilm records. The few entries on the card told a fascinating story. He was accompanied by a thirty-four-year-old brother, Elias, and Elias's wife and two children. The immigration card for Uncle Elias indicated that he had lived in America for five years, from 1892 to 1897, and had returned to Lebanon to bring over more of his family. Elias must have lived a long and extremely productive life, because when I told his daughter—my cousin—Sylvia Sophiea, who lives in Flint, Michigan, about the family Elias brought with him, she nearly had a seizure. "My God," she exclaimed, "he must have been married *three* times." Sylvia knew of two marriages—the one to her mother and the other to the mother of Albert and Josephine Abourezk, but the family in Lebanon came as a complete surprise.

Charlie crossed the Atlantic on the *S.S. Bordeaux* and landed in New York with $42.50 in his pocket, telling the immigration officer that he was on his way to live with four older brothers in "Cattsburg," South Dakota. There is no Cattsburg in South Dakota, but the word "Cattsburg" was obviously what the immigration officer heard when Charlie struggled to say "Gettysburg, South Dakota," which is where he ended his journey. Moreover, he had only two brothers, Michael and Elias, and, to further correct the record, he was the eldest in the family.

Charlie did a lot of different things to survive in turn-of-the-century South Dakota. He homesteaded, sold snow cones during the land rush in Gregory, South Dakota, and peddled spices, linens, and other notions from a pack on his back throughout the Indian reservation. A number of years ago an old Indian, Bob Moran, who lived south of Wood, told me that he still remembered my father walking through that part of the country peddling, on occasion staying overnight with Moran at his cabin, then walking on to the next human habitation in the morning.

Charlie finally decided to return to Lebanon to find a wife. Back in the village of Kfeir, which today is just a few kilometers from Israel's northern border, he sought out and married my mother, Juliana "Lena" Mickel, then an eighteen-year-old distant cousin. (One imagines that most everyone in that small village was somehow related.) My older sister, Helen, and my older brother, Chick, were born, in that order, after which Charlie decided to leave Lebanon again, telling my mother that he would send for the family when he got the money.

Charlie's economic position slowly improved after his return from Lebanon. From walking peddler, he moved up to riding a horse as soon as he could afford it, then to a buggy, and finally, in 1913 after his return from Lebanon, he opened his first store in Wood. In 1920, the year my mother finally arrived in South Dakota with Chick and Helen, he opened a second store in Mission, Todd

County, which is twenty miles south of Wood, very near the Nebraska border.

I was born in the family home in Wood, which started out as a one-room house, but by the time of my birth it had grown into a thirteen-room, two-story rambler, each room built on as needed over the years by my father. I was born in the house, because by the year of my birth in 1931, there was no hospital. My mother was attended by a midwife, there being no doctor available at the time.

Before World War II broke out, it seemed that, except for the grinding poverty in which people found themselves, Wood's most critical problems centered on preventing drunks from burning mattresses in the city jail and trying to keep enough gravel on Main Street so that it could be navigated during the rains that came infrequently. When you hear of the semi-arid West, think of Wood, the most semi-arid of them all. For those who lived off the land it was strictly hardscrabble farming, trying to make do with very little rainfall, with no rivers nearby from which to irrigate, even if the farmers had been able to afford it. One of my most powerful remaining memories from the 1930s is the sight of an endless number of giant tumbleweeds, or "Russian thistles" as they were sometimes called, rolling across the prairie and down Main Street. Tumbleweeds grew in the pastures to a height of three or four feet, quickly dried out, and then were pulled up by the strong South Dakota winds to roll on and on, stopping only when they caught on a fence. They are today a symbol for me of the pervasive harshness of the weather on the Great Plains, the inescapable poverty that resulted from the lack of rainfall, and the inability to stop the wind from blowing, eternally carrying its cargo of dust into both homes and nostrils.

Living conditions for Indians around Wood were worse than for whites, except that the government managed to get food to them part of the time. At best, Indian homes were plain small shacks, made from either logs or sheets of tin. At worst, they were white canvas tents that simply could not keep out the bitter winter cold. One family—Ed Stranger Horse's—for some reason is burned into my memory. They lived in a canvas, army-style tent for as long as I can remember. Ed was quite old when I was a child, and what I remember most about him were his periodic wintertime trips from the tent to my father's store to buy one or two items, all he had money for, struggling desperately to keep warm in the thin jacket that was his only barrier against the cold. I remember that his eyes perpetually watered and his nose continually ran, much like that of a small child who had been in the cold too long. My father gave him credit whenever he needed food and had no money.

Until 1953, it was illegal to sell Indians alcoholic beverages. The federal law prohibiting the sale of liquor to "hostiles" dated from the time when white traders took unfair economic advantage of Indians after plying them with booze. It appeared to me to be a self-defeating law. The poverty that afflicted Indians, combined with the psychological defeatism that the white occupation imposed on them, created a class of Indian alcoholics desperate to escape their condition. The law never stopped Indians who wanted to drink from drinking, yet it often dangerously forced them to drink anything they could get their hands on. Because vanilla and lemon extracts contained alcohol, they were, in our store, big-selling items to Indians. Several white bootleggers made a living selling illegal wine and whiskey to Indians. Occasionally, the ingestion of wood alcohol would either kill or blind someone who couldn't get his hands on ordinary booze.

Both Indians and whites scraped to stay above the poverty line, trying to keep warm by picking up coal along the railroad track and by cutting wood along the creek east of town. I don't remember our family ever being short of food or fuel, so I never felt the sting of poverty as did much of Wood's population. Neither did I have an appreciation of how badly we whites treated the Indians. I grew up believing it was permissible, even heroic, to ridicule the Indians of Wood. Most of them, like Ed Stranger Horse, tried to stay out of everyone's way, there being no profit in finding oneself on the receiving end of a white's misdirected anger. The most visible Indians were the public drunks, those for whom alcoholism was a shield of armor. Until I left the reservation, I never understood the damage my own racism was doing as I joined the community in its uniformly bad treatment of Indians. I scoffed at Indians who would spend what little money they had on sweet rolls and cold cuts, taking them from the store to their cars to feed small children waiting there. The antics of Indian winos were the staple of our running jokes. We had no sympathy and very little mercy for those less fortunate than we. I belittled Indians until I left the reservation and attended college, where a friend, Peggy Goodart, figuratively slapped me in the face one day, forcing me to realize how destructive my attitudes were.

The flatness of southern Mellette County was broken only occasionally by a butte protruding here or there out of the prairie's expanse. In a way that makes one think of California as two states, South Dakota is sliced in half by the Missouri River, its two parts called West River and East River. The Missouri was created a few millennia ago by the western edge of a glacier that left in its path wonderfully fertile soil east of the river, and to the west, where it did not flow, hardpan prairie. The extreme western part of the state is blessed, however, with the gently rising Black Hills, spectacular granite mountains whose name comes from the black hue created by the massive stands of Ponderosa Pine that blanket the mountains. Just east of the Black Hills are the multicolored Badlands, fossil-filled lumps of red, yellow, and purple clay exposed by erosion over the centuries. But the rest of the West River country is mostly plain, flat grassland.

There is an interesting difference in political outlook between South Dakotans from the West River and those from the East River. For whatever reason, the flat, rich farmland east of the Missouri has created a more liberal kind of voter, one who does not shun government programs, whether for farms or for social needs. West of the Missouri, where there is a greater concentration of cattle and sheep ranches, is the base for all sorts of right-wing political movements, from the Posse Comitatus to the John Birch Society. But there is also a streak of antiauthoritarian radicalism in the West that the East cannot match. I once held a town meeting in the isolated sheep-ranching country of the West River and listened in amazement as a rancher rose to his feet to ask when we were going to get enough gumption to overthrow the federal government. Other ranchers exist out there—not many, however—who preach socialism for the masses. One of the great liberals of America, ninety-year-old Homer Ayres, a retired rancher, still writes lucidly about the sorry state of the nation's politics.

South Dakota has a relatively brief, but interesting frontier history. In 1876, Wild Bill Hickok was shot in the back of the head while playing poker in Deadwood, a mining town in the northern Black Hills. Butch Cassidy and the Hole in the Wall Gang robbed their first bank in Belle Fourche, just north of the Black Hills, and General Custer's place in history was established when he led an expedition to the Black Hills in 1874 and discovered gold. The gold rush that he precipitated led directly to the government's violation of its 1868 treaty with the Indians. The treaty, which promised that the Sioux would be left alone on lands conceded to them, was broken so that white gold-seekers could enter Indian country. When pressure from the gold hustlers was more than the Grant Administration could withstand, the president sent out a team of negotiators to try to revise the treaty with the Indians. When the Indians refused, Ulysses S. Grant ordered the army to round them up and drive them onto reservations. When Custer, among other army commanders, proceeded to carry out the order, it resulted in the Custer massacre in 1876, prompting the Sioux Indian intellectual, Vine De Loria, Jr., to announce to the white man a century later that, "Custer died for your sins."

I never really knew why Charlie settled in South Dakota. Today it's a most pleasant place to live, with its beautiful, sometimes spectacular mountain scenery in the west and along the river banks, and its peaceful, rolling farmland in the east. Cold winters are now much easier to take with modern technology's new ways to keep warm. But in 1898 there was none of that, making it all the more puzzling when one tries to fathom why people from Norway, Germany, Sweden, Czechoslovakia, Ireland—and Lebanon—settled there rather than in, say, San Diego or San Francisco. Its character as a settler society has derived from those people who gathered from all parts of Europe and the Middle East—people escaping from poverty, from forced military conscription, from religious intolerance, from whatever it was that brought them to America. Life in South Dakota was always a marginal one for these exiles from the older civilizations overseas, but it was much less marginal than the life they lived in the old country, wherever that might have been. There was, of course, nothing romantic about their existence on the edge, but there is a great deal that is admirable about it.

By the time Charlie made enough money to bring the family over from Lebanon, World War I had intervened. Because Syria was still part of the Ottoman Empire, an ally of Kaiser Wilhelm's Germany, there was no communication between the United States and the village. Charlie tried to send Lena money, but it never arrived, leaving her no choice but to raise the children by herself, keeping them in line by threatening them with punishment by the Turkish army, which was enough to make anyone behave. The Turkish army in those days was not at all reluctant to confiscate food from Lebanese peasants to feed itself. My mother's memory of constant near-starvation in Kfeir contained for her enough vividly remembered trauma to prevent her from ever wanting to return for a visit. When asked, she would simply say, "I don't want to go."

The only story that I ever heard my father tell about the old days was one describing Lena's arrival in Wood. Beyond that he refused to discuss the past, choosing to speak only of life in South Dakota and America. I took his attitude, in later years, to mean that there was nothing he wanted to remember about the old days. Whatever family history of the old country I had heard came from my mother, or from my sister Helen.

Charlie delighted, however, in telling of the welcome the Sioux Indians gave to my mother and siblings when they arrived. Because they liked my father, the Indians decided to stage a powwow in honor of the family's reunion, dressing in full costume and war paint. When my mother came out of the house to see what the fuss was about, she saw what she perceived to be hostile Indians about to do her in. She scooped up her children and locked herself in the house until Charlie convinced her that it was safe to come out.

Charlie was a 260-pound, one-man threshing crew when it came to eating. During the 1920s and 1930s, Lena spent most of her time cooking meals for him, as many as six a day. He was so gregarious that whenever a traveling salesman came through Wood, he would drag the poor fellow from the store, across the street to the house for a meal. They were usually drummers with such names as O. C. "Pop" Castor, who sold wholesale groceries for the Ulry-Talbert Company, and Put Putnam, the Portis hat salesman, who passed out business cards identifying himself as "Everlastinglyatit Put." Offering such Lebanese hospitality not only allowed Charlie to show his generosity, but it worked as an excuse for him to eat one more meal during the day.

Charlie remained a big man, even in his sixties and seventies when I knew him (he was sixty years old when I was born). By then he had lost most of his hair and all of his teeth. He was still quite tall, but after decades of ingesting Lena's splendid butter and olive oil–based cooking, he had managed to construct a magnificent stomach. I think he overate at every meal, at least when I was present. Each time he did he would curse himself with his trademark broken-English profanity, a delightfully accented, "Gotdam me! Gotdam me, I ate too Gotdam much," a signal to Lena that she had cooked another great meal, causing her to turn away to smile to herself.

The empty lot across the street from the house today contains only a concrete foundation, the sole remnant of the old movie theater, another of my father's enterprises. It was one from which I greatly benefited, because a requirement of every lease agreement that he signed with the various movie exhibitors who were tenants was my unhindered passage, without charge, into any movie shown.

About a hundred feet or so east of the theater is my father's original store building, now boarded up and crumbling. In its glory days it was known as C. ABOUREZK MERCANTILE, which Charlie owned from 1913 until he gave it to my adopted brother and blood cousin, Albert Abourezk, upon his discharge from the army in 1946. After Cousin Abie died prematurely from spleen cancer, the city fathers of Wood bought the building and converted it into a combination on-sale bar and off-sale liquor store. The city liquor store was then moved into the building.

At its earlier location, Pitsy Jaros had managed the liquor store. He was assisted by his second wife, Gloria, who ran it by herself during farming season when Pits took to the fields, working to supplement what little he made as a store manager. The empty lot next to the old Abourezk's Store building was where the post office stood for most of the years of my young life.

The only commercial buildings remaining today on Wood's main street are Dewey Larson's Mobil station and the grocery store and adjoining post office, both run by Warren Sinkler. Sinkler's store is now in the building that once held the Central Market, owned in the old days by my cousin Eli Abourezk, a bachelor who had come to Wood from Lebanon, by way of Brazil, sometime in the 1920s.

Moving westward in the earlier part of this century, the Chicago & Northwestern Railroad line reached Wood in 1931. Some three thousand souls poured into the little town that year searching for prosperity. Some came looking for work on the railroad line, but most came because they believed that a boom would accompany the railhead. The line was built, but somehow nothing happened. Within a year some 2,500 of the 3,000 moved on to look elsewhere for relief from the depression.

I don't suppose Charlie made much money off the whites around Wood during the depression. What kept his head above water, despite going bankrupt a couple of times during the 1920s and 1930s, was the U.S. government and the Indians. We had what was called a "boss farmer" in Wood—Mr. Lindbloom—a government Indian agent whose job it was to teach the Indians how to farm. Creating Indian farmers was another of the government's failed experiments with the Indian tribes they had subdued in the last thirty years of the nineteenth century. Sioux Indians, who had spent most of the previous two hundred years living in unrestrained freedom as deer and buffalo hunters, looked curiously at the farming implements that the Bureau of Indian Affairs provided them, their silence communicating something like, "Don't call me, I'll call you." The result was that the boss farmer's job became one of issuing government purchase orders and vouchers to the Indians, who would bring them to our store, among others, and spend them on groceries, hardware, and dry goods, all of which Charlie offered for sale. Charlie would present the purchase order to the government, which would then reimburse him.

Not long ago a dealer in antique artifacts, Douglas Ball (coincidentally, former diplomat George Ball's son), sent me a copy of a small coupon that read:

25 cents
C. Abourezk
General Merchandise
Wood, South Dakota

He had been offered the coupon for sale and wanted to know its background. My best guess, I told him, was that it was scrip printed by my father, illegally of course, and given as change for a government purchase order when an Indian customer fell short of spending the entire amount. I learned later that Ball sold the coupon for $900, a sum that would have made Charlie's heart glad.

The stores in Wood and Mission were similar in appearance. They were each 24-feet wide and nearly 100-feet long. Until 1946, when my brothers took over the management of the Mission store, both it and the Wood store were the old clerk-behind-the-counter type, in contrast to the more modern self-service markets and supermarkets. The customers would ask the clerk for, say, a can of beans, which the clerk would fetch, put on the counter, write down both the item and price on an order pad, then go for the next item, and on and on. The shelves were stuffed with groceries on one side and dry goods on the other. At the rear of the store was the meat counter with its free-standing butcher block, and adjacent to it were shoes and hardware. Except for canned goods—fruit and vegetables—nearly everything was sold in bulk. Nothing was prepackaged. Flour, sugar, prunes, raisins, peanuts, whatever were all sacked up in paper bags by the clerk and sold by the pound. Vinegar was sold out of a wooden barrel stored in the back room, provided, that is, the customer brought his or her own empty bottle. Although most stores in that part of South Dakota are today self-service operations, there has been one holdout. Linehan's store in Oglalla, on the Pine Ridge Reservation was, the last time I was there, still caught in a mercantile time warp. It had glass counters full of items that could be fetched only by a clerk. Horse collars for sale were hanging on the wall, and a posted sign read:

For Prosperity
On The Reservation
Trade Here.

The floor in Abourezk's Store was wood planking, which occasionally had to be sloshed with oil to keep it from cracking, and there was the obligatory potbellied wood stove located in the center of the store. The few fresh vegetables available were kept in unrefrigerated bins. Fresh eggs were piled in a cardboard box on the floor without dividers to protect them. A local wag once walked into the store in Wood and offered to bet Charlie twenty-five cents that he could jump into the box of eggs with both feet and not break a single one. Unable to resist the challenge, Charlie called his bet, then watched in horror as the fellow jumped into the box, smashed every egg, and threw his quarter to Charlie as he ran out the door. Charlie, the story goes, recovered sufficiently to retaliate with a can of tomatoes that narrowly missed the fellow's head.

Charlie's temper, I'm told, was ignited in part by my own childish antics throughout the 1930s and 1940s, such as the time when, immediately following a funeral held in the theater building, I jumped onto the running board of Charlie's 1940 Buick, demanding that I be allowed to ride to the cemetery with him and the carload of pallbearers he was transporting. "Gotdamit, Jimmy," he exploded, "Get off the Gotdam car. Can't you see I've got to take these Gotdam *ball players* up there?"

Somehow my mother's real name, Juliana, was shortened to Lena, which was all I ever knew her by until after her death. She was, to say the least, straightlaced; she eschewed makeup, never once drank a drop of whiskey, never smoked, and never swore, except for one historic moment when I witnessed her trying to make trouble for a woman in town she didn't like. I was playing nearby when I saw her sit a friend of hers down and ask, referring to her enemy, "How do you like being called 'sonofabitch' by Mrs. So and So?" Lena was a tough woman, an attribute which derived, I'm certain, from her never-ending struggle for survival, from protecting and finding food for my older brother and sister, Chick and Helen, back in Lebanon. Add all that to the hereditary Mickel stubbornness and the product could be nothing other than a most formidable woman.

My mother struggled to adapt herself to an American society defined by the small town of Wood and its surroundings. The leap from the culture and life of a peasant woman in a small Lebanese village to that of "society matron" in a small South Dakota town was for her a gigantic one. She did not learn to speak English for a number of years after she arrived. In the first four or five years of my life I spoke mostly Arabic because that was all I heard from my mother. Eventually she began to entertain the Wood Ladies Aid Society in her formal living room, cooking for them the staple of meat and potatoes, the standard cuisine in that part of South Dakota. Although Lebanese cooking was vastly superior, she never offered it to the Ladies Aid Society, perhaps fearful that, unable to adjust their palates to it, they might ridicule it. But when the Ladies Aid or the Eastern Star were not around, she cooked mountains of Lebanese food, in particular on Sundays—in fact, every Sunday— when Sam and Albert Abdnor and their families drove down from Kennebec and Presho to spend the day with us. They were usually joined by my Uncle John Mickel and his family who drove down from White River.

The Abdnor family had originated in Ain Arab, a small Lebanese village just north of Kfeir. Sam Abdnor settled in Kennebec, north and east of Wood, where he ran a store and made a great deal of money as a wheat farmer. His brother Albert lived and ran a store in Presho, ten miles west of Kennebec. Sam's son, Jim, became a Republican, as was Sam. Although Jim was nominally a high school athletic coach, he moved steadily upward in the South Dakota Republican Party, serving first in the state legislature, then as lieutenant governor, and eventually was elected to the U.S. House of Representatives when I moved over to the Senate. He made it to the U.S. Senate by defeating George McGovern, staying there until 1986, when my former legislative director, Tom Daschle, defeated him. Ronald Reagan then appointed him as National Director of the Small Business Administration. Although Jim's mother, Mary Abdnor, was my godmother, and his uncle Albert was my godfather, I never let that divert my attention from doing what I could to campaign—unsuccessfully—for George McGovern in 1980.

During all those family visits in the 1930s, we behaved very much as I supposed people in the old country did—eating a huge meal, listening to Arabic music on the wind-up Victrola, the adults talking until nightfall, or as late as they could before the visitors had to start driving back home. Interestingly, I remember no talk of Middle East politics, but only of the store business, the Orthodox Church and its leaders in New York, and of the hardships endured by family members who remained behind in Lebanon.

Cousin Eli's personality was much like my father's—volatile, yet generous and warm. If anyone needed anything, food, money, whatever, both Charlie and Eli would hand it over if they had it. But there was something uniformly strange about Lebanese immigrants, at least those in my family—they tended to reject advice and strenuously avoided changing positions, a trait that some people define as stubbornness. It was especially true of my mother's side of the family, in particular of my Uncle John Mickel, who was a world-class hardhead. In my entire life I don't remember ever hearing him, or my mother, admit that they had been wrong about anything.

Cousin Eli worked in the store for my father after he emigrated to Wood, until 1936, that is, when he argued violently with my parents and resigned in anger to open his own store down the street. His first store, the original Central Market, had a dirt floor and was no bigger than 10 feet by 15 feet. But he prospered and eventually moved to the bigger and better building across the street, where he stayed until his first retirement. Eli later moved to Winner, population 3,500, some forty miles east of Wood, to open another Central Market there. After retiring a second time, he opened his third store—again a Central Market—in the small town of Witten, located between Winner and Wood. The townspeople and farmers around Witten had pleaded with him to open the store there—a previous one had closed sometime before—guaranteeing that they would buy everything they could from him. Good to their word, Eli prospered again until he finally and fully retired.

Eli was crabby, especially with small children. But on occasion he was given to prolonged bouts of good humor that made him as lovable as a teddy bear to everyone within his reach. He was the adventurer in our family, sometimes driving 250 miles in his car— usually the newest, most sporty model on the market—just to eat a sandwich with a friend. He was mad about American baseball, and absolutely nuts about the New York Yankees back in the days when they were winning with great regularity. I never knew how he managed it, but one fall he wangled a World Series ticket from Yogi Berra, went to the Yankee-Cardinals game in St. Louis, and was invited by Yogi to fly with the team in their plane to the next game in New York. Of course, that resulted in Eli becoming the undisputed hero and social leader of Mellette, Tripp, and Todd Counties.

Next door to Cousin Eli's first store was the famous "Bloody Bucket" saloon, formally known as "The Rosebud Club." I say famous, because when I grew up I was certain that everyone in the world had heard of it. It was old George Wang's pool hall and beer joint, so named out of someone's romantic notion of what a tough Western bar ought to be. When I was old enough to pull the door open by myself I started hanging out there, learning to shoot pool and trading stories about how dangerous old George Wang was. We—the boys around Wood—used to tell Bloody Bucket stories to anyone who would listen. One of our favorites involved the time a drunken Indian tried to reenter the saloon after being thrown out. George Wang shot through the door, so the story went, and with perfect aim shattered the drunk's kneecap. He was once offered a pistol for sale, brought into the Bloody Bucket by the hopeful seller. George asked if he could test fire it, then shot into the wall over the seller's head. Whether the stories were true or not, they made George Wang someone to fear and respect. But it never occurred to me that his ferocity might be less than met the eye. I later learned that he was really just a gentle old man who spent most of his days sipping beer and collecting a dime a game from eight-ball customers.

I spent a lot of my youth in the Bloody Bucket, becoming accustomed to the permanently unventilated, malodorous smell of stale urine and rancid beer, and to the perpetual blue haze of a hundred cigarettes. Behind the bar hung a print of Custer's Last Stand, the romanticized version of the massacre that the Budweiser beer company distributed to bars all over the country. George Wang was very old when I was very young, always sitting in a chair behind the bar, forever unshaven, dressed in clothes so shabby and grimy that it was obvious he never changed them. Today the old building that housed the Bloody Bucket is the Masonic Lodge.

Charlie was a Democrat. He was elected mayor of Wood about the same time Franklin D. Roosevelt was elected president, and he resigned at about the time Roosevelt died. He deviated from his usual Democratic politics, however, the year Tom Dewey was running for president and rode on his campaign train through Valentine, Nebraska. Charlie dressed up in cowboy boots and a wide-brimmed hat to go see Dewey, who waved at him and yelled, "Hi there, cowboy," with the result that Charlie voted Republican for the first and only time in his life.

Charlie was famous for his unlimited generosity. Not only did he find it hard to refuse credit to both Indians and whites needing groceries, but he carried cigarettes and candy in his pocket to offer to people he met on the street or in the store. In the words of the local Indians, he let them *ikazo* (sign) for their groceries. Whenever anyone, Indian or white, gave him a hard-luck story, he would fill a box with food staples and send them on their way. While his benevolent spirit endeared him to its recipients, it totally exasperated my mother, who was determined never to go through a period of starvation again as she had in Lebanon. She saw every penny he gave away as one that brought the family that much closer to the poorhouse. In fact, his charitable tendencies were the only real bone of contention between them. That, and his occasional ventures down the street to the Bloody Bucket.

The incident I remember most vividly took place when he was seventy-three years old. He initially went to play poker in the Bloody Bucket's back room, but drank too much beer and surrendered to the temptation of dancing with Ramona Balfany, Bill Balfany's widow. I heard about his carousing and went down to the Bloody Bucket to take him home. It was not enough that Lena locked us *both* out of the house, but she stood just behind the locked door screaming bloody murder—in Arabic—at Charlie for his transgressions. I had no idea what I'd do with my tipsy 260-pound father if I couldn't get him into his own bed. Apparently the lack of alternatives gave me a special eloquence in pleading his case, because my mother eventually relented and let him in.

History sort of passed by Wood, though World War II created radical change. Those men who weren't drafted into the military moved to California to work in the defense plants. My brothers, Tom and Chick, and Cousin Abie all went into the service, and because my Uncle John had earlier opened a store of his own in White River, Charlie had to move to Mission to run the store there after the war broke out. He made his home in the living quarters attached to the back of the store. My mother, who was no longer obliged to cook Charlie's daily six meals, had to take charge of the Wood store, assisted by Olga Sully and Abie's wife, Frances. Although Lena could neither read nor write English, she had no trouble counting the money taken in at the end of the day and entering the amount into a ledger book.

The war changed things very little for me. I still ran free in the graveled streets of Wood, much the same as I had ever since I learned to walk. Except that now, I could escape both Wood and my mother and hop over to live in Mission with Charlie whenever I felt the urge. He paid less attention to me than my mother did, which was just fine with me, because it allowed me almost total freedom. I joined everyone else in their concern over gasoline rationing, mostly because I had only recently learned to drive at the tender age of eleven and found myself restricted by the shortage of gasoline.

I experienced one major change, however. I read every comic book that I could find on the subject of the war, conjuring up dreams of becoming a war hero, as either a fighter pilot or machine gunner—dreams that I did not shed until years later. My brother Chick, a combat engineer, was in Europe and brought back a picture of himself shaking hands with Russian soldiers at the Elbe River in Germany. My brother Tom was a U.S. Marine master sergeant, the ground crew chief for Pappy Boyington's First Marine Air Wing. And my cousin Abie was an ordinary infantry grunt in the Pacific theater. When his unit was sent to Peleliu Island in the Palau chain to "mop up" the Japanese army after the initial landing assault by the marines, Abie heard that Tom's unit had set up operations on the island. So he made his way over to visit him. When Abie finally came home from the war, I asked him to describe the visit in detail, expecting his story to be as exciting as I had dreamed it would be ever since I read his brief V-mail letter about it. All he said was, "When I got there Tom was roaring drunk."

We once saw a bomber flying low near Wood, presumably on a training mission from one of the dozens of airbases established by the Army Air Corps throughout South Dakota and Nebraska. In December 1943, a B-17 bomber crashed some forty miles west of Mission near a small Indian settlement called "By The Way," killing ten airmen on board. I was awed by stories of the kids from Mission who had hurried out to pick up pieces of the airplane as souvenirs. I was especially impressed by the plexiglas ring that one of them had made from the bomber's cockpit window. This created a problem for me. I desperately wanted a bomber to crash near Wood, but I didn't know how to make it happen without killing one of our servicemen. The Indians living in the community ultimately changed its name to "Soldier Creek," in honor of the airmen who died there.

In 1946, Chick, Tom, and Abie came back from the war unharmed and took over operation of the two stores, giving my parents time to travel. Abie and Frances ran the Wood store. Chick and his wife, Elda, and Tom and his wife, Twila, took over the

Mission store. My sister Virginia had moved to Winner during the war, and I was now the only one left at home.

Charlie, Lena, Uncle John, Aunt Carrie, and I went to West Virginia to visit Helen and her family that year in Charlie's new Dodge. On the way back, passing through Indianapolis, Uncle John decided to buy his first new car. Because he had no idea how to make his way in city traffic, I announced that I would drive, taking the wheel of the new Ford coupe for the entire trip back to Wood, with Uncle John riding shotgun and aunt Carrie stuffed into the narrow back seat with their belongings. Because I was driving my uncle's car, my father had to drive the Dodge, an act that caused great consternation all around, especially for my mother. Every trip Charlie made behind the driver's wheel was a scrape with death, and that was in the days when he was healthy.

During his later years when his faculties were failing him, he was an absolute menace on the road. Returning to Wood from Winner one night, my mother persisted in telling Charlie that he was driving on the left side of the road. "Gotdamit, Lena, I'm on the right side," he insisted. But when she finally talked him into stopping the car, he got out of the driver's seat and immediately fell into the ditch on the left side. Even during the 1930s when he was presumably alert, Charlie was still dangerous. He had built a garage next to the house for his cars. Because he consistently forgot to put on the brakes, he crashed through the garage wall so frequently that he ultimately installed thick, squat guard rail posts just in front of the wall to retard his forward progress.

During his seventy-fifth year, Charlie drove to his ranch south of Wood to make sure that his cattle had enough feed to last through a snowstorm that had been predicted. He had no hired man at that time, and had to feed them himself. Unfortunately the blizzard struck, stranding him on the farm. The storm was so severe that we could not get out of Wood to take supplies to him for a full week. When the weather finally cleared, my uncle John came down from White River to help. We drove as far south of Wood as we could make it in the deep snow, then we started out on foot. I was given the honor of carrying on my back a bulging gunny sack full of food for the two-mile trip to the ranchhouse. We fully expected to find Charlie frozen to death, but we were delighted by, although not quite prepared for, the sight of the defiant seventy-five year old who met us on our arrival. We found him sitting in the house, swearing a blue streak because the only food he had found in the house was a bag of flour. Charlie had tried to make biscuits, but his recipe caused them to take on the consistency of concrete. Because he had forgotten his false teeth in town, all week long he had been forced to suck on the biscuits to make them soft enough to swallow. When he saw that we had brought fresh food, he threw one of the biscuits against the wall where it left a permanent dent.

In 1947, I once again traveled in the summer to Beckley, West Virginia to stay with my sister Helen and her family. Suddenly things were changing there as well. The prosperity that Beckley had experienced over the years was beginning to wane. It was the center of the coal mining country, and coal was gradually being replaced as a heating fuel by natural gas, even by those in Beckley whose living was dependent on the mines. Whereas I couldn't see poverty right under my nose in South Dakota, I began to notice it in West Virginia. The most graphic experience for me was watching a blind coal miner play a guitar with a tin cup attached to the end as his wife guided him up and down the sidewalk on Beckley's main business street. It was one of those incidents that I never forgot. He moved slowly sideways, one step at a time, staring straight ahead with eyes that could not see, and singing "Just A Closer Walk With Thee." I knew nothing of the economics or the politics of poverty and hard luck, but my stomach churned at seeing someone humiliated into begging for a living. He turned out to be only the tip of the unemployment iceberg that was to envelop the coal fields in the years following the war.

But while I was just beginning to build a mental opposition to the mistreatment of vulnerable and weak people, I was still self-centered enough to be more concerned about finding my own place in the world.

2

My Life as a Sailor

I attended school in Wood from grade school through high school, with the exception of a semester in the tenth grade, when I felt like living in Mission, and the last half of my senior year, when I was expelled for tying a teacher to a radiator by the Wood superintendent and principal, Mr. Nibbelink. My parents, by now tired of my attention-getting escapades, decided to kick me out of the house. Homeless and without money, I hitchhiked to Mission and asked my brother Tom to take me in so that I could finish school. I was sixteen years old and could not, even with parental permission, join the navy. When I begged the principal in Mission, H. D. Redfern, to allow me to graduate, he agreed to do so, but warned me that even the slightest infraction would leave me without a high school diploma. I moved in with Tom and his wife, Twila, who had taken over the living quarters in the back part of the Mission store. I worked in the store every day after school and all day on Saturdays and also babysat for them in return for room and board and two dollars a week spending money.

Unlike Wood, Mission had dormitories to house the kids brought in from the far reaches of Todd County, and that was where I hung out in the evenings after the store closed. It was also where I learned how to fight; I should say that this was where I *should* have learned never to fight again.

One evening the crowd at the boys' dormitory was passing its time bullying one of the Zinema boys. The Zinemas were an unusually poor farm family, burdened not only with poverty, but also with a fat, eccentric, and aggressive mother whose looks and behavior drew mocking snickers behind her back wherever she went. Picking on the Zinemas seemed grossly unfair to me, and I shouted at them to stop. Then, to show my courage, I foolishly challenged the group of bullies to pick on me instead. They were happy to oblige, designating their toughest member, Harold Peed, to do the honors. I fought Harold out of desperation, wishing with every blow I took that he had not called my bluff. I ended up losing the fight, my right eye blackened, but in the process I managed to punish him some. The upshot of it all was that, while I was no great shakes as a fighter, neither the Zinemas nor I had any subsequent trouble. It turned out that no one was anxious to tangle with even a sure loser—one crazy enough to stand his ground, that is.

In the summer of 1945, I worked as a farmhand for Joe Assman on his land east of Mission. For one dollar a day plus room and board, I milked seven cows twice a day, drove a tractor with various machines attached to its rear end, and cooked most of the meals. Joe's brother and partner, Nick, had been drafted into the army, and because it was still wartime and hired help could not be found, we worked long hours to get all the work done.

I was physically short and stayed that way all through high school, but I went out for the basketball team in Wood anyway. In my second year, the Wood Bulldogs were scheduled to travel to Dallas (South Dakota) for a road game. The coach, Arnold Distad, who was also the school's superintendent and principal, announced that he could take only six players in his car. Because there were seven of us on the team that year, it meant choosing between Milo Koskan and me as the sixth man—or boy—to go on the road trip as the lone substitute. We drew straws and I won, traveling to Dallas with the first team.

Not very many minutes into the second quarter of the game, as we were losing badly to the Dallas team, Pitsy Jaros fouled out, prompting Coach Distad to push me out onto the floor to substitute for him. It was the big chance I'd been waiting for. I was going in to save the game. However, the most unusual thing happened, something I had never seen before. Immediately perceiving that I would probably make the game much less interesting, the Dallas coach looked me over and said, "Let the other guy stay in."

I did marginally better as a musician. Somehow, while I was still in grade school, old Mrs. Bridgeman, the music teacher, recruited me for the school band and I learned to play the drums. After playing for a time for the school, I joined a local dance band in 1943 called "Junior Bair and His Cubs," led by trumpet whiz Junior Bair, who was the depot agent's son. I wanted to be a musician, but I was also attracted to the possibility of being near Junior's sister, Jacqueline, who was, I thought, as beautiful as any young lady could be. But Jacqueline, who was the band's vocalist, somehow succeeded in totally ignoring me. Junior, in later years, achieved a measure of success as a semi-big-time band leader. I heard him one Saturday night on the radio, broadcasting from the rooftop of the Roosevelt Ballroom in New Orleans. By then he was calling the band "Buddy Bair and His Orchestra," specializing in a musical style reminiscent of Lawrence Welk's, complete with the sound of corks popping followed by the fizzing of champagne.

I played a few of the dances booked by Junior in the surrounding tri-county area, that is, until the return of his original drummer, Fuzzy Elsasser. Now a free agent, I was picked up to play a few dances by Jimmy Scull's band, which was based in White River, and in 1946, I played drums for Tom Kerns and his Tom Kats, a clarinet genius who played dances out of Winner. We worked mostly in small country dance halls in communities with names like Keyapaha. My musical career was short-lived however. I had been a Tom Kat for only a few months when Tom folded his band and moved to Yuma, Arizona.

The war ended, but that didn't stop Calvin Schaefer, who was two or three years older than I, from leaving Wood and joining the navy as soon as he was eligible. When he came home on leave he was full of stories about the plethora of women in California. "They love the uniform," he told the admiring gaggle of high school boys gathered around him. "It's just a matter of telling one of them that you want to go to bed, and it's done." Pointing at his sailor's uniform, he said, "You can't believe how easy it is to get this front flap open when the time comes."

My heart pounded at the thought of this West Coast Valhalla. I was unable to believe my good fortune at having discovered the secret of being a great lover. Boy-girl social life in Wood, for me at least, was nonexistent. Actually, that's understating it. It was more like an involuntary pledge of celibacy. There were not very many girls to begin with, and of those who lived there, not one showed an interest in me.

The day after I was given my high school diploma in Mission I went to see the navy recruiter. Because I was still only seventeen years old, all I had to do, he said, was to get my parent's written permission to enlist. My father, who was seventy-seven years old at the time, nearly broke his arm trying to sign the papers. I was happy to be gone, but not as happy as he was to have me gone.

Calvin Schaefer must have joined a different navy. I do not recall his mentioning twelve weeks of exhausting training in boot camp, of never having enough sleep, of constant close-order marching, of being ordered to do push-ups on boiling hot pavement in the peak of the San Diego summer, of trying to roll up, squeaky tight, every piece of clothing the navy issued me so that it could be either laid out with great precision on my bunk or packed into the seabag designed to hold the clothing. Or of having my head shaved, which I was sure would act as a deterrent to the potential oncoming rush of California girls.

With boot camp over and my hair growing out, I enrolled in Electricians' Mate School in San Diego, pushed my hat back on my head and swaggered into San Diego, anxious to introduce myself to all those women whom, I was convinced, had been waiting for my first shore leave. Nothing happened. There were no San Diego women interested in me, so I was reduced to attending, as frequently as my money allowed, the last remaining burlesque show in the world, which had the funniest comedians and the most beautiful women anywhere, although quite untouchable.

My luck with women never changed, at least not in San Diego. I finished electricians' training in January 1949, and shipped out to the navy's transient station on Yerba Buena Island in San Francisco Bay. From there I was ordered to Tokyo, Japan, to the APL 46, an old barracks boat tied up to the dock on Tokyo's Sumida River. I was transported on a Martin Mars flying boat from Alameda Air Station, near San Francisco, to Honolulu, and from there on a four-engine DC-6 propeller plane that island hopped the rest of the way across the Pacific.

Tokyo had not yet recovered from the B-29 raids that had nearly flattened it three and a half years earlier. Everywhere one looked there was the rubble of buildings destroyed by the relentless pounding of General Curtis LeMay's B-29 bombers. My own thoughts were more instantly focused on the hordes of women—petite, cute, friendly Japanese girls, my vision of what heaven should be like, who ultimately taught me, among other things, to speak a semi-fluent kind of Japanese.

The APL 46 was not a complicated ship, in fact it was not really a ship at all. It could not move on its own power and had to be towed from the United States to Japan after the war ended. It was connected to electricity from ashore, and so those of us in the "Black Gang"—sailors working below deck—had only to make certain that the hot water boilers were in repair. Beyond that, we changed light bulbs and watched as the Japanese civilian electricians repaired electric motors.

One of the responsibilities of Electricians' Mates on the APL was to run the 16-millimeter movie projectors at night in the mess hall. When I was assigned the job I was paid one dollar a night extra, a windfall, which, when added to the $52 the navy paid me each month, made me almost a rich man.

The APL's reason for existence was to provide a floating barracks for the staff of Admiral Berkey, the Commander of Naval Forces Far East, or COMNAVFE, as the official navy called him. However, the admiral himself was not required to bunk on the APL 46; he lived in a fine Japanese mansion expropriated for him in another part of Tokyo. Part of my job was to drive there once each week to make certain the five refrigerators in which he kept food and booze were operating properly.

The APL was commanded for a time by a naval aviator, a full lieutenant named Cutair, who routinely ordered the ship's company into a lineup in order to deliver a lecture on taking both life and the navy seriously. "You must recharge your moral batteries," was his favorite and oft-repeated challenge to us, an admonition better tried in theory than in practice, since I cannot recall even one sailor on the APL converting to Cutair's brand of Christianity during his tour. Everyone always listened politely, then went right back out to the same bars and bawdy houses against which Lieutenant Cutair sermonized.

I once asked to see him to tell him that I spoke a fair amount of Arabic, and would I not, therefore, be of better use to the navy if I were transferred to, say, Lebanon? His response was my first, but not my last, exposure to the strange ways of the U.S. military, where Ph.D.s are routinely assigned as truck drivers. The captain unflinchingly informed me that I was much more valuable to the navy right where I was.

Navy logic came to the fore one more time shortly after the

Korean War broke out in June 1950. I received the news that I was to be assigned as a movie operator on a small hospital ship, one of several the navy had activated to carry wounded soldiers from Korea to Taiwan. When I reported to the personnel officer to pick up my orders, he asked me where I had attended movie school. "I've never been to movie school," I confessed.

"What?" he shouted, in what I thought was a tremendous overreaction. "You can't take this transfer. It requires someone who's been to movie school!"

His tone was accusatory, even though I hadn't asked anyone for the transfer. Moreover, the fact that I'd been running movies for more than a year mattered not at all to him. Without certification the navy said I simply wasn't qualified. Then, as if to prove that the navy is capable of matching jobs with the qualifications of their men, I was immediately transferred to Yokohama as an electronics inspector with the Military Sea Transport Service (MSTS), actually a civilian organization created by the navy to transport men and equipment to the war in Korea. There have been a great many mysteries in my life; chief among them are the workings of those little lines and squiggles called electronics diagrams and the decision-making policies of the U.S. Navy. Nonetheless, I stayed in Japan a total of thirty-five months, spending a great deal of my non-working time in beer halls drinking green Japanese beer and fraternizing with the friendly ladies who frequented them.

Having demonstrated their perceptive powers in making my first Yokohama job assignment, the navy brass eventually decided that I should become the chief engineering officer at the MSTS boat pool, situated at the end of the city's outer breakwater. The boat pool provided small boats—LCMs, LCPLs, and ordinary whale boats—for the naval officers whose job it was to greet each MSTS ship entering Yokohama's port. Fortunately for the war effort, a former Japanese admiral who had commanded a fleet of five miniature subs during World War II, and who actually understood how to repair diesel engines, was assigned to work for me. His presence, of course, left me free to do whatever I pleased, such as learning how to run the boats in the boat pool.

A certain fatalism descended on everyone in Yokohama during the first weeks of the war. As we watched the North Koreans closing in on the Pusan perimeter before reinforcements could arrive, one old salt in our unit warned us that the Communists were certain to finish off Korea in short order, after which they would take Japan, then in one final blow, wipe out the United

States. We were fools, he said, for not canceling our life insurance policies so that we could spend the premiums on liquor. There would be, he assured me, no insurance companies in America left standing to pay off the policies. What he said had a certain insane logic to it, so I immediately canceled my National Service Life Insurance policy, enabling me to spend the monthly $3.15 premium on Japanese beer. After our side started winning, I had become so accustomed to the extra income that I failed to reinstate my insurance policy, convinced that drinking beer was the wisest course.

I finally saw my chance to be a war hero, and at least twice a month I volunteered for duty in Korea. I had heard about a program in which sailors could exchange places with GIs assigned to combat duty. Although my requests to go into combat were always refused, I continued to insist that I be sent to the front. But I stopped asking when winter came and I saw wounded infantrymen evacuated back to Japan with shrapnel fragments and bullet holes in their bodies, or with their feet amputated because of frostbite.

In February 1951, I learned from the Red Cross that my father had died. He was seventy-nine. When I realized that he was gone, it suddenly dawned on me that I had not really known him at all. I began a long struggle to get out of Japan on emergency leave. Those were the days before jetliners could make it across the Pacific in only a few hours, and travel by propeller plane took two or three days. I had very little money and the Red Cross refused to loan me any. So when I finally landed in the States, I began a series of hitchhiking, bus, and air trips that ultimately ended in a flight to Pierre, ninety miles from home, where my brother Tom and other family members met me. I had missed the funeral; the family, not knowing exactly when I would make it home, held it without me. After Charlie's condition of the last few months was described to me, I had no regrets about not getting there in time.

Cancer, combined with a worsening case of diabetes, made his final months and weeks abominably miserable. His doctor had ordered strict compliance with a severe diet, depriving him of all the food he loved. When Lena clamped down the refrigerator door in a desperate effort to keep him alive, he would leave the house and find someone to drive him the forty miles to Winner, where my sister Virginia lived. There he was able to eat what he wanted, returning to Wood only after he had eaten his fill and had begun to miss Lena. At the time of his death, cancer had wasted his 260-pound frame to under 90 pounds, not the way I wanted to remember him.

Charlie had braved Lebanese poverty, survived the American

frontier and the bitter South Dakota winters, and had withstood the economic disasters of the depression. To have someone of his physical strength and endurance struck down by this deadliest of diseases was a tragic ending to a most remarkable life. We get very few chances to remedy omissions in our own lives, which is why I have never lost the regret I felt then that I didn't spend even a fraction of the time with my father that I really should have. I was never mistreated by him, and although his advanced age prevented him from paying a lot of attention to me as a child, I loved him. I honestly thought that there would be plenty of time to see more of him. Like most other people, when I was young I believed very strongly in my own indestructibility and that both my father and I were immune to the erosion of time and age, until it was far too late to recapture the opportunity, lost and forever irrecoverable.

When Tom met me at the Pierre airport he had with him my uncle John and another uncle by marriage, Joe Nasser. I had never met Uncle Joe before, but I had heard plenty about him over the years from the family. He was a Catholic originally from a village in Northern Lebanon, and had married my father's sister, Mahiba.

Joe had owned a beer joint and pool hall in Winner in the 1930s, but he eventually moved to Omaha, Nebraska. Chick told me that he had once driven through Omaha with Uncle Joe, who pointed out one tall building after another, claiming that he had once owned them. Joe had a storied career as a hustler during his tenure in Winner. Legend had it that he would sweep the floor of his beer joint at night, then sprinkle the cigarette butts and other trash along the bar as soon as he opened up the next day to make it appear as if his early morning business was bustling. He always had a poker game going in the back room, and because he profited from the rake-off, he never stopped urging new players to join in the game. There is no letter "p" in the Arabic language, and, like most immigrants from the Arab world, he could not pronounce it. Joe gave away his immigrant status each time he tried to lure new poker players, when he would say, "Come on boys," to the kibitzers, "get in the game. We 'blay' loose."

After my father's funeral, I returned to Japan and stayed until December 1952, when I was sent back to San Diego, this time assigned to the *U.S.S. Skagit*, a slow-moving cargo ship that stayed fairly close to shore for most of the remaining six months of my enlistment. Although I had signed up for three years, my enlistment, like everyone else's, was extended for one year by President Truman because of the Korean War.

Aside from giving me a few years of supervision while I continued to grow up, I can say, without fear of contradiction, that the navy taught me little more than how to withstand the routine of military life. I also learned that I had no interest in subjecting myself to much more of it.

Ownership of my father's ranch fell to my mother after his death. It was a conglomeration of pieces of land that were located south of Wood and south of Mission. After my discharge from the navy, Lena wanted me to work the ranch, which I agreed to try to do. I began in the summer of 1952, but I found out within a short time that I couldn't stand the isolation. After a couple of months of cutting hay and taking care of the cattle herd, I told her I could no longer take it. I quit and moved back to town.

3

College

I first met Mary Ann Houlton in 1946 while working at her parent's farm. I did not see Mary again until I was home on leave from the navy in January 1952, but when I did, lightning struck. She had grown from a gangly teenager into a beautiful woman. I saw her at a community dance in Colome, a small town east of Winner, and asked her if I could take her home. She agreed, first giving the news to the fellow who had escorted her to the dance.

During that leave, and after my navy discharge in May, we saw a great deal of each other. In December 1952, we ran off—eloped is the word—to Pierre, South Dakota's capital. I asked my best friend, Vernon "Pits" Jaros, to stand up for me. He agreed, but on the condition that he be allowed to take with him as bridesmaid Betty Maas, a woman he was sweet on. During the ninety-mile drive from Winner to Pierre, I suggested to Pits and Betty that it would be quite extraordinary if they would join us in the ceremony, making it a double wedding. I was only joking, but I was stunned to hear them say that it was a splendid idea. To my everlasting surprise they had their blood tested and took the wedding vows with us. Clearly, they were a bit too impulsive. They filed for divorce only a few weeks later.

Mary bore our first son, whom we named Charlie, after my father. Our only daughter, Nikki, named after Ellery Queen's secretary, followed a year later. I had been reading Ellery Queen mysteries before her birth and was taken by what I then thought was an unusual name.

I began working a series of different jobs. At first, we lived for a time with my mother in Wood, then we moved to Winner, where I started work as a bartender in the Pheasant Bar. It seemed like the right thing to do, because I had been spending a lot of time sitting on the other side of the bar, contemplating my future.

I eventually moved from there to work at the Stockmans' Bar, just down the street. The clientele at the Stockmans' was a bit rougher than the Pheasant's, the job requiring nearly as much bouncing and breaking up fights as it did pouring drinks. In any of the bars in Winner, however, you couldn't remain a bartender for long if you refused the many offers to fight. You didn't always actually have to fight, but if you wanted to maintain your respectability you were expected to accept an offer to go outside. Fortunately, whoever was challenging had usually drunk too much, and in most cases simply accepting the offer to fight was enough to calm the aggressor. On occasion I was forced to go through with a fight. But most of the time work at the Stockmans' required only that the other bartender, Harold "Mutt" Berendes, and I go over the top of the bar to stop disputes between customers. I learned a lot about street fighters during those years, mainly that anyone who really was tough never started a fight because he had no need to prove anything. It was only the semi-toughs who felt the need for aggressive behavior.

There were enough unusual characters in Winner to populate at least one John Steinbeck novel, most of them to be found in Winner's four bars. For a time an itinerant hay baler named Ray Pennico terrorized the patrons of the Stockmans' Bar, taking on anyone who accepted his offer to fight. He made the near-fatal mistake of challenging Paul Cavanaugh one night. Cavanaugh was an easygoing Irishman whose favorite pastime was drinking and laughing at both his own jokes and others'. But he was also probably the best street fighter in Winner, if not in the entire Rosebud. When he and Pennico—accompanied by all the Stockmans' clientele—went outside to settle their differences, Cavanaugh hit Pennico, knocking him down. Pennico's wife, who always accompanied him during his search-and-destroy missions, happened to be standing behind him when he was leveled by Cavanaugh. The result was that Pennico landed on his back on top of his wife. The irate Cavanaugh leapt on top of Pennico and began using his head as a punching bag. After delivering a few blows to Pennico's jaw, Cavanaugh shouted, "Have you had enough, you sonofabitch?

"We never have enough," Pennico's wife screamed defiantly, from beneath her battered husband. Cavanaugh's state of mind prevented him from realizing that it was Pennico's wife who wanted to keep fighting, so he obliged by delivering additional blows until someone advised him that Pennico was unconscious.

Winner also boasted a local sign painter whom I will call Red Comeaux. Red was a veteran of World War II who had seen too much action, and who, upon his return to Winner, began swilling great amounts of liquor to forget the trauma of his combat duty. On the rare occasions when he was sober his hands shook enough to prevent him from painting a straight line, so his bouts of sobriety became fewer and fewer.

Red took up with an Indian woman whom I will call Samantha White Buffalo. During a drinking bout one day in the Pheasant Bar, Red and Samantha decided to get married. They asked Wilbur Smith, a gigantic farmer who had come to town that day wearing greasy bib overalls, to stand up for them as their best man. With a staggering Wilbur Smith in tow, they made their way up the street to the Philips Hotel, there to find Paul Goodwin, who was both the hotel's owner and the justice of the peace. Lurching into the lobby, Red and his coterie told Goodwin, who was sitting behind the reception desk, that they would like him to perform a wedding ceremony.

"So you finally decided to do it, huh Red?" Paul commented, trying hard to be friendly.

"Well, we already done it, Paul," Red responded with great honesty, "now we want to get married."

Mutt Berendes' brother Glen was half owner of the Stockmans' Bar. His partner was a little fellow appropriately named "Shorty" Billings, who had an intense dislike for Mutt. One snowy cold December night in 1953, when Glen was out of town, Shorty decided to fire Mutt. I became immediately indignant, telling Shorty that he couldn't do that to a friend of mine. I took off my white apron and threw it at him as I stomped out of the bar. In my anger I had forgotten that I was supporting a wife and two constantly hungry kids, and that it was mid-winter in South Dakota. There was, I soon discovered, no work to be had in Winner at that time of the year. When I couldn't find a job, I traveled for a time with Glen Berendes, selling "carbonic dispensers," at that time an innovation for bars that used carbonated mixes in highballs. I was eventually saved from starvation by a job offer from Earl Dodson and Mark Wingerd, who had sold the Pheasant Bar and bought the much bigger Peacock Bar up the street.

The town of Winner had gained its name from an election decades earlier to determine where the county seat of Tripp County would be. The county's voters had to choose between Lamro, a settlement a few miles to the west, and the yet unnamed area that won the election, hence the name "Winner." Over the years drinking became one of Winner's major pastimes, resulting, I suppose, from the lack of other diversions, though in the 1930s, '40s, and '50s it was a center for pheasant hunters who came in from all parts of the United States. Apparently Clark Gable had stayed in Winner during one pheasant season, giving the town a reputation happily accepted by the chamber of commerce.

Because of the annual influx of pheasant hunters, setting up a gambling enterprise—illegally—in some of the bars seemed like a highly profitable idea to the bar owners. Winner had been running high stakes poker games since the 1930s, resulting in the creation of a gambling class whose locus was Winner, with offshoots reaching out to Wood, Mission, White River, and other points. The continuing hard times of the 1930s provided few other options for honest work, making gambling, both honest and dishonest, one of the few methods of economic survival.

One of the great gambling legends in Winner was a fellow named Stein Standish, a card mechanic of the first order, who had a reputation for hustling anyone willing to become his victim. Playing poker one night in the late 1930s, Stein took a farmer for all his money. Because it was so late when the game ended, the farmer commented that he could not drive home that night, but would have to sleep in his truck until morning. Ever hospitable, Stein invited the farmer to spend the night in his home, a small, crude cabin at the edge of Winner. The farmer watched with great interest as Stein, also tired, undressed in preparation for bed, absentmindedly exposing the holdout machine that he was wearing under his jacket. A holdout machine, at least for a right-handed card mechanic, consists of a string running from the knee to the left arm, with a hidden card held by a clip that opens when the string is pulled taut by the action of the left leg. When the card of the player's choice is deposited into the palm of the gambler's hand, it generally converts what could be a losing hand into an assured winning hand.

Upon seeing the machine attached to Stein, the farmer asked, "What's that?"

Without hesitation Stein replied, "It's a truss. I've got a rupture, you know." The farmer said, "Oh," and went off to sleep, waking the next morning to watch Stein again putting on the strange looking truss for the new day's work.

When Winner's businessmen decided to support a semi-pro baseball team in the 1950s, the project was financed by "smokers," poker games to which everyone was invited, with the house rake-off used to hire college baseball players. The smokers were held in the city auditorium, the only place large enough to contain the fifteen or twenty poker games going on at the same time. I had neither the money nor the card playing skill to participate in the smokers, and so I worked as a house man, raking off a percentage of each pot for the cause of semi-pro baseball. Occasionally the games were invaded by road agents—sometimes called "crossroaders"—professional card cheats who traveled from town to town looking for easy marks.

These unfortunate men were usually unaware that Winner was home to some of the finest card players in America. I saw two crossroaders sit down at the same table one night in 1954, proceeding, against the odds, to deal each other consistently winning hands. The game was attracting a lot of attention from the kibitzers who were gathered around the table. Then two of the hometown gamblers at that table gave up their seats to my brother Chick and Mark Wingerd, who wasted no time in reversing the flow of winning cards. It soon became obvious to the crossroaders that they were outclassed. After losing several hands in a row, they politely excused themselves from the game and left town, never to return.

Chick learned to play poker soon after he arrived from Lebanon at the age of eight. Some of the cardsharks in Wood discovered that Chick, by the time he became a teenager, had access to the cash register in the family store. Their plan was to open a continuous flow of money from Charlie's cash register via Chick to them by getting someone they thought was a "dumb immigrant kid" hooked on poker. What they didn't bargain for was Chick's quickness. After initially learning by losing to them, Chick advanced his card knowledge far beyond those who sought to teach him. During the 1930s he teamed up with a crossroader named Chump Willingham, and the two of them spent the depression traveling throughout the Midwest looking for poker games to hustle.

Gambling in Winner's bars eventually advanced over the years from serious poker games to the addition of crap and twenty-one tables. By the 1970s the Pheasant Bar was one of the more popular spots, its back room usually bustling with gamblers until dawn. One had to say that, whatever else, its owner, Wally Laudenslager, was meticulous about obeying the liquor laws. While the lights were blazing and the chips were flying in the back room, anyone who wanted a drink after the legal closing time of 1:00 A.M. was told, with a straight face, that state law required the bar to shut down at one in the morning.

Gambling in Winner came to an end one night in 1979, when South Dakota's Attorney General Mark Meierhenry, accompanied by State Treasurer David Volk, both good Republicans, took to drinking in the Pheasant, then to gambling in the back room. It was during pheasant hunting season, when out-of-state hunters flooded the illicit gambling halls. The *Sioux Falls Argus Leader*, South Dakota's biggest city newspaper, had sent a reporter to Winner to investigate reports of illegal gambling and to write a story about its presence there. It was a journalist's dream catching two high officeholders breaking the law. When the reporter walked in, Meierhenry and Volk recognized him, and took him off to the side to convince him that they, too, were checking out Winner's sinful reputation. To prove his point, Attorney General Meierhenry walked back into the room where the tables were raking in money at flank speed and announced that he was closing down the operation. The trouble was, no one recognized him.

Believing Meierhenry to be only a loudmouthed troublemaker, the gamblers shouted at him to get lost. "Who in the hell are you?" one asked. A couple of customers, weighted down with drink, offered to fight South Dakota's chief law enforcement officer, but Wally quickly calmed them down, telling Meierhenry that he, the owner, would close the place on his own, and that Meierhenry should leave before he caused more trouble.

Meierhenry's ploy ultimately failed, however. Nobody believed his story that he was on duty that night, and public pressure eventually forced him to confess his guilt and to pay a hundred dollar fine to the local authorities. But Wally Laudenslager, a life-long loyal Republican and former state heavyweight boxing champion, never forgave him for causing the permanent closure of gambling in Winner. Wally lost interest in Republican party politics, even voting for a Democrat once or twice after that.

When I lived in Winner, my children, like most during their early years, became magnets for all strains of bacteria and viruses. We chose as our family doctor, Joseph Studenberg, a native of Cincinatti, Ohio, who came west bringing his radical East Coast ways to the Rosebud. Dr. Studenberg was given to chain-smoking and pacing the floor for twenty or so hours each day—and talking the kind of liberal politics not at all acceptable in Winner. When I first brought my howling children to his office for treatment, he introduced himself by asking, over their screaming, what the hell a smart guy like me was doing tending bar. I was unable to give anything but the obvious answer, "Because that's what I do." He must have seen in me a convert. He began handing me strange reading materials, such as I.F. Stone's Weekly, The Nation, and The New Republic (thank God long before Martin Peretz bought it and made it the in-house journal for the Israeli lobby).

For the next three years, we sat together in his house, as his wife, Lorraine, cooked meals, he talked, and I listened and learned about politics. Dr. Studenberg had prints of Albert Einstein, Sigmund Freud, and Jesus Christ hanging on his office wall, to which at least once each week he would point and ask, "Isn't it amazing that the three most brilliant men in the history of the world were all Jews?"

It's hard for me to describe the awakening I experienced during those years. So anxious was I to escape the narrow confines of my world in Winner that I soaked up every bit of knowledge Studenberg dished out and more. I began reading everything I could get my hands on. The erudite and curious Studenberg, who, during his lifetime, had thoroughly explored every facet of American society, was force-feeding me with the intellectual nourishment that he had stored up over the years. We read and discussed Philip Wylie, Fred Hoyle, and Aldous Huxley, among other writers. We cursed Senators Joseph McCarthy and Karl Mundt, and, of course, Richard Nixon, who was the arch criminal of those times as well. We listened with great joy to the pro-labor and anti-McCarthy songs of Joe Glazer, and over and over again we played a recording of the Canadian Broadcasting Corporation's program, "The Investigator." "The Investigator" was an expertly done radio show, an allegory, detailing the fictional death of a U.S. senator, obviously Joe McCarthy, in a plane crash. He went to heaven, wormed his way onto an investigating committee that gave him the license to accuse everyone in heaven of subversion. When he tried to call God before his committee for questioning, he was stripped of his power and sent back to Earth.

From Dr. Studenberg I not only learned about politics—the right kind—but about other matters of importance as well, such as public service. He charged no more than two dollars for an office call, cheap even in the 1950s. He often charged no more when he made an occasional house call. When the Salk polio vaccine first became available for mass inoculation, the Rosebud Medical Society—all the doctors in the area—held a meeting to determine how much to charge patients for the immunization series. All of the doctors agreed on a charge of five dollars per person until Studenberg stood up and said, "Charge what you like, but my charge will be a dollar." That did it. Although the medical society had seen an opportunity to make a lot of quick bucks, they didn't dare exceed Studenberg's charge. In his view, given the dangers of polio, the vaccine was an absolute necessity, not a luxury. To him, gouging low-income patients for an essential vaccine would have been unconscionable.

Dr. Studenberg died of a heart attack in 1967 while I was in West Virginia attending my brother-in-law's funeral. I was unable to get back to Winner to bury someone who was my closest friend as well as my teacher. Sadly, he was not around to witness my entry into politics.

During my first year in the Senate in 1973, the notorious journalist, I. F. Stone, came to the Hill to have lunch with me. "So, Abourezk," he asked, "how did you get to be such a liberal?" I told him about Dr. Studenberg, emphasizing how frequently I had read *I.F. Stone's Weekly*, which prompted Stone to respond, "Is that right? What was his name again? I'll go look it up in my records. You see, I only had one or two subscribers in South Dakota."

Mary and I struggled to make a living. My salary as a bartender ranged from $60 a week to as high as $70. When I worked in the Pheasant Bar I also sold Mason shoes out of a catalog to my bar customers. I tried selling cars for a Ford dealer for a while, but failed to make any money. Although I rode on a hot streak for a time, selling a great number of new cars very quickly, I learned that the sales manager had lied about how much commission I was to be paid. So I quit and returned to tending bar.

In 1956, I worked for a year traveling as a wholesale grocery salesman for the Ulry-Talbert Co., headquartered in Grand Island,

Nebraska. My salary was $50 a week, plus commissions to be paid on sales over a certain dollar figure, which I don't recall ever reaching. My vision was still pretty much limited to my immediate surroundings—Wood, Winner, Mission, and some of the other small towns on the salesman's route that I traveled with increasing monotony each week. Suddenly, my brother Tom, who was one of my customers, suggested that if I would pick out a college and apply for admission, he, my brother Chick, and my mother would chip in to foot the bill.

I was then twenty-six years old, with a wife and two children, and imbued with a feeling that I didn't have too long in which to achieve all my ill-defined objectives. I was desperately frightened that I would not have enough years to do everything I wanted to do, the most obvious of which, at the time, was to provide for my family, and to stop jumping from one lousy job to another. I sensed that there was a new world out there somewhere and I needed to find a way to become part of it.

It was 1957, and there was a great deal of interstate highway construction underway around the country. So, I reasoned, why waste time on anything but an engineering degree? Certainly I would never be out of a job as long as construction projects were being funded. I settled on engineering as the quickest ticket out of town, although I had no idea what the work would be, whether I would take to it, or even whether I could understand it well enough to be competent. Liberal arts I eliminated as not offering a decent living. A couple of years earlier I had bought a correspondence course in law from the La Salle Correspondence School of Law in Chicago. I paid for it, but, even though I finished a couple of lessons, I never understood it. Consequently aiming for a law degree seemed too remote and would, I thought, take too long. Instead I went straight to Rapid City to enter the South Dakota School of Mines & Technology and began a four-year struggle to complete what were for me the immensely difficult courses required for a degree in civil engineering.

I lacked a working knowledge of mathematics and took a required noncredit course in algebra the first year at the School of Mines. Even this failed to relieve the great difficulty I had with any course requiring a facility in math, which, unfortunately, included pretty much all of the courses offered during the four-year degree. My interest in studying law was rekindled by a retired lawyer, Alex Patterson, an old Chicago lawyer who taught contract law at the School of Mines, and whose stories about practicing law thoroughly fascinated me. I also found a home in the liberal arts curriculum, principally inspired by Professors Rena and Kelvin Van Nuys, and Professor Bill Raff, who, when he taught his course on American literature, told the class how much he envied our being able to read all those wonderful books for the first time.

The School of Mines was a natural breeding ground for conservative politics. The majority of the faculty were engineers who upheld the social status quo. The alumni were largely successful engineers and members of other professions who saw no need to change the country's methods of doing business. The most celebrated alumnus in those days was Homer Surbeck, who had gone on to be a Wall Street lawyer. He was known for his financial contributions to the school and for his reactionary politics, which he clearly enunciated in the articles that he wrote for the alumni magazine. We were, in fact, "Homer Surbecked" to death during the four years I spent there.

I organized a college Young Democrats group and kept it going until I graduated. I also used what little spare time I had to do "grunt" work for the Pennington County Democratic Party. I issued press releases to the wire services, wrote letters to the editor challenging the newspaper's Republican bias and South Dakota's one-party rule, and ran local campaigns. Being a Democrat in an overwhelmingly Republican state had the disadvantage of making me an automatic underdog, but it was a role that I relished. Because the Democrats had nowhere to go but up, I was free to experiment with techniques for winning elections. I became permanently hooked on politics

Of no additional help to my studies was the job I took at night as a bartender in the Rapid City American Legion Club. Things were happening in Rapid City back then that brought people into the bars in great numbers. There was a Strategic Air Command base ten miles east of Rapid City—Ellsworth Air Force Base—and the beginning of a great deal of construction of missile silos around the base that would house Atlas ICBMs. Most of the hard drinkers at Ellsworth AFB and at the missile site poured into the Legion club every night. For a salary of two dollars an hour, I poured drinks as fast as I could, and several times a night another bartender and I had to leap over the top of the small horseshoe bar to separate aspiring fighters. As Yogi Berra once said, it looked like "*déjà vu* all over again." I knew that I was fighting a losing battle. There were more of them than there were of us, and they believed that fighting was the only proper form of entertainment.

My most effective tactic for stopping fights was to immobilize a contestant by grabbing him from behind, gripping his biceps and pinning his arms to his sides. I could then either talk him into calming down, or, if he wasn't too tough, throw him down the flight of twenty or so stairs that led to the front door. Once I grabbed a musclebound fighter and the club's manager, Del O'Daniel, a short, brave Irishman, seemingly negligent of his own safety, reached over my shoulder to hit the tough repeatedly with a blackjack—a weapon that I never used, nor wanted to. I had had him under control before Del came along, but Del's clubbing increased the fellow's strength and anger to the point that I worried about what would happen after I released him. "Who's hitting me with that fucking beer bottle?" he shouted. Then he turned his head partly around and said to me, "Turn me loose, or I'll kill you when I do get loose." I suddenly lost my commitment to peacemaking, and seeing no reason to continue holding him I said, "Whatever you say." I released my grip and prepared to undertake the fight of my life. Fortunately he ignored me, choosing instead to look around to find whoever had been clubbing him, but Del had wisely decided that it was time to get back to work and was nowhere to be seen.

I eventually became adept at avoiding fights. One of the first things I had done when I arrived in Japan in 1949 was to take judo classes at Tokyo's Kodokan Judo University, and though I never became too proficient at the art, it turned out to be a valuable aid in more than one way. Judo is a technique that allows one to defend oneself. Beyond that it is a fine sport that teaches civilized values. When I studied in Japan under Mr. Ishikawa, then the world champion, we were taught never to use the sport to harm anyone. One of the tenets of judo is to initially give way to an opponent's aggressive attack, then to use his inertia to defeat him. Knowledge of it allowed me to avoid being punched out by street fighters, permitted me to throw them out of bars when necessary, and enabled me to refuse fights when I wanted to.

I had spent part of my time when I was stationed in Yokohama— insanely, now that I look back on it—duking it out with various members of the military services who were also street fighters. But as I grew older it seemed so unprofitable, that I swore off fighting, except in self-defense. On one or two occasions, while drinking beer in a working-class bar in Rapid City, I was invited outside by one of the customers for a one-on-one fight. I would give my stock answer: "I'd love to, but you know, I'm a judo black belt and my hands are registered with the police." I wasn't, and they weren't, but it always worked like a charm. One such challenger, impressed with my phony credentials, even offered to buy me a beer.

My limited knowledge of judo also helped finance my schooling. I began teaching the sport at the School of Mines, charging a dollar a lesson per student and also selling judo uniforms at a profit of about four dollars each. I teamed up with a sergeant at Ellsworth Air Force Base, Ted Pozdzioch, a 275-pound Polish giant who actually had earned a third degree black belt.

To promote our judo classes, I arranged to have Ted appear on KOTA-TV to demonstrate his ability to break boards with his bare hands, a skill that is actually a part of karate. It was early in the evening and everyone at the American Legion Club gathered around the television to watch Ted do his stuff. Whether he was hung over, or whether the boards were reinforced with metal, no one knew, but after five minutes of Ted's unsuccessful hammering—a television eternity—the host of the show announced that, although he was sure Ted could break the boards, now he had to cut away for the commercial.

Mary, the kids, and I lived in a campus veterans' housing unit, a tiny two-bedroom apartment for which we paid $35 a month rent. It was one of the most enjoyable times of my life, although the routine never allowed for enough sleep. I attended classes and labs all day beginning at eight in the morning, ate a quick dinner at five or so in the afternoon, then went to work in the Legion club until 1:30 A.M., studied at home for three or four hours, slept two or three hours, then returned to the School of Mines where I dozed through the first two morning classes. The walls in the campus apartment were so thin that while studying in the middle of the night I could hear the neighbors next door making love. It became so distracting that I exchanged bedrooms with the kids.

I spent summers during those college years working at whatever job I could find. I worked nights in the American Legion Club the first summer I spent in Rapid City, but in the daytime I landed a job with the Brezina Construction Company building a Catholic school. During the second summer I worked days as a laborer, carrying boxes and choking on cardboard dust in the Kraft cheese warehouse, and again I worked nights at the Legion club. Because the pay was so low, and although I was getting some help from my family, there was never enough money to keep food in the house, even with two jobs, so I routinely sold my blood to the blood bank for a price that was somewhere around $12 a pint.

On the recommendation of Bob Dardis, a friend who was the head bartender at the newly opened Gay Lady Bar and Restaurant in Rockerville, I was hired in the summer of 1960 as a bartender by the club's owner, Tex Fletcher. Tex came to Rapid City the summer before my last year at the School of Mines, opening the night club in nearby Rockerville, an old gold mining town that had been restored by Terry McCullen for the purpose of fleecing Black Hills tourists on their way to Mount Rushmore.

When you meet someone with a name like "Tex," your first assumption is that he's a WASP from Texas. That's what I assumed, but I was wrong. Tex Fletcher turned out to be an Italian who was born and raised in New York City Hell's Kitchen. His story was that his family was so poor that he left Manhattan at the height of the 1930s depression and hitchhiked west, somehow landing in Harding County, South Dakota, in the extreme northwest corner of the state. Tex worked on a ranch for a time. Then, discovering a previously hidden talent for music, he learned to play the guitar left-handed and upside down. He also began writing cowboy songs, ultimately over two hundred of them. They were not country western and bluegrass mind you, but genuine cowboy songs about real cowboys who had lost their cows and horses.

When he was younger, Tex looked an awful lot like Victor Mature. He eventually began traveling the Western rodeo circuit, playing music well enough to be noticed by a newly opened Hollywood film studio, Grand National Studios. Grand National hired Tex and scheduled him to star in six cowboy movies, but he made only one film before the studio went bankrupt—a clinker named *Six Gun Rhythm*. World War II broke out at about the same time Grand National Studios went bellyup, taking Tex from Hollywood to the U.S. Army. He did a children's show on ABC television for a time after the war, among other show business gigs, and then decided to move to Rapid City to open The Gay Lady.

When he opened The Gay Lady in 1960, Tex hung all of the memorabilia from his film days on its unfinished wood walls—publicity stills from *Six Gun Rhythm*, records he had cut, and a pair of shiny pearl-handled forty-five Colt pistols that he said John Wayne had given him as a gift after the filming of *Stagecoach*. Also hanging on the wall near the bar was a well-worn, moth-eaten stuffed moose head with a small red light bulb shining out of the socket of its left eye.

One busy Saturday night we both had a chance to perform, using the shiny chrome, pearl-handled John Wayne pistols that hung behind the bar. A customer with too much to drink began bullying those around him, and Tex, although by now too old to fight, ordered him out of the bar. The tough guy said, as his type usually did, "Come and get me." Tex turned to me—I was still behind the bar—and shouted, "Give me those guns."

Now, the guns had no bullets and the firing pins had been removed, probably by the Duke himself. In any event, I thought it would be nice to add a little drama to the scene, so I shouted with great emotion in my voice, "No, Tex, you don't want a murder rap against you."

"Goddamit, I said give me those guns." Tex was a menacing figure, reminiscent of his publicity stills from *Six Gun Rhythm*.

"All right, but for God's sake, don't shoot him," I pleaded, thrusting both pistols at him, handles first, as though we were in the movies. But the last part of our act was unnecessary, because the tough was just then shifting into high gear on his way out of the The Gay Lady's swinging doors.

The American Legion Club offered opportunities for advancement as well. In my last year in college I moved up from bartender to twenty-one dealer. Although gambling was illegal in South Dakota, the Legion club, presumably because it had status as a civic organization, was never raided. I not only was paid better as a twenty-one dealer, but the work was easier, meaning I no longer had to break up fights, at least not on weekends when I was dealing. One of the municipal court judges was a regular customer, and my sense of public relations, and of survival, told me that when the judge played at my table, he should not be charged for chips when he lost, which was frequently.

Not content with the heavy odds in favor of the house, one of my bosses, whom I will call Errol Flynn, consistently cheated twenty-one players when he was dealing. He was, at best, a crude cheat, bending the corners of certain cards so that he could deal seconds to the customers when he saw that the top card would give them a good hand. Errol temporarily relieved me one night, and when I returned to my table to resume dealing I saw that he had bent the deck nearly out of shape. I had intended to deal one more hand with it, then bring in a new deck, but that plan was aborted when one of the players, a huge missile construction worker, shouted, "This deck is marked!"

It's hard for me to describe my feelings. I had never cheated anyone in my life, and never wanted to, but I was about to get the blame for someone else's hustle. But Errol, who was still standing at the table after relinquishing the deck, calmly stepped over, grabbed the questionable hand, and said, with great authority, "Let me see those cards."

The construction worker, now thinking he had an ally in Errol, said, "Do you see the diamonds on the back of this card? One of them is larger than the other."

A wave of relief spread over me. There was, of course, nothing wrong with the diamonds on the back of the deck, and the fellow had totally missed Errol's crudely bent corners. Errol, continuing with his magnificent act, then said, "I'm confiscating this entire deck to investigate it, and if I find that anyone has been cheating, there'll be hell to pay." Then he looked around at all the players and asked, angrily, "Did any of you have anything to do with this?" Everyone was immediately defensive. His performance was so convincing that even the construction worker held up his hands and said, "Not me."

In 1961, the only job that was offered to me as I prepared to graduate with a civil engineering degree was with the State of California's Division of Bay Toll Crossings in San Francisco. I accepted and we moved to the San Francisco Bay Area, settling first in Pinole, then later moving to Mill Valley, in Marin County. Although the city was beautiful, the job was unpleasant and undesirable. No engineering work needed to be done while I was there, and I was working for the most difficult boss in the entire state. I had been assigned to work on the initial stages of construction of a new Hayward–San Mateo Bridge, designed to replace an old bridge that connected both sides of San Francisco Bay. The design was completed by the time that I reported for work in the summer of 1961, and the only real work remaining for civil engineers was what was called construction inspection. I spent the first few weeks standing out on the "mole fill," the massive mound of dirt being dumped into San Francisco Bay into which the pilings would be placed when the bridge was completed. My job was to collect load tickets from each truck driver as he drove onto the fill to dump a load of dirt. Never having worked as an engineer before, I restrained myself from complaining aloud, but wondered if this was the proper and customary way to exploit the four hard years of engineering school that I had just completed. Somehow, my fantasy of an engineering career did not include collecting load tickets from truck drivers.

To make it even more unbearable, the supervisor, Mike Uhl, was perhaps the most small-minded, wretched person I had ever met.

He was inefficient even at assigning nonsense work designed to make us look busy. When not collecting dirt tickets, we ran redundant transit surveys on the old bridge nearly every day, wearing down what little patience I had left. One day, unable to abide it any longer, I challenged Uhl over one of his petty outbursts. He was, it appeared, quite surprised that someone would refute his illogic, but rather than argue with me, he walked away. I couldn't leave well enough alone, so I followed him, continuing my harangue, which amounted to a circuitous way of saying, in the words of the immortal country western song, "Take this job and shove it." The result of the confrontation did not become evident for another two weeks. Earlier in the summer, I had asked and received permission from Uhl to attend night law school at the University of San Francisco. But after challenging him, I suddenly found myself assigned to a night job. Forced to quit law school, I immediately asked to be reassigned to the California Division of Highways. I worked for a few months in its planning department, but quit in the summer of 1962, returning to Rapid City.

Vic Bay called me from Vernal, Utah, where he was working in the oil fields as a roustabout. The parents of his wife, Butch, lived in Vernal. Vic and Butch at one time owned Vic Bay's Salad Bowl Cafe in Winner, where we first met and became fast friends. Vic, who was originally named Vic Tabacco, was from Rochester, New York, where he spent his late teens and early twenties working as an apprentice for a race track tout, and for a time, in a Howard Johnson's restaurant.

Vic and Butch had landed in Winner by accident, or by stroke of fate, depending on one's point of view. He was training race horses on the Midwest low-rent race circuit, and just as they reached Winner, Vic was ruled off the track for some sort of infraction. To survive, he took a job tending bar, and Butch worked as a waitress. They took their meals in Winner's "finest" restaurants. Restaurant food, which had never before bothered anyone in Winner, due primarily to the lack of comparison, was not at all to their taste. They borrowed money and opened Vic Bay's Salad Bowl Cafe, which was for Winner a humdinger of a steak house, offering food the likes of which the locals had never before tasted.

Winner's restaurants traditionally provided a bottle of Kraft Salad Dressing for the customers' salads. But Vic made his own assortment of salad dressings from scratch, sweeping the Winner gourmet crowd off its collective feet. His salad dressing was tasty enough to entice several local investors into what became Vic's further venture into capitalism—manufacturing Vic Bay's Salad Dressing.

While the stuff he bottled was good, something went wrong with the marketing and the company went bankrupt, taking Vic's local popularity right along with it. He and Butch eventually sold out and left town. But by the time he called me from Vernal, Utah, he was anxious to get back into business, and so we agreed to quit our respective jobs and meet in Rapid City to make our fortune.

There was a problem, one we didn't think about until after we had burned our bridges and landed in Rapid City: we had no money. I took a job with the Peter Kiewit Construction Company as a construction engineer, building Minutemen missile silos, and Vic began work as a butcher in a small meat packing plant. I bought a trailer house on time—some people call them mobile homes—and worked for Kiewit until December 15, 1962, when Tom Wilson, the assistant project manager, fired me, a Christmas gift that I will always remember.

On the day that I was fired I went back to the trailer to discuss with Mary the possibility of my trying to get into the University of South Dakota's law school in January. Before I could make any inquiries in that direction, my brother Tom called me from Mission to ask if I would be interested in working in the Mission store. It seems that he and Chick wanted to open a couple of other businesses, and they thought that I could learn how to manage the place for them. Tom offered me one-third ownership in the Mission store as compensation. My response was, what the hell, why not? I'd think about law school another day. Besides, I had no other work and I needed a job.

I had the trailer pulled to Mission, but I was unable to find an empty trailer hookup in town. About eight miles west of Mission, very near the Indian agency town of Rosebud, a rancher by the name of Bill Meyer had a number of hookups, left over from a once busy construction project nearby. I hooked ours up, but our trailer sat alone on the Todd County Prairie, unbanked, and, as a result, bitterly cold. (An unbanked trailer, meaning one without bales of hay or other protection from the wind around its base, is even colder than a banked one, which is plenty cold enough.) A school bus passed by the trailer court each weekday morning and took Charlie and Nikki to the school in Mission. Paul was two years old and of course stayed home with Mary. I went to work, learning to manage the store, which by now was a major business operation, vastly expanded from the time my father ran it.

The weather grew colder and the wind blew stronger as the winter of 1963 set in. One bitter night in January, when the temperature reached 38 degrees below zero, both the trailer's water and sewer lines froze, and to give double emphasis to what I saw as a warning of things to come, the electrical power went out. The trailer used a forced air heating furnace fueled by propane gas, which was stored in a tank outside. One can never begin to understand the flimsy, vulnerable character of mobile homes without this kind of wintertime experience. It quickly grew very cold inside. We turned on the propane gas oven, left its door open, and all of us huddled around the stove, bundled up, trying our best to stay warm through the night by soaking up what amounted to a baby's breath of heat. The next morning I went to a phone and called a trucking company that specialized in moving trailer houses, found a newly empty hookup in Mission, and moved as quickly as I could.

It was not long before Tom and I began arguing about how to run the store. Although I was presumably the manager, Tom objected to my wanting to experiment with new ways to sell groceries. He had been so successful in the store that I can now understand why he was reluctant to change the operation, although I couldn't see it then. My biggest mistake was not realizing how expert he was in running the business. So in 1963, when spring came, I resigned and, at Chick's invitation, pulled my trailer home and my family to Hot Springs to work in the Evans' Plunge, another of the partnership businesses that Chick was managing.

As fall approached, I worried that there would be no work in Hot Springs after the tourist season ended, so I once again pulled up stakes and moved the trailer to Rapid City, where I was certain there would be year-round work. What I hadn't counted on was the severity of the economic recession that had hit Western South Dakota that year. There were no jobs for engineers, so I looked for a position as an engineering draftsman. There were none. Then I applied for a bartender's job, but the bar owner, who knew me, said that I was too highly educated and not apt to stay around too long.

Getting more desperate for work, I answered an ad for construction laborers—the pay was $1.50 an hour—on the new interstate highway twenty miles east of Rapid City. I was told to report to the job the day after Labor Day, which I did. It had rained the night before, and the construction foreman, ignoring the four or five new laborers with whom I was waiting, paced up and down in front of us, stroking his chin. Finally I shouted, "Hey, are you going to put us to work or not?"

"Come back out tomorrow," the foreman said, "I think it's rained too much for you to do anything," although it was obvious that the rain had not stopped his regular crew from working.

I was livid. No money and no work had made me cranky. "What do you mean, come back out tomorrow?' It's twenty miles each way." I looked at the others and said, "Come on. Let's all walk off this goddamn job."

I'll never forget the look on their faces. They stared sheepishly at me, then at the ground. I hadn't realized until that moment that times were so tough and work so scarce that the men were afraid of losing a $1.50-an-hour job.

I walked away, cursing the foreman, and drove back to Rapid City. I stopped to complain to Vic Bay at the packing plant, and, on an impulse, asked to use the phone in his office. I called the dean of the University of South Dakota law school, John Scarlett, and asked him if it was too late to be admitted. Although I was unknown to him, he asked if I could quickly send my college grades to him. I called the School of Mines and asked them to forward my transcript. On the next day, Wednesday, I called Dean Scarlett again, who told me that my grades had arrived. "Can I be admitted?" I asked.

"Why not?" he said.

4

Shoot All the
Lawyers
First

The trailer house made its last trip that year, 1963, taking us the four hundred some miles from Rapid City to Vermillion where the state university's law school is located. Earlier I had borrowed some money from a friendly banker in Hot Springs, and I now informed him that the only way to protect his investment was to loan me enough additional money—unsecured—to put me through law school. He had no choice but to agree. That, combined with the $1 an hour salary Mary earned as a clerk in Nate Horowitz's Piggly Wiggly supermarket in Vermillion, and some more financial help from my mother, made it possible for me to finish three years of law school.

I worked in Hot Springs in the summer of 1964, following my first year in law school. Some of the businessmen in this old resort town in the southern Black Hills had put up the money to finance an outdoor play called *The Crazy Horse Pageant*, a live production staged on several acres of ground near Highway 79 east of Hot Springs.

The pageant was a dramatization of the life of Chief Crazy

Horse, the great Sioux warrior known for his brilliant military tactics and for resisting the white man's advance until the bitter end. It was written and produced by one Raw Hyde, born Robert Hyde in Huron, South Dakota. Raw Hyde earlier tried to peddle the idea of a pageant to businessmen in Rapid City, but they weren't buying. Spearfish had its Passion Play, the life of Jesus Christ, and Rapid City had its location adjacent to Mt. Rushmore and other tourist attractions. Other than the Evan's Plunge, a warm spring water swimming pool that Tom and Chick owned, Hot Springs had nothing else to attract tourists until it took on *The Crazy Horse Pageant*. The play employed local volunteer talent as actors, both on horseback and on foot. The actors were not required to speak, but only to gesture in synchrony with the professional voices that boomed out of the loudspeakers. Raw Hyde took some of the money put up by the show's backers and hired velvet-voiced Hollywood actors to record the script on tape.

I was the pageant's business manager that summer. Among my duties was insuring that the gift shop was fully stocked with cheap souvenirs. I was also responsible for the money both from the shop and from the ticket sales. Very quickly, I was able to double sales in the gift shop, but I saw a clear need to attract more tourists to the pageant. I proposed to the board of directors a three-day Indian dance, to be called *The Crazy Horse Powwow*, which would consist of an Indian encampment and dance contest that would award prizes on the final day. When I assured them that the cost would be minimal and the profits great, they agreed.

I advertised to all the Indian reservations in South Dakota that the dance contest would offer a $100 first prize, a $50 second prize, and a $25 third prize. I was not prepared for the magnitude of the response. Hundreds of Indians showed up from all over the great American West. They came from South Dakota, North Dakota, Montana, Wyoming, Utah, Oklahoma, Texas, California, and Nevada. What I hadn't realized, until then, was that Indians all over the Great Plains spent their summers traveling from powwow to powwow. It was the only vacation most could afford, and an inexpensive one at that. Their only overhead was gas money, because most brought along their own tents, and most powwows provided free food. Additionally, good Indian dancers travel all over the West to enter dance contests, partly for the money and partly as an excuse to travel. Those who came to Hot Springs without a tent that year merely slept on the ground, using their arms as pillows.

Earlier in the summer I hired an Indian named Ben Black Bear and his family. They were the pageant's resident Indians, acting in the pageant at night and providing local color for the tourists by day. I appointed Ben as the chief judge for the Indian dance portion of the *The Crazy Horse Powwow*, and asked him to choose two other distinguished Indian elders to assist him. There were some terrific Indian dancers, both in the traditional and in the fancy dance categories. Also, a number of singing groups showed up as volunteers, simply for the pleasure of drumming and singing during the contest. While non-Indians may derive pleasure from watching Indian dancers in their colorful costumes, it is the singing groups, made up of four or more Indian singers, that really turn on the Indians. Pounding the drum as they sing, Indian singers recite the most beautiful poetry during their performances, in much the same way Christian chanters do during High Mass. I learned how to distinguish between tribes by the tempo of their singers. For example, the Oglala Sioux had a faster beat than the Minneconjou band of Sioux, reflecting, I thought, the fact that Oglalas were much more aggressive. The singers who came to the *The Crazy Horse Powwow* put on a show both for the tourists and for the other Indians that would not be forgotten for a long time.

As the culmination of the dance contest approached on Sunday night, I walked over to Ben Black Bear and asked if he had decided on the contest winners yet. "Yes." he said.

"Who did you pick?" I asked.

"The winner of the first prize is Lloyd One Star."

My blood froze. Lloyd One Star was Ben's brother-in-law. While Lloyd was a decent journeyman dancer, he was no match for some of the younger fancy dancers who had been wowing the audiences all weekend.

"What about second prize?" I croaked.

"I'm giving it to Joyce Crow Flies High," he went on, in his measured English, "because she needs the gas money to get home on."

My bodily fluids iced up. Joyce was also a good dancer, but the reason for her prize? Hold everything, Ben. The third-prize winner was chosen on the same grounds, that is, Ben wanted to do a favor. I said nothing to Ben, partly because I had no idea what to say. At the end of the contest when Ben announced the prizes publicly in the dance circle, Mary and I were in the gift shop, closing it down and trying to count the money we had taken in that day. There were about forty or fifty Indians milling around the shop, looking over the souvenirs to see if they had been made in Hong Kong or in Indian country, when I heard a series of shouts outside. Someone burst into the gift shop and said, "Sidney Whitesell just hit Ben Black Bear in the jaw."

I jammed the several thousand dollars I had been counting into the metal cash box, shouted at Mary to stand on top of the box, and ran outside to try to break up the fight. By the time I reached the scene of the fight, it was all over. Sidney Whitesell, young, tall, and musclebound, perhaps the best fancy dancer of the weekend, having taken his satisfaction from Ben, was turning to leave and Ben was rubbing his jaw.

But the *The Crazy Horse Powwow*, despite the rumble, was a great success, prompting the board of directors to host it again in the summer of 1965. I was pushing drinks and steaks in The Gaslight Cafe (formerly the Gay Lady) then, but Roland Grosshans, who was married to my niece Linda, Chick's daughter, and who was a year behind me in law school, became the new business manager for the pageant.

I drove down from Rockerville to Hot Springs on the first day of the powwow to reminisce. Roland approached me as soon as I walked onto the grounds to complain about Frank Fools Crow, the Oglala Sioux holy man. It had started raining that morning, and the forecast was for rain all weekend, threatening to prevent the influx of tourists upon which the pageant depended. "I asked Fools Crow to say a prayer to stop the rain," Roland told me, "and he retreated behind that billboard by the highway, pointed his pipe at the sky for a while, and then wanted me to pay him for it."

"What did you do?" I asked.

"I told the old phony that it was still raining and that I refused to pay him a penny."

It was still drizzling as I talked to Roland, but no more than twenty minutes had passed when the drizzle stopped and the sun began wedging its way through quickly scattering clouds.

About ten minutes later, Frank Fools Crow saw me and came over. "Jeem," he said, "I make the rain stop, but they woont pay me." His English was halting, heavily accented, but his meaning was clear—he had done the trick, had defied the forecast, and had saved the powwow. My suggestion to Roland, who agreed, was that it would be wise to give Fools Crow something, either money or food, for fear that he might make the rain start again.

Years later, in 1975, to be exact, I arranged for Fools Crow to say the opening prayer in the U.S. Senate, hoping that he could somehow create a similar miracle for the United States, but as hard as he tried, and as we now know, nothing happened.

The summer following my second year in law school I worked again in Rockerville. This time I leased The Gas Light Restaurant. My entire family moved into the rear of the building. Mary and I had one small room for a bedroom. Nikki and Paul, then eleven and five years old, respectively, slept in the big room next to ours, along with the three university coeds who worked as waitresses. Charlie, age twelve, slept on the dance floor with the bus boys and Bill Janklow, the bartender. In later years, when Bill was elected governor of South Dakota, he somehow neglected to put that particular summer job on his resume.

Janklow and I were close friends in law school. We studied together, hung out together, and talked politics together. After getting his law degree, Janklow first worked as an Indian Legal Services attorney, based in Mission, the center of the Rosebud Sioux Indian Reservation. Indian defense law was a new concept in Todd and Mellette Counties in the late 1960s, and to his credit Janklow began challenging every legal precept that had been for years the basis of white discrimination against Indians. Community attitudes about Indians were clearly expressed, while Janklow was there, by Howard Piper, who ran a gas station in Wood. When I returned to Wood for a visit, Howard complained to me of this new radical, Janklow, who, he said, was making it difficult, "even to throw a drunk Indian in jail anymore."

Janklow virtually risked his life challenging the discriminatory customs and practices of a now angry white population. His legal successes ended decades of gross mistreatment of Indians by the white authorities, but tragically, his attitude dramatically changed when he decided to run for state attorney general years later. His flip-flop was incomprehensible to me, although it probably made sense to him politically. I had thought before then that Janklow was one of the more principled people I knew. Almost overnight opportunism overcame his principles. Janklow began inserting code words in his speeches that signalled to whites that he was against the Indians and on their side in the ongoing Indian-white conflict. His run for office coincided with the beginning of the rebellion by leaders of the militant American Indian Movement, providing him with a convenient target. When I first saw him after his turnaround, I characterized his decidedly anti-Indian rhetoric as a blatant racist attack. "I'm not against Indians," Janklow answered, "I'm just for obeying the law."

He went on to win two terms as attorney general, and following that, two terms as governor. He rode into office, I once told him, on the backs of the extremely vulnerable Indians, a fact that reveals at least as much about the state of mind of some of the whites in South Dakota as it does about Janklow's opportunism.

Across the street from The Gas Light was the Rockerville "Mellerdrammer" Theater, a summer theater stocked with aspiring actors from all over the United States. Each play in the Mellerdrammer's repertoire included a variation of the hero, Dudley DoRight, besting the villain whose name, I think, was Black Bart. The theater made as much money selling peanuts to the audience to throw at the villain as it did on admissions. Kenny Eulo, a highly accomplished actor from New Jersey who played the villain, once told me, with only a tinge of anger, that my son Charlie had the meanest arm in the audience. I had to tell Charlie to ease up on the peanut-throwing, or he might lose his free pass to the Mellerdrammer.

Three of the actors from the Mellerdrammer comprised the band I hired on weekends at the rate of $15 each per night plus a free meal. Years before Tiny Tim began trilling "Tiptoe Through The Tulips," one of the women in the Mellerdrammer cast did her rendition of that song in The Gas Light at least once a night when the band played. It was a delightful song and dance routine, and the customers loved it. But after the 150th performance of "Tiptoe" that summer, I began to hate the sound of it.

Beyond spending an interesting summer at the Gas Light, I made enough money—$2,200—to finance my third and last year in law school.

* * *

In the spring of 1966, as graduation threatened, I began to worry about finding full-time work. Mayer Kantor, Stuart Van Mevren, and I drove to California to look for jobs during Easter break, but we came away empty-handed. All my life I'd been told that the more education one had, the better off one was, but each of the interviewers I talked to on that trip told me that I was too highly educated for an entry-level position. I was baffled. The Del Monte Company interviewer said that I was not likely to stick with them for very long because I had too much education, very much the same thing the Rapid City bar owner had told me three years earlier. The only job that I was offered came from a lawyer in Rapid City, Frank Henderson, then a Republican state senator embroiled in a primary fight to keep his seat. Henderson was called a maverick by the Republican party bosses who were out to get him that year, successfully as it turned out.

Henderson's worries did not end with his primary loss, however. His associate, Frank Wallahan, decided leave him to open his own law practice, taking several clients with him. By the time I started work in early June, just after the disastrous primary, Henderson had secluded himself on his farm in the Black Hills, nursing a heavily damaged ego. He withdrew more and more from his law practice, leaving me to handle the myriad clients and ongoing cases, which as one might guess, was not the thing to do with a novice— though it certainly accelerated my learning process. Because Henderson showed up in the office with less and less frequency, my lack of experience required that I work more and more hours just to keep up.

My employment in Henderson Law Offices ended ten months after it started under somewhat wild circumstances. I had become a cigarette smoker in the navy at the age of seventeen. By the time I started engineering school I was smoking anywhere from three to five packages of unfiltered cigarettes every day. In 1960, I quit cold turkey, promptly gaining over fifty pounds. In 1966, brother Chick advised me to start chewing on cigars—not lighting them but chewing them—which, he said, would cause me to lose weight. I took his advice and started chewing cigars. The next day I decided to light one. It tasted so good I lit another, and when that was gone another, and another. Then I began inhaling the smoke, and by 1967, I was smoking up to fifteen or twenty cheap cigars a day. My mouth began to taste like the inside of a sewer line.

During the tenth month of my employment with Frank Henderson, I stayed up most of one night writing an appeal brief for a murder case that Frank was defending. During the night I decided to quit smoking cigars, and by the next day I was climbing the walls, both from lack of sleep and from nicotine withdrawal. Henderson chose that moment to walk into the office for the first time in days. He looked around and said, "Jim, we've got to start working nights to get some of this work out around here."

Henderson was six foot six and weighed over three hundred pounds, a menacing figure even when he was not angry. But he posed no threat to me, because I was crazed from nicotine withdrawal. Crazed is not really the word for it; I was downright suicidal and my usual restraint had dissolved. "Start working nights?" I shrieked, "Start working nights? You sonofabitch, you can take this job and shove it up your ass." I got up, stomped out, went home, and stewed for several days before I finally returned to Henderson's office and asked if he would rent my old office to me so that I could set up my own law practice. To my everlasting surprise, he agreed.

Under my original agreement with him I was to be paid a salary of $500 a month plus one-third of any new business that I brought in on my own. I had brought in enough paying clients in the previous couple of months to surpass my salary. The first month that I practiced on my own, I grossed $700, and the money increased each month thereafter. Of necessity Frank began working more and hiding out less, and together we moved to a building with cheaper rent. I remained his office partner until I moved in with Bob Varilek, another lawyer in solo practice. Henderson had lost interest in his practice, and I wanted to move on.

Varilek's original partner, Bill Brady, had been shot and killed in court during a divorce proceeding. Brady represented a Mrs. Ray Blevens. Her husband brought a gun into the divorce hearing, whipped it out, and sprayed the courtroom with bullets. Besides killing Bill Brady, Blevens also killed his wife and wounded Tom Parker, the presiding judge. Parker, despite the gunshot wound, picked up the heavy chair behind the bench and threw it at Blevens while he was still shooting. I later officed with attorney Bob LaFleur, an arrangement that lasted until I was elected to the U.S. House of Representatives.

Some of Rapid City's Indians came to me with strange stories about the unexplained deaths of Indian prisoners in the Hot Springs jail. Seven or eight had died in a very short time. Additionally, there was a report of a sheriff's deputy who had beaten an Indian, David Gillespie, to death on a lonely stretch of highway in Shannon County. I began challenging the authorities in Hot Springs over the deaths, and I demanded that the attorney general investigate the beating death of David Gillespie. I could get neither the state authorities nor the media interested in the case, which, I thought, would ultimately bring about some kind of official action. The coroner's jury investigating Gillespie's death announced that it was "non-felonious," letting the sheriff's office off the hook and foreclosing any further investigation. But one of the jury members years later confided to me that they had all agreed to a cover-up, because the Indian was dead, and it would do no good to stir up the matter again.

It might be unwarranted nostalgia, but I don't remember being happier than in the few years I spent practicing law in Rapid City.

Perhaps it was the variety of cases that came into my office that kept boredom from setting in. I found time to do *pro bono* work for hard-pressed Indians and to get involved in local political campaigns. It was all great fun, except for a narrow scrape with death involving my whole family.

I should have known better. Mary and I were caught in a Nebraska blizzard in 1953, on the highway between Valentine and Mission, forcing us to walk to a nearby farmhouse where we were allowed to spend the night. Although I had always believed that there is nothing left to learn from the second kick of a mule, I failed to heed my own advice. It was precisely on April 30, 1967, a warm spring day in most climes, that my family and I were driving back to Rapid City after having visited my mother in Mission. Snow warnings had been broadcast on the radio, but I chose to ignore them, pushing on westward, hoping to get home before the blizzard hit. A highway patrolman was trying to stop traffic on the highway, but I ignored him and kept driving.

The snow started, wet and thick, about seventy miles east of Rapid City, not far from the town of Wall. It was difficult to see because the flakes were being driven directly into the windshield by a wind that was clocked by the weather bureau at a steady seventy-five miles an hour. Because the temperature started out relatively warm, the snow began melting on the highway, creating before long a solid sheet of ice some two or three inches thick. My car slid off the highway and into a steep ditch. We abandoned the car, climbed up to the road, and flagged down the first car heading toward Rapid City, a small Plymouth containing a middle-aged couple and their two Mexican Hairless Chihuahua dogs. Although we added five people to their car—Mary, Charlie, Nikki, Paul, and me—they generously invited us to ride with them into Rapid City. We had driven no more than a mile when we came to a fairly steep grade. The ice on the road was so thick that the car would no longer move forward. For eighteen hours the seven of us, and the two dogs, huddled together in the small car. I had to go out with Mary and the children when they relieved themselves to prevent the seventy-five-mile-an-hour wind from blowing them away. The kind gentleman who had picked us up had an injured foot and was blown over by the wind on one of his trips out, forcing him to crawl back to the car on his hands and knees.

Since we had no idea how long we would be stranded, we agreed that we would start the car and run the heater for only a few minutes every hour to save gasoline. The periodic warming was a bit of a comfort, but at about four o'clock in the morning the car refused to start. I struggled outside to inspect the engine and discovered that the alternate melting and freezing of the snow on the radiator had created a block of ice running from the radiator all the way down to the ground, totally immobilizing the engine. It grew colder and colder, and there was no help from the heater. I eventually took the blankets away from the two shivering dogs and gave them to my children, suggesting to our hostess that she snuggle the dogs under her coat. She reluctantly agreed.

In all, we spent eighteen hours in the car, ultimately rescued by a snowplow operator who came along the following day. He took us to a motel in the small town of Wall where we recuperated before going home. I never traveled in winter in South Dakota again without a complete emergency package in the trunk of my car—blankets, food, candles, and other items designed for blizzards.

The clientele in my law practice varied widely, probably because I hustled business from many walks of life. The first thing I did upon setting up my own practice was to call all the established law firms in Rapid City, telling them that I was now on my own and asking them to send all their "low grade ore" cases to me. This brought in divorces, bankruptcies, and criminal cases—everything that the big firms had no time for, or that paid too little. They of course kept their "high grade-ore," the rich, well-paying clients, but I was happy with anything that would help me make a living. I spent many nights in Rapid City's bars, meeting a lot of new people. Inevitably I would enter my office in the morning to find in my waiting room one or more of those I had met the night before who wanted to hire me as their lawyer.

I asked all the trial judges in Rapid City to appoint me to defend criminal cases, taking as many as I could get. There was no money in it—$25 to $50 per case in those days—but it was great experience, and like most lawyers who weren't busy, I gave the accused intense representation. When a personal injury victim retained me, I made it a policy never to settle the case, especially for the low prices that the insurance lawyers consistently offered. It was always their practice to try to buy out of these cases as cheaply as they could. I tried case after case, winning most and always getting a jury award much bigger than the settlement offer. Bill Porter, an insurance defense lawyer, complained that, after all the cases we had tried against each other, the companies he represented had bought me a house, a car, and all the clothing I owned since I left law school.

When I worked for Frank Henderson, he assigned me to represent one of his clients, a gigantic black man whom I will call Tyrone Jefferson. Tyrone was periodically charged by city officials with bootlegging, because of the activities he conducted in his home along Rapid Creek, at the edge of Rapid City. Tyrone introduced black airmen at Ellsworth Air Force Base to Indian women of his acquaintance. The introductions took place in his house, which was furnished in much the same way a small night club would be. He had a juke box, booths, and alcoholic beverages—illegal—that were profitably served to the singles-hoping-to-be-doubles who patronized his home. Tyrone, who called these events "parties," always paid his attorney's fees in rolled up coins taken from his juke box. I thought it was funny, but he always paid.

He escaped one bootlegging charge when several prisoners in the city jail destroyed all the prosecutor's evidence in his case, requiring a dismissal of the charges against him. The prisoners' cell was next to the evidence room. They somehow found a long wire which they used to seize the evidence, a case of whiskey confiscated in the raid on Tyrone's house. Some of the bottles broke as the case was pulled off the table, but the rest were promptly emptied by the delighted prisoners.

Years earlier Tyrone had worked in a night club for black airmen called The Coney Island where he was implicated in a killing, although he was totally innocent. At that time Rapid City was still segregated and blacks were not allowed in bars and restaurants, hence the need for a social outlet like The Coney Island. Tyrone showed up for work one night gnashing his teeth. Sam Marras, the club's owner, knew this meant that Tyrone was upset about something, but he restrained his curiosity. After a couple of days of high decibel teeth-gnashing, Tyrone finally asked Sam, "What would you do if you knew where there was a dead guy?"

"You sure the guy's dead, Tyrone?"

"Yeah, I'm sure."

"Go back and check it out. Maybe he's just sick," Sam told him, so Tyrone left, returning shortly to say, "He's dead all right."

Sam asked to see the body. They drove to a house at the edge of town and went inside. There on the floor, dead as a doornail, lay the Diamond Duke, a black airman known to Sam. The Diamond Duke earned his name from the many diamonds he wore, including two implanted in his front teeth. He had been fatally stabbed in the back with a butcher knife while sitting at the kitchen table. After rigor mortis set in, his body fell over backwards onto the floor, and his arms, which had been lying flat on the table at the time of his death, were now aimed grotesquely at the sky. The Diamond Duke's immense diamond finger ring, now a trophy displayed at the end of a cold, stiff arm pointing upward, glistened in the light.

Sam reached for the ring, but Tyrone said, "Uh, uh. It won't come off. I already tried it."

Sam called the police, and, as they waited, he extracted the story from Tyrone. It seems that Tyrone, a few days earlier, was on his way to the Duke's house to collect five dollars owed to him, when he saw the Duke's Indian girlfriend running from the house in a state of panic. Tyrone stopped his car to pick her up, and she blurted out that she had stabbed the Duke and thought she had killed him. "Get in," he shouted, "we've got to get the hell out of here," and he started driving out of town. They drove some 150 miles east of Rapid City before it dawned on Tyrone that he had done nothing requiring him to run from the police. He turned around and drove back to Rapid City, eventually telling his story on the witness stand during the trial of the Duke's murderous girlfriend.

Tyrone was out on bail, facing a bootlegging charge, when a hapless Indian named John Ernest Bird Necklace robbed a Rapid City liquor store in the wee hours of a cold winter morning in 1967. Bird Necklace, obviously under the influence, broke out the store's plate glass window and stole three bottles of the worst rotgut in the inventory. The ground outside was blanketed with fresh snow, providing the police with an unmistakable trail leading from the liquor store straight to Tyrone's house. Upon reaching the house, Bird Necklace broke out the window just above Tyrone's bed, crawled inside, stepped over a soundly sleeping Tyrone, and collapsed onto a sofa in the living room, the three bottles of rotgut resting on the floor beside him. Since Tyrone had hosted a "party" the night before, he had imbibed more than his share of the sauce and was dead to the world, which is what the police learned when they arrived at his front door. They pounded on the door for a long time before Tyrone finally woke up to answer it.

"Can we come in?" the police asked Tyrone. Because he knew that all his guests from the night before had left, he said, "Sure." They walked in, finding John Earnest Bird Necklace still passed out on the sofa, the evidence of his crime on the floor beside him. He was promptly arrested and taken to jail.

Attorney Frank Wallahan was appointed to represent Bird Necklace. Because Tyrone was then under indictment for bootlegging, I accompanied him to Bird Necklace's trial to try to prevent him from incriminating himself during his testimony as a witness. It was Wallahan's strategy to point the finger of guilt at Tyrone in order to get John Earnest Bird Necklace acquitted, so Tyrone was called as the first defense witness.

"Please state your name," Wallahan said.

"Tyrone C. Jefferson, sir."

"What is your occupation?"

"I'm a heavy 'quipment operator, sir."

Wallahan was momentarily stunned by the answer, but the judge, who was well acquainted with Tyrone, could barely conceal his outburst of laughter. The humor did not end there.

"I refer you to this floor plan of your home, Mr. Jefferson, and ask you if this accurately represents it?" Tyrone agreed that it did.

"Now," Wallahan said, "What is this item that I've drawn here in your kitchen?"

"I believe that's a juke box sir."

"A JUKE BOX?" Wallahan shouted incredulously, mostly for effect since he already knew what the object was.

"Yes, sir."

"And what is this item here?"

"That's a kitchen table, sir."

"WHAT DO YOU MEAN, KITCHEN TABLE?" Wallahan shouted once again. "That's a booth, isn't it?"

"That very well could be, sir."

One of the major points of the arresting officers' testimony was that the burglar was easy to track because he was wearing a high heeled Italian-style boot with a pointed toe, approximately size seven. As it happened, Tyrone was just then wearing boots of this description, so Wallahan tried to exploit the opening. He began questioning Tyrone about his boots and his whereabouts during the time of the burglary, but his entire strategy fell apart when the prosecutor, on cross-examination, asked Tyrone what size boots he wore. "Size twelve, sir," Tyrone answered, holding them up for the jury to see and removing all doubt about his involvement in the crime. Bird Necklace was convicted of burglary, and Tyrone was left to answer the bootlegging charge later in a different court.

Of all the Indian clients I had, my favorite was Noah Helper, a young athletic Sioux Indian who spent most of his time drinking and fighting in the bars of Rapid City, when he wasn't fighting with his wife, Mary Belle.

Mary Belle sued him for divorce, and a dispute arose over custody of their three children. I first met Noah on the day Mary Belle's lawyer, Mike Driscoll, sent out a notice for a default divorce and child custody hearing. Noah didn't hire a lawyer when he was served with the lawsuit, and his failure to answer the initial complaint over a three-year period ultimately prompted Driscoll to set the hearing.

Noah ran into my office at 11 A.M. with the notice of Driscoll's intention to take a default judgment. The hearing was set for one o'clock that day. I called Driscoll to tell him that I would be appearing for Noah, then at one o'clock we both went before the judge. I discovered that, as ill-prepared as I was, Mike was even less prepared, fully expecting the hearing to go.uncontested. I saw that it was to my advantage to agree to the divorce, but to contest the custody part on the spot, a tactic that would not give Mike time to prepare. Somehow I was able to convince Judge Lampert that the hearing should proceed.

Just before he was to take the stand to testify, I noticed that Noah had an ace bandage wrapped around his right hand. He explained that he had hurt the hand during a fight the night before. "Take it off," I whispered, not wanting him to have to answer questions about his unconventional night life. He stood up and in full view of the judge, who was watching, removed the bandage and dropped it on his chair.

In order to have any chance of winning custody of his three children, I had to establish that Noah was fully able to take care of them, so I asked him a leading question, one which suggested the answer. "Now, Mr. Helper," I said in the most patronizing voice I could summon, "if the court sees fit to give you custody of these three wonderful children, you fully intend to get a full-time job, to stop fighting, and to quit drinking, don't you?" It was, of course, totally improper procedure, but Mike Driscoll, still stunned by the suddenness of the whole affair, let it pass without objecting.

Taking my earlier admonition to tell the truth completely to heart, Noah thought a minute, then answered, "Well . . . I'll cut down."

I was stunned. I glared at him, then shouted an involuntary, "WHAT?" prompting him to immediately change his answer. "No, no, I'll quit," he promised, but it was too late. After hearing testimony from Mary Belle, the judge awarded the children to the state welfare agency, making *Helper vs. Helper* perhaps the first case in history in which both lawyers lost.

* * *

I was working harder than ever and enjoying my law practice, but I couldn't get politics out of my mind, and by 1968 I was becoming more deeply embroiled in it.

In 1968, I became a candidate for delegate to the Democratic National Convention in Chicago, committed to Robert F. Kennedy's presidential race. I spent a great deal of time helping in his South Dakota campaign, learning the basics of political organizing from the likes of Matt Reese and Rosalie Whalen, who came to South Dakota to help out. Reese, West Virginian-born but Washington-based, was one of the best political consultants in the country at that time, an expert in organizing door-to-door campaigns, always turning out heavy votes for his candidates. Rosalie Whalen, also from Washington, was a specialist in setting up and running telephone banks.

Our taste of victory on primary night—also the night of the California primary—turned sour as we watched Robert Kennedy's assassination. The Kennedy slate won in South Dakota over both Eugene McCarthy and Hubert Humphrey, so we went to the Democratic National Convention in Chicago pledged to George McGovern, who had picked up Kennedy's organization and had run a seventeen-day campaign for president. The 1968 Chicago convention was my first, and, after watching the riots and Mayor Daley rig the convention in favor of Hubert Humphrey, I wondered what the Democrats could possibly do for an encore.

I also ran a losing campaign for attorney general of South Dakota in 1968. It was a dismal year for South Dakota Democrats, except for George McGovern, who, despite little success at the Chicago convention, ran for and won reelection to the Senate. Bob Chamberlin was our candidate for governor, and I was the candidate for attorney general. The Democratic candidate for the U.S. House of Representatives in the Second District was a relative newcomer to South Dakota by the name of Dave Garner.

Dave was an employee of the Standard Oil Company, but he did not fit the mold of an oil man. He had a superb sense of humor and a dislike of corporate bullies. Dave's moment of glory came during a talk show on KOTA radio in Rapid City. Each political party, including the George Wallace party, was offered four hours of time by KOTA to answer questions from its listeners. When the Democrats' turn came, we agreed that three of us would represent the Party on the air. Homer Kandaras, a local lawyer and chairman of the Pennington County Democrats was one. Because I was running for attorney general, I got a spot, and then, of course, Dave Garner was on as the congressional candidate. Joining us in the small studio as an observer was Jeff Smith, a bright Arizona native who had been on Bobby Kennedy's staff, but after Kennedy's death had stayed around to help McGovern in his reelection campaign for the Senate.

It was a time of great political confusion in South Dakota. Passion over the Vietnam War was at its height, and the country was deeply divided. The listeners' telephone calls came in steadily during the four hours that we held forth, but there were four calls that dealt directly with an issue that surfaced unexpectedly that night:

First call (a man's voice)—"Why did George McGovern vote against the appropriation for B-52 sorties in Vietnam?"

Not one of us knew the answer, but Dave Garner, who knew a hostile question when he heard one, grabbed the microphone and said, "Because B-52 bombers are not effective in Vietnam, that's why."

"Good answer, Dave," I said when our mike was turned off.

Second call (a woman's voice)—"I wouldn't vote for that man for dogcatcher. If he doesn't think B-52s are effective in Vietnam, he should ask our boys in the marines. The B-52s saved their lives during the siege of Khe San."

She clearly dealt Dave a body blow with this statement. Dave was now grasping. To try to bail him out, Jeff Smith scrawled out in large letters on a yellow pad, "F-85," holding the pad up so that Dave could see the message. "They used these at Khe San," Smith whispered to Garner, pointing to the letters.

His confidence renewed, Dave drew himself up to the microphone. "They used F-85s at Khe San, not B-52s," he said as though he had known the answer all along. When the mike was turned off again, I told Dave that I thought he ought to downplay the issue. "They used F-101s, not F-85s," I told him.

Of course, we were both wrong. In 1968, an F-85 was an extremely popular Oldsmobile compact car. To make matters worse, just ten miles east of Rapid City stood Ellsworth Air Force Base, where several thousand experts on air warfare both worked and lived.

Third call (a man's voice)—"If you don't think B-52s saved our boys at Khe San, just read *Time* magazine, the issue back in May.

They have pictures of B-52s during the siege bombing the Commies at Khe San."

Unrepentant and without hesitation, Dave responded, "What I meant to say was that they used *both* F-85s and B-52s at Khe San."

Fourth call (a man's voice, heavy with a border state twang)—"I'd like to congratulate them Democrats for their courageous stand on the state income tax and on those other issues. Oh, by the way, I also want to say that I've been in the U.S. Air Force for twelve years and I've never heard of an F-85."

KOTA's announcer, Bill Goodhope, who was taking the calls and moderating the program, tried to bail us out. "Isn't that a navy fighter or bomber, or some sort of navy plane?" he asked.

"No," the gentle voice said. "It's not a navy plane, and it's not in the air force inventory either—at least *not in our air force.*"

Garner finally gave up. He ended the episode by telling the folks in radioland that he actually should be congratulated for not knowing anything about weapons systems and armaments. The incident had no effect on his share of the votes. He received around 30 percent of the vote that year, about the same as any Democrat got when they ran against E. Y. Berry.

* * *

Ronnie O. Goode was a black airman stationed at Ellsworth Air Force Base in the late 1960s. He had been living with a Rapid City woman—she was white—and her two-year-old son. The child died and the medical examiner said that the death was the result of beatings administered by a person or persons unknown. The result of his report was that both Ronnie and the woman were charged with manslaughter.

Both Ronnie and the woman were represented by her family's lawyer, which would have been all right, except for two problems. He had never tried a criminal case—he was essentially a real estate and probate lawyer—and his representing both defendants was a severe conflict of interest.

Ronnie Goode's family in Petersburg, Virginia asked their minister to help. The minister contacted the Southern Christian Leadership Conference, which in turn asked the American Civil Liberties Union to intervene. I was contacted by Marv Bailin, a lawyer in Sioux Falls, who, I think, was the ACLU stringer in South Dakota. He asked me to take the case on a *pro bono* basis, to which I agreed. I would, he said, be co-counsel with an attorney from New York, a fellow by the name of William Kunstler.

Kunstler and I began conferring on the case by telephone, deciding to attack it on the basis that Goode was essentially deprived of his right to counsel. As I read the transcript of both trials—his and that of his female companion, I was shocked. The woman was tried first. Their lawyer advised Ronnie to confess during her trial that he had beaten the child just before it died. She would be absolved, the lawyer assured him, and he, the lawyer, would be able to prevent that admission from being used in Ronnie's own trial on Fifth Amendment grounds. Ronnie did what the lawyer told him to do, and despite his damaging admission, the woman was convicted anyway. Then, at Ronnie's subsequent trial, the prosecutor simply read into evidence the part of the trial transcript in which Ronnie had admitted contributing to the child's death. I had talked to Ronnie at length, however, and I was convinced that he had not abused the child. He was totally non-aggressive, even wimpy in character. He had, he told me, confessed at the woman's trial, because the lawyer had convinced him that it was the right thing to do.

I wrote the appeal brief, then sent it to Kunstler. He asked me if I wanted him to come out to argue the case before the South Dakota Supreme Court. I was emphatic in telling him yes. He was not yet fully in the public spotlight—this was before the Chicago Seven trial had started—but I had heard of his ability as a lawyer, and I felt that I had something to learn from him.

Kunstler came to Rapid City one day before the argument, which was to be made before the South Dakota Supreme Court in Pierre. I took him to an Indian community center in Rapid City where he gave a talk to a small gathering of Indians, advocating resistance to the government's handling of Indian affairs. As I dropped him off at his motel for the night, he asked if he could review the trial transcript and the appellate brief for the argument the next day. I gave both of them to him, and by morning he had digested it all. He even had his hair cut short before coming, "in honor of the South Dakota Supreme Court," he told me.

Kunstler made the initial argument on the case the next day, and despite the court's conservatism and his reputation as a radical, I noticed the justices sitting on the edge of their chairs, absorbing one of the best oral arguments that any of us had ever heard. They ultimately decided in Ronnie Goode's favor, agreeing totally that he had been deprived of adequate counsel. The prosecutor declined to recharge Ronnie and dismissed the charges against him. When he was released, he left the state, never to return.

I drove Kunstler to Sioux Falls, some two hundred miles east of Pierre, so that he could catch a plane to begin what he described as a "political trial" in Chicago arising out of the 1968 Democratic Convention. We talked by phone once or twice a week updating each other on Ronnie Goode's appeal and on the Chicago Seven trial, which was by then generating headlines, a result that Kunstler wanted. Political prosecutions required a political response as much as a legal one, he told me. He said again and again that the prosecution was being directed from the White House. Only later, during the Watergate disclosures, did I learn how prescient he was.

* * *

In 1967, I was appointed by the South Dakota Circuit Court to represent a client whom I will call Billy The Kid. Billy rustled cattle for a living, operating out of Shannon County. Although Billy lived on the Pine Ridge Indian Reservation, he was not an Indian. His specialty was loading the cattle he stole into a house trailer that he had adapted by cutting open the sides and top of the trailer's back wall to form a loading ramp. He would then, according to legend, load other folks' cattle up the ramp, into the trailer, and drive down the road to find a market for the purloined beef.

He was finally caught on a day when he got a flat tire, prompting a friendly highway patrolman to stop to offer help. Naturally, the officer became suspicious at the sound of cattle mooing inside the lace-curtained house trailer and he arrested Billy, who began what was to be a long journey through the criminal justice system.

He was first tried and convicted in federal court on several counts related to the trailer incident, and sentenced to three concurrent three-year terms in Minnesota's Sandstone Federal Prison. He was allowed to be out on bail before his term began, so that he could appeal the conviction as well as respond to his lawyer's demand for legal fees. In Billy's case, the money that he intended to pay his lawyer happened to be locked inside a safe belonging to a business in Rapid City. Moreover, Billy neglected to ask permission of the safe's owner when he removed the safe from the premises in order to open it.

He and two friends drove the safe to a barn some ten miles east of Rapid City, where they were interrupted by the arrival of the sheriff's men as they were peeling it open. The law never actually saw them peeling the safe open in the barn that night—they escaped when they heard the posse coming. They were arrested, however, at a roadblock set up by the sheriff, then charged and tried for burglary in the South Dakota state courts. The partially picked safe was left behind in the barn as they fled, and the sheriff found paint scrapings from the safe in the trunk of Billy's car. When, at the trial, a witness from the FBI lab in Washington was asked how he knew the scrapings came from the safe, he disclosed that the FBI tells safe manufacturers what kind of paint to use specifically for the purpose of tracing.

Billy's court-appointed attorney, Bill Rensch, disputed the State's contention that Billy and his two accomplices were capable of lifting the safe in and out of the car's trunk. During his closing argument he issued a challenge to the jury that if any two of them could lift the safe, they should convict his client. His strategy collapsed when one of the jurors, a strapping Indian woman, came down from the jury box and lifted the safe, cart and all, by herself. When Billy was convicted of the burglary charge, Rensch suggested that I be appointed to handle the appeal.

I appealed the case on the grounds that the evidence against him—the paint scrapings—was gathered by means of an illegal search and seizure. Although my appeal to the South Dakota Supreme Court was ultimately successful, the entire process took a little over twenty-eight months. Because the court agreed with me that the search was unconstitutional and the evidence therefore inadmissible, the case against Billy had to be dismissed. But instead of releasing him, the South Dakota authorities notified the federal authorities, who were waiting at the gates of the South Dakota Penitentiary to arrest him. They immediately took him to Sandstone Federal Prison in Minnesota to begin serving the three-year cattle rustling sentence that he had been appealing.

Although Billy had very little education, he was highly intelligent—street smart I believe is the proper description. He wrote on prison stationery a writ of *habeas corpus*, demanding his release on the grounds that the federal authorities should have given him credit for the time he served in the South Dakota Penitentiary.

The federal judge, a Norwegian immigrant named Axel Beck, phoned me to ask if I would represent Billy. By then I had announced my candidacy for the Second District congressional seat.

"I've served my time with Billy, your Honor," I said. "I handled his appeal for over two years and all I got was the $50 fee the state paid me for the appointment." The judge gave up—temporarily.

A few days later he called back to tell me that no one else wanted to represent Billy, and that because I did such a good job on his last case I should really represent him on this one. I was afraid to push my luck any further, so I lied a little and told him how happy I was to be able to do it.

I prepared both a brief and my argument, and on the appointed day of the hearing in late January 1970, I flew to Aberdeen, the location of Judge Beck's court. Billy was brought down from Sandstone for the argument, looking pale from the long months spent in prison. When both the U.S. attorney and I finished making our opposing cases, Judge Beck announced that he would need to review more case authority before he could decide the matter. He directed us to come back with a more complete legal memorandum on the point of law that was the centerpiece of the matter. My policy had always been that when I represented criminal defendants, I saw it as my responsibility to get them released from prison on bail. I decided to take a chance on getting Billy out on bail at least during the time that Beck would be considering the case.

"Your Honor," I said in my most rational, and hopefully convincing, voice, "Billy has been wrongfully imprisoned for more than two years now, and I think that he's entitled to be out on bail until your decision comes down."

"I'll grant that request," Judge Beck said.

Everyone was shocked, including me. The U.S. attorney was immediately on his feet, shouting his objections to the judge. The U.S. marshal who had brought Billy from Sandstone shook a sheaf of papers in the judge's face.

"Judge—you can't turn him loose," the marshal screamed, turning blue with rage. "Nebraska wants him, everybody wants him. I've got the hold from Nebraska right here."

The marshal forgot the unbridled power of federal judges. "I don't care vot Nebraska vants," Beck said, crashing his fist down onto the desk, "he's gonna stay loose until I'm done vit him."

I hurriedly signed the bond form for Billy, hustled him to the Aberdeen airport, and bought him a ticket back to Rapid City before the prosecutor could think of a reason to have him arrested again. We landed at the Rapid City airport just after noon, and as we got into my car, I told Billy that I wanted to stop at a restaurant where the Democratic Forum was having a lunch meeting. The Democratic Forum was a sort of political Rotary Club, a group that I had organized, where business and professional people who were Democrats could meet once a week to listen to a speaker discuss an issue related to politics. In heavily Republican South Dakota, it was a way of making Democrats feel somewhat respectable.

"Our new candidate for governor, Dick Kneip, is speaking today, and I'd like to try to hear at least the last part of his talk. Is it okay with you?" I asked.

Billy couldn't say "yes" fast enough. I had the feeling that he was so happy about being out of prison that he probably would have rubbed out someone had I asked him to.

We were too late for the speech, and as we walked into the crowded dining room, Gene Bushnell, the president of the Forum announced that "our candidate for Congress has just arrived," prompting applause from the partisan audience.

As Billy and I found empty seats, I could hear Bushnell over the public address system saying, "Jim, I see you have a guest with you today. Would you like to introduce him?"

I winced. Although Billy had been out of the news for a couple of years, his name had become a household word because of the publicity surrounding his burglary trial and his other escapades. He was so colorful that the newspaper and television newsmen had practically made a living running Billy the Kid stories.

"Yes," I said, suppressing an impulse to run out of the room. "I'd like to introduce Billy the Kid, my client, who just returned from Aberdeen with me."

As the applause started, Billy stood up, obviously feeling a bit awkward and appearing unsure of himself. As it continued, however, he clasped his hands together in the same way that victorious prize fighters do, and held them above his head, acknowledging the audience's welcome.

Fortunately, only the lawyers in the room remembered his name, as evidenced by the flurry of whispers going back and forth between them when his name was announced.

But the hapless Dick Kneip (who was elected governor that November) had no idea who he was. He came over to us after the meeting adjourned, greeting me and shaking my hand. He was equally effusive when he turned to Billy.

"Where are you from, Billy?" Kneip asked.

"From Shannon County, sir." Billy responded with a mumble, all the while shuffling his feet and looking down at the ground.

"What kind of work do you do?" Kneip pressed on, unsuspecting.

"Uh . . . I'm in the cattle business, sir." Billy was clearly uncomfortable with this overly curious politician.

"And where are you from, did you say?" Kneip was relentless.

"Well, actually, sir, I just got out of federal prison in Sandstone, Minnesota." Billy couldn't take the charade any longer.

Kneip gulped, turned and literally ran to his car, unable to deal with what he surely saw as a negative association, something that might destroy his candidacy.

Billy's story doesn't end there. As my congressional campaign became more serious, I had to turn his defense over to Bill Janklow. After I was elected and started serving in the U.S. House of Representatives, I got a letter from Billy, written on Sandstone stationery, telling me that Judge Beck had ruled against his writ, then asking if I wouldn't mind carrying the enclosed writ of *certiorari* over to Justice Bill Douglas at the U.S. Supreme Court. I begged off. But somehow, I never knew how, Billy sent in the writ himself and won his point, eventually getting released from prison.

Later, he ran into my brother Chick. As they were visiting, Billy commented that he had used a lot of lawyers in his day, but that "your kid brother, Jimmy, was the best of the lot. He did more for me than anyone else who ever represented me."

"In fact," Billy said, "I'm gonna do him a big favor down in Shannon County some day."

"Like what?" Chick asked.

"I'm gonna hang a jury for him."

5

Getting
Political

Who knows why people get into politics? Probably only deep psychoanalysis can determine what really drives politicians. I suppose that, besides my own ego drive, I entered politics for a combination of reasons. I had an abundance of physical energy. In addition, I had accumulated during my adult life a set of beliefs for which only political activity provided an outlet. A private life was not enough for me, fueling my desire to move into public space.

After losing the attorney general's race in 1968 to Gordon Mydland, the Republican candidate, I tried to concentrate on law for a time, but found it difficult, unable to shake the political virus that gripped me. In 1969, Harlan Severson and Jim Webster, who worked for East River Rural Electric Cooperative in Madison, asked if I would agree to act as statewide cochairman of a referendum committee. The rural electric co-ops wanted to kill a bill that Republican Governor Frank Farrar had rammed through the Republican controlled state legislature, a bill that favored the private power companies and was, therefore, extremely unpopular with the rural co-ops. I couldn't wait to say yes.

I spent a great part of 1969 making speeches around South Dakota, trying to build support for referring the Farrar bill to a vote of the people. Sensing that Farrar had ruined himself politically with his controversial legislation, I began to think more and more of running for governor. That thought ended in October, however, when Mary packed up and left, thoroughly disgusted with my chronic traveling. After a week or so of separation, we reached a truce of sorts. I agreed not to run for governor and she agreed to come home.

I moped around the house, practiced law—listlessly—until just before New Year's Day in 1970. Congressman E. Y. Berry, the incumbent representative in the Second Congressional District, announced that twenty years in the House was enough and that he would retire at the end of his term. I suggested to Mary that she really ought to withdraw her objections and allow me to run for the House. "I won't win anyway," I told her. "And besides, if I do, Washington would be much more interesting to live in than Pierre (South Dakota's capital city, which we pronounce 'Peer')."

More out of weariness than desire, she relented, concluding that such a race might get it all out of my system. So, when Bob Williams, one of the Teachers Union's political activists, called me to see if I was interested in the race, I was ready.

"Other candidates have called," Williams said, "asking for our support in the congressional race. We'd rather support you, so I'm asking if you're going to run."

Expecting me to ask for time to think it over, I gave Williams his New Year's shock by immediately responding, "Why not?" I made a public announcement shortly afterward, and began lining up my campaign in January 1970.

Campaigning for attorney general was one thing, because it required only speechmaking. Running a House race, I learned, was an entirely different matter. Speechmaking was only a small part of it all. Matt Reese used to say, "Find out where the cherries are, then go pick 'em." He was referring to the process of determining voter sentiment toward each candidate through both telephone and door-to-door canvassing, then getting out on election day those who intended to vote for you, and ignoring those who did not. I knew I would have to follow Matt's advice if I had any chance at all.

In addition to me, there were two other candidates in the Democratic primary for the House seat in 1970—Elvern Varilek, a farmer from Geddes, who was minority leader in the South Dakota House of Representatives, and Don Barnett, a young army veteran who had been a hospital administrator in Vietnam.

Barnett was a good speaker who appealed to a lot of people and who, in the end, almost won the primary. Varilek started the race vastly overconfident because of his position in the state legislature. He believed, erroneously as it turned out, that because he was well known in the legislature he would carry the state. He told George Cunningham, who was then George McGovern's administrative assistant, that he knew he was ahead in the race because he had handed out several thousand Elvern Varilek balloons (dubbed ever afterward as the Varilek "balloon poll"). Elvern only momentarily frightened me, when, at his kickoff banquet, he brought in Billy Martin, the famous baseball player and New York Yankees manager, to make a speech for him.

My campaign manager was Ian Brooks, a young Canadian college student who, along with his partner, Greg Smith, had first appeared in Rapid City during the 1968 presidential primary election. We had put them to work in the Kennedy campaign, and they loved American politics so much that they couldn't wait to return in 1970. We had virtually no money to spend for the House primary, relying mostly on personal contact and what little free press I could get from the newspapers.

I barely skimmed past Barnett on primary election night, winning with just a few hundred votes. I won, most likely, because I had started out better known than he. Elvern Varilek came in substantially behind Barnett. On the day after the primary my prospects for winning the general election already looked utterly hopeless. There were far fewer Democrats than Republicans in the Second District, traditionally the most conservative of the two districts in South Dakota. The Second District had elected a Democrat only once before in the history of the state, in 1932, when Theo "Dates" Werner rode in on FDR's landslide. I was totally out of money, having used all of my personal funds during the primary campaign, with no hope of finding any more. After having fed both my family and a platoon of campaign workers for weeks, there was no food left in the house.

With the history of Republican party domination in South Dakota, especially in the Second Congressional District, no one cared to invest in a sure loser. Well, almost no one. As I sat in my law office staring at the wall and wondering how to carry on with the general election campaign, and at the same time, how to buy groceries so that my family could eat, Earl Brockelsby walked in and plunked down $300 in cash on my desk. "I figure you could use this about now," Earl said. It was an amazing gift, made with perfect timing. I thanked him profusely, and after he left, I went straight to the Safeway and stocked up on food.

With food worries temporarily out of the way, I began thinking again about the general election campaign. Fred Brady, who beat Jim Abdnor in the Republican primary, was to be my opponent in the fall. Abdnor had spent several years toiling in Republican party politics, first as a state legislator, then as lieutenant governor. Brady was a newcomer, a civil engineer from Spearfish whose shock of white hair made him look more distinguished than Abdnor.

I called George McGovern at his Senate office in Washington to ask if he would lend one of his staff members to run my campaign. I specifically named Pete Stavrianos, whom I had met in 1968 when he was working McGovern's "boiler room" operation in Sioux Falls. McGovern agreed and, I'm thankful to say, so did Pete. Pete was, and is, a political natural, a very quiet operator who got out McGovern's vote in 1968 with great efficiency. Before working for McGovern in 1968, he had been doing graduate work at the University of California at Berkeley. His father, Leften Stavrianos, who had been George McGovern's history professor at Northwestern University, is a brilliant historian. Although now in his seventies, he still publishes a new book every couple of years. His mother, Bertha Stavrianos, before her untimely death in 1987, held a Ph.D. in psychology and was a specialist in children's education.

Pete's first directive as campaign manager was to order me to get out of our headquarters, actually my law office, telling me that I had clinched every vote *there*, and that now I should start working on the rest of the voters in the district. He took over the scheduling and sent campaign workers off in every direction to begin canvassing voters' intent. Beyond his superb organizational abilities, he soon demonstrated that he could also see around corners politically.

When I first began campaigning for the House in early 1970, John Thorne, the news director for a Rapid City radio station, KIMM, had interviewed me a couple of times for his news program, telling me that he was a pilot and that if I ever wanted to fly anywhere, he'd be happy to pilot the plane. I took him up on the offer, at first renting a small, single-engine plane. Unfortunately, on our initial trip to Aberdeen, a blizzard struck shortly after we landed there, snowing us in for several days. After a few flights, we began talking about his working full time. I had no money to pay him, but just as we were about to give up on the idea, a contributor from Omaha, Nebraska, Warren Buffet, donated a stock certificate to the campaign. It was valued at about $2,000, so I offered it to John as salary for the rest of the campaign. He accepted, and quit his job at KIMM, becoming, for official purposes, campaign press secretary and chief pilot.

We borrowed a small, single-engine Mooney aircraft from a contractor for whom I had worked when I was in engineering school. The plane was ordinarily used to carry spare parts and oil cans to construction jobs. Its condition was so bad that it should have been grounded by the FAA. The instrument lights didn't work, requiring me to hold a flashlight over the instruments during night flights so that John could read them. We didn't complain, however, because the plane worked most of the time, and, of course, it was free.

Thorne was also creative as press secretary. He developed a system of taping "live actualities" of my voice, which he would surround with his professional announcer's voice, producing a "live" news broadcast that he then provided to radio stations around the district. The stations were all small with no independent news staff, and so they were delighted to get a live feed from a politician, even though they knew it was totally self-serving.

Because we would have little or no money to spend, there remained only one way to run a campaign in the district: by making personal contact with as many people as possible prior to election day and by canvassing voters to get the pro-Abourezk people out to vote when the time came. We also had to use as much free press as possible, such as John Thorne's "live actualities." Television commercials were out of the question, simply because we lacked money for them. I made it a point—publicly—to campaign in every single town and city in the district, which was my own version of the gimmick some candidates were using of walking through the entire state. About once a week, Pete would send out a news release to the press announcing that I had now visited x percent of the towns in the district.

Since I started out virtually unknown in the district, I was willing to go anywhere and do anything to meet people. Well, almost anything. I was taken to a meat packing plant in Mitchell to shake hands with the workers. I was not prepared for the smell, however, which quickly overpowered me and sent me flying out in search of fresh air. The union steward followed me out and laughed gleefully as I vomited on the ground. I told Pete never to schedule me to visit a packing plant again. It occurred to me, however, that while I was able to choose whether or not to visit a meat packing plant, real people—not the rich and the powerful—were forced to lead their lives in such deplorable conditions each day.

Day after day I went in and out of main street stores in every town in the district shaking hands. My favorite campaign locations were bowling alleys, which were open after most other businesses had closed. They contained the closest thing I could find to a captive audience. I adopted the practice of working my way up and down the lanes, shaking hands and bantering with the bowlers, who seemed to enjoy a chatty politician for the brief time that I stopped to talk. I would make one round through all the bowling alleys in those towns that had more than one, then return to work the second shift of bowlers.

I became known both in and out of South Dakota as an anti-war candidate, ultimately prompting hundreds of students from all over the United States to volunteer to work in my campaign. The first volunteer to drift in was Tom Pokela, a student from Minnesota. Randy Fredrickson, the son of an American Baptist minister in Sioux Falls, came to work after dropping out of Harvard Divinity School. Marge Stavrianos, Pete's sister, joined the campaign as well. Amy Vance, Cyrus Vance's daughter, and two of her friends came in from Mt. Holyoke College. Buddy Paul, who had been teaching cinema at Northwestern University, spent weeks knocking on doors as part of the canvassing effort. The biggest contingent came from Carleton College in Northfield, Minnesota, where working in the Abourezk campaign became a campus project, all of it organized by two Carleton students from St. Louis, Jimmy Kolker and his brother Danny.

These were paranoid times, with Richard Nixon's demagoguery about crime, criminals, and hippies flooding the airwaves, forcing us to require haircuts of the young campaign workers. At Mitchell, the entry point for the Carleton students, the campaign's representative would stop each male student with long hair and direct him to a barber shop for a haircut. I told one student, who bitterly complained, that even Bill Kunstler had gotten a haircut before coming to South Dakota in 1969, which seemed to mollify him.

All of the volunteers in Rapid City slept at our house, mostly on the floor. Mary cooked a huge pot of something different every day to feed them—beans, rice, stew, whatever was cheap and filling. In other towns, the volunteers piled into homes of local Democratic supporters to eat and sleep.

The South Dakota newspapers, with the exception of Mitchell's *Republic*, saw it as their solemn duty to keep South Dakota Republican. Their editorial columns reflected this attitude, and in a way, so did the news columns. Coverage of the campaign was generally slim, making name identification much more of a problem for Democrats than for Republicans, who had a surfeit of money and had been much better organized over the years. In the five campaigns that I ran in South Dakota, not once did I get the endorsement of my hometown newspaper, the *Rapid City Daily Journal*. The South Dakota daily newspapers had for years sponsored a poll of voter preference for candidates. The poll had always shown Republican candidates, no matter who they were, in the lead. The newspapers sponsoring the poll were undeterred by the frequent criticism of their polling method—it was done by mail and counted only those responses mailed back in. In spite of the gaping hole in their procedures, they continued to trumpet the poll's efficacy each election year. Their method of polling favored the better organized Republican party, and the results of the poll, when made public, always dried up campaign funds for Democrats.

In 1970, I wanted desperately to get the *Journal's* endorsement, as much for reasons of ego as for political gain. It is the most powerful paper in the Second District, and one that had never, to my knowledge, endorsed a Democrat for anything.

Pete made an appointment for me to meet the editorial board for the ostensible purpose of deciding whom they would endorse. On the appointed day I was in the northwestern part of the state campaigning, and I returned to Rapid City less than an hour before the meeting was scheduled to begin. Pete was nervously chewing the inside of his mouth when I ran into the headquarters and asked him what he thought I should say to the board.

He handed me a reprint from the Congressional Record. It was a speech that George McGovern had earlier delivered on the Senate floor on the subject of agriculture and the family farm. It was a brilliantly written statement, one that had obviously received a great deal of work from McGovern and his staff, particularly from his speechwriter, John Holum. I memorized as much of it as I had time for, then went to the *Journal's* editorial office.

I was placed at one end of a semicircle, fully realizing that I was the long shot in the race for endorsements by the *Journal*. In fact, the *Journal* had an institutional hatred of George McGovern, and they saw me as one of his progeny. For the better part of that year the *Journal's* editorials had been ripping off McGovern's skin, using as an excuse his renewed effort to run for the presidency. I felt akin to the victims of the Spanish Inquisition as I sat there, facing a lineup of stalwart Republican partisans, opposed both to me and to my politics.

Jim Kuehn, the managing editor, opened with, "Now, tell us what you'll do for South Dakota if you're elected, Jim."

I was frightened enough to be superbly articulate that day. I regurgitated virtually the entire agricultural policy speech over which George had labored so hard, reaching heights of eloquence that even I could not have imagined.

When I finished there was a long silence. Then one of the editors broke the lull with a sigh, saying, "You know, Jim, that was fantastic. Now why can't McGovern come up with something like that?"

I could only croak, "I'm sure he has." I managed to escape before they could ask any more questions. The *Rapid City Journal* endorsed Fred Brady.

Someone named Bob Colodzin mysteriously appeared in Rapid City one day during the campaign. Apparently George McGovern had told him I was against the Vietnam War, that I was a decent candidate, and that I deserved support, so he had come out to look me over. Colodzin had been a television producer in New York City, and apparently knew everybody in the advertising business there. He offered to help make television commercials for me, and more importantly, he said that he could make them at little or no cost.

Under Colodzin's direction, John Thorne bought a hand-wind Bolex 16-millimeter movie camera, rented a lens from somewhere in Chicago, then gave them both to Buddy Paul. Using black-and-white film—we couldn't afford color—Buddy followed me around South Dakota for several days, doing nothing other than filming me as I campaigned. Buddy refused to have his long hair cut, and combined with his ambush-like filming techniques, aroused great suspicion among the folks in one small South Dakota town. I overheard one say that she thought Buddy was "one of them there hippies that come to blow up the Corn Palace."

We sent the undeveloped film to Bob Colodzin in New York, who in turn gave it to Evan Stark of the Doyle, Dane and Bernbach advertising agency. Evan found the technical help needed to develop, edit, and narrate the commercials, and produced two or three in black and white that were highly attractive and extremely effective. (For several years, South Dakotans would mention the commercials to me, usually singling out the one where I chased down a farmer who was driving a tractor, forcing him to stop and shake hands.)

While we now had the commercials "in the can," as they say in the trade, we had no money to put them on the air. But just then Morrie Clarkson, a semi-retired banker and once a losing Democratic candidate for the same House seat, came riding in like the Lone Ranger to save the campaign. Morrie and his wife, Gless, agreed to loan me $10,000 to buy television time. I told them that if I lost, my law practice would enable me to pay them back, and if I won, I would be able to raise the money. They took the gamble, an act of great charity—and faith—on their part, considering the slimness of my chances. Aside from the Democrats who had won during the Roosevelt landslides, only Ralph Herseth for governor and George McGovern for U.S. House of Representatives in the First District had been elected during the 1950s. When anyone contributed to a Democrat's campaign, it was more symbolic than serious. And I was even more of a long shot than most.

In January 1970, Fred Brady, my Republican opponent for the Second District House seat, printed and distributed thousands of small handbooks, entitled, *This—I Believe*, advertising his views on the issues of the day. Since he was a newcomer to politics and no one expected him to beat Jim Abdnor, little attention was paid either to him or to his handbook during the primary race. Brady sort of crept up on Abdnor with a late surge, inhibiting any real debate on Brady's views.

One point in the pamphlet was of particular interest to me. Brady had proposed "Compulsory Citizenship Training" as a first step in obtaining a "professional service force." He meant, I think, that the draft should be ended and that the country should have a volunteer army that would be fed by a compulsory youth corps. What caught my attention was the part of Brady's proposal requiring "every citizen of the United States under 26 years of age to serve a minimum of two 90-day periods of Compulsory Citizenship Training."

It was an amazing statement. The handbook said that,

> "Many hundreds of thousands of young men and women would enjoy ninety-day summer camps of recreation, schooling, discipline, good food, and warm quarters. Most of our young people have never had the opportunity to be properly disciplined."

Brady believed, and said so in his booklet, that many youth would be anxious to sign up for an extended period, after which they would elect to make a career out of service to their country as members of our "well-paid professional service force." Brady saw his program as an answer to the civil rights demonstrations rocking the nation and as "a solution to the present dissent that wracks our colleges and universities." He also wanted survival to be taught in the program, seeing this kind of training as a deterrent to an external enemy who might be contemplating invasion. Like most politicians in those days, Brady failed to see that the political polarization was caused, not by undisciplined youth, but by the president and the Congress ignoring public demands to end the Vietnam War. It was clear to me, at least, precisely who Brady had in mind when he talked about lack of discipline.

As I campaigned around the district during the summer, I asked different voters what they thought of the idea. Virtually everyone I asked made a similar comment: "Sounds like a Hitler youth program to me."

Bingo!

Pete, John, and I prepared a campaign on the issue, timed for the fall, after Labor Day when people turned their attention more to politics. I let go the first salvo in early September, releasing a public statement blasting Brady's compulsory youth training program. The release was buried in the few newspapers that chose to run it, giving it no more than a column inch or two. My heart sank. Here was the best and only chance to engage Brady in any kind of debate, and the newspapers were not being very cooperative. Certainly Brady would not be stupid enough to respond. Or would he?

Nothing happened for three days, and then bingo again. Brady rose to the bait, issuing a statement denying that he favored compulsory youth training. I responded, once again charging him publicly with authorship of the proposal. This time he answered immediately in the press, now insisting that he meant to say something different from what the booklet said.

It was his biggest mistake, and my biggest break, because it suddenly aroused interest on the part of the press. It was a genuine controversy, and at the same time it called into question Brady's political judgment. Now, in addition to nonstop campaigning on various issues, we had found a loose thread that, if properly pulled, threatened to unravel Brady's entire campaign. All of us continued to tug away at the youth camp proposal. We ran ads reprinting that part of his handbook, and at one point, because the booklet was becoming hard to find, Pete bought classified advertising in some of the daily newspapers offering a reward of ten cents a copy for Brady's handbook. A supporter in Belle Fourche volunteered the use of an offset printing press located in the basement of his home, which we immediately commandeered, reprinting and distributing the youth camp proposal by the thousands.

Brady and I appeared in a face-to-face debate only once, before a League of Women Voters' forum in Rapid City. He used most of his allotted ten minutes to describe, in what I thought was a corny presentation, his South Dakota upbringing. He droned on about how he was born in South Dakota, the son of pioneers, educated as an engineer at the South Dakota School of Mines, and had served in the Pacific theater during World War II (actually in Alaska). I couldn't resist. When my turn came I announced that I too was born in South Dakota of immigrant pioneer parents, that I was also educated as an engineer at the South Dakota School of Mines, and that in addition I had received a law degree from the University of South Dakota, and had served in the Pacific theater during the Korean War. However, I said, holding my index finger high in the air, I possessed one quality that even my distinguished opponent could not claim. I paused for effect, then said, "I am also a highly skilled notary public," to the roar of the assembled audience.

There was a story going around that Brady was so confident of winning that he had sold his home in Spearfish *before* the election, and had already been looking for a new home in Washington, D.C. I never knew whether the story was true, but it was a good indication, at least, of Brady's overconfidence.

We Democrats swept all three major races in 1970. Dick Kneip won the governorship, Frank Denholm the First District House seat, and I won in the Second District. The newspapers' poll had shown Kneip ahead, but Denholm and I dramatically upset their predictions. The final result of my election, reported to me through growing waves of euphoria as election night progressed, was in my favor, 51.3 percent to 48.7 percent.

The euphoria of the victory lasted only so long, however. I was soon brought back down to earth. Before the campaign started, I owned several credit cards—mostly oil company cards, and one from American Express. When the campaign got under way, I shuffled and dealt them out to the campaign staff, keeping the American Express card for my own use. At the end of the campaign, although I had paid the bills whenever I could, I owed money on every one of the credit cards.

In January 1971, after I was sworn in as a House member, I began receiving dunning letters and threatening phone calls from a collection agent regarding the $600 I still owed American Express. I tried to explain to him that I would get a paycheck at the end of January from the government, but that I currently had no money and couldn't pay until then. He was not interested in waiting, and continued calling me at my congressional office in the Cannon House Office Building. He seemed especially aggressive, and I knew of no way to get him off my back. So with the liberal use of some threatening profanity of my own, I invited him to come in person to collect, telling him that upon his arrival I would personally handle his case. As an alternative I invited him to sue me. I had anticipated him correctly. He chose the latter option.

Sometime earlier John Thorne had applied for an American Express card for himself, giving my name as a credit reference. At about the same time that American Express's computer was about to file a collection lawsuit against me, it sent a letter asking me how John's credit was. I wrote back saying that, "John Thorne's credit is every bit as good as mine." It must have been a convincing reference because John promptly received a credit card, just before American Express demanded that I return mine.

There were backup money systems available, however, if I had only chosen to use them. A delightful Indian woman named Millie Chasing Horse and I had become friends when I practiced law in Rapid City. She would come into the office occasionally for a loan of a few dollars whenever she ran short. She made one of her periodic visits and requests for money just at the beginning of my campaign for the House. I told her that I just didn't have any money to give her, that I needed it for the campaign.

"Campaign? What campaign?" she asked, totally surprised, "I never heard of any campaign."

"I'm running for the House of Representatives," I told her, "and I need to use what little money I have to buy advertising and to pay other expenses."

"But you don't need any money," Millie insisted, seemingly shocked that I would not have talked to her about my problem earlier. "I'm gonna do a *Yuwipi*—prayer to the great spirit of the Lakotas—for you and you'll win without any money."

I smiled, inwardly, of course, and as she left, empty-handed, I thanked Millie for her prayer.

The day after I won the election in November, I was in my law office when Millie came charging in. "You see," she said, smugness permeating her voice, "I told you I'd do a *Yuwipi*, and that you'd win, didn't I?"

I dug in my pocket for what money I had and gave it all to her.

Both of my brothers, Tom and Chick, had been, in spite of my father's Democratic party leanings, strong Republicans. In fact, I have always believed that both of them voted against me in the 1970 elections, doing so for two reasons—one, I was a Democrat, and two, they found it impossible to take their kid brother seriously, either as a candidate or as anything else.

Shortly after my upset victory for the House in 1970, Tom drove from Mission to Rapid City, two-hundred miles west, to conduct business. Down around Mission, where they had operated the famous Abourezk's Store since 1945, Tom and Chick were quite well known because of their long-time, extensive roadside advertising campaign, promoting free ice water and other inanities.

Everywhere Tom introduced himself that day in Rapid City, he was asked, "Are you related to Jim Abourezk?"

He fumed, his anger increasing with each inquiry. Finally, as he and his wife entered a restaurant to eat dinner, the hostess asked for his name.

Without hesitation he replied, "Tom Fox."

6

Running for the Senate

I was a member of the U.S. House of Representatives for about a month when I decided to run for Karl Mundt's Senate seat. In all the years that he was in the political arena, Mundt had been unbeatable. He was, you may recall, one of Senator Joe McCarthy's minions and a political ally of a young and hungry Richard Nixon during their Red-baiting days. When Mundt was thought to be the most vulnerable, in 1960, George McGovern gave up his First District House seat to run against him. Among other things, Mundt produced a televised endorsement by J. Edgar Hoover during this campaign. And when Drew Pearson tried to nail Mundt with allegations of illegal profiteering from the placement of a federal interstate highway on Mundt-owned land, the *Sioux Falls Argus Leader* provided Mundt with front-page space to refute the charge even before readers could look inside the paper to learn what the story was all about.

What a series of political challenges could not accomplish, however, a paralyzing stroke in November of 1969 did, taking Mundt out of the race and out of politics for good. Even though the stroke completely incapacitated him, his wife would not allow him to resign before his term officially ended. Had he resigned during the period between his stroke and January 1971, when Democrat Dick Kneip was sworn in as governor, incumbent Republican Governor Frank Farrar could have appointed a Republican replacement for him. Because he did not, there was no Senate incumbent running for the seat in 1972, and more importantly, no Republican incumbent.

Pete Stavrianos and I were discussing the Senate race while walking through the underground tunnel from the House floor one day in February 1971, when I told him that I thought I would run for the Senate seat. What seemed like a simple decision just then turned into eighteen months of living on extreme fast forward. For me, life became a montage of day and night campaigning, while at the same time I was trying to carry out the responsibilities of a freshman House member. I soon discovered, however, that the two jobs were not mutually exclusive, that a member of Congress spends most of his or her waking hours campaigning either for reelection or for election to a new post. And most of that campaign time is spent raising money. In a sense, I would not have found myself doing things much differently had I been running for reelection to the House.

I requested appointment to the House Judiciary Committee, chaired by Manhattan Congressman Emmanual Cellar, and to the House Interior Committee, chaired by Colorado Congressman Wayne Aspinall. My timing, although accidental, was nearly perfect. By starting my term in 1971, I stumbled into a backbencher's fantasy—a revolt of the reformers in the House, something that thoroughly delighted my dissenting bones. That year the reform leadership decided to challenge some of the entrenched and encrusted committee chairmen, such as John McMillen of South Carolina. In the Interior Committee, Phil Burton, a San Francisco Democrat, took on Chairman Aspinall, hoping to soften his dictatorial rule.

There was also anger building at Nixon's refusal to get out of the Indochina war. I joined what was then a small group of House members trying to cut off funding for the war—Bella Abzug from Manhattan, John Conyers from Michigan, Bob Eckhardt from Texas, and Don Edwards and Phil Burton from California, among others. As a group we would periodically march into House Speaker Carl Albert's office to demand an end to the Vietnam War, always, however, coming away empty-handed.

I attended a meeting called by one of the anti-war groups to hear a speaker named Daniel Ellsberg, who was so eloquent about the damage the war was doing not only to America, but also to the Vietnamese peasantry, that I returned to my office extremely shaken. I circulated a memo to my staff suggesting that none of us were really doing enough to try to end the war, and that we needed to think of new ways to attack the problem.

The next day, Ellsberg called me and asked if I could set up an appointment for him with George McGovern. He had been unable to get a response when he requested it directly. I agreed to help him, and called John Holum, McGovern's speechwriter, asking him to set up a meeting. Holum said he would.

Then, several days later Holum called to tell me that Ellsberg had offered to give McGovern what he described as "top-secret" documents dealing with the Vietnam War. Without divulging their contents, Ellsberg stressed to McGovern that they would dramatically affect the progress of the war. "What do you think, Jim?" Holum asked. "Should we take them?"

Neither of us knew what was in the documents, which of course turned out to be the Pentagon Papers, but the words "top-secret" frightened me. I told him that my best judgment would be not to take them, because divulging them would bring the authorities down hard, especially under Nixon. I later learned that Ellsberg had offered the Pentagon Papers to Bill Fulbright, who also turned them down, before *The New York Times* decided to publish them.

As a congressman I began a program of "Town Meetings" throughout the Second Congressional District. I would announce a schedule of meetings in virtually every town of any size in the district, by news release and in a mass mailing of our office newsletter. The meetings were generally well attended by South Dakotans, although there were occasions—an assault on the ego—when only two or three people showed up. Typically, a meeting would start with a question-and-answer period on issues of current interest, followed by a one-on-one session with anyone who had a problem with the federal government they thought I could resolve.

Most people could not afford to travel to Washington to get the government to behave properly. It soon became obvious to me that only the well-off, or the well-organized, knew how to bend the government to their point of view. Taking the complaint table out to the people was, from my perspective, the only way to open up the system to those who either had no money or never knew how to ask for anything.

The meetings became quite popular in South Dakota, and I think

South Dakota politicians have been expected to hold them ever since. I had mixed feelings however, because the meetings were pure drudgery. There was considerable boredom in dragging myself the often great distances from town to town on weekends and congressional holidays. But the physical and emotional discomfort was vastly outweighed by the sense that I was fulfilling a great and solemn responsibility to my constituents. I had seen too many politicians get elected, only to operate subsequently with the "I've-made-it, too-bad-for-you" attitude that has always given politicians a bad name.

It was such a frenetic time that both the staff and I sometimes forgot the larger context in which we were operating. In 1971, I held a meeting in Gregory on Easter Sunday morning without realizing that it was a holiday, until someone in the surprisingly sizable audience mentioned it, causing me to ask out loud, "What am I doing here? In fact, what are we all doing here?" But the meetings turned into an unusual combination of real public service and pragmatic reelection politics.

I spent so much time in South Dakota that my congressional office pretty much ran without me. My staff once agreed to cosponsor a bill named something like the Crime Prevention and Control Act of 1971. They did so without telling me, while I was campaigning in South Dakota. I first heard of the bill—and my cosponsorship—when I stopped in at radio station WNAX, the "farmer's friend," 560 on the AM dial. I asked if the announcer would like to interview me, and he said yes. The first question he asked was, "Let's discuss this bill you've sponsored—the Crime Prevention and Control Act of 1971. Now, Congressman, will you tell us what is in this bill?"

Inside I began dying a slow, agonizing death, but I responded in my most soothing radio voice, telling the audience, "It's far too complicated a piece of legislation to go into in the short time we have here, but I can tell you that if it's passed, it will go a long way toward solving the problem of crime in this country."

Hoping to God my apprehension was not noticeable, I looked up at the announcer. Highly pleased with the answer, he said "thank you" and went on to another subject, as anxious as I was to abandon such a complex issue.

Early in my House term, Senator Hubert Humphrey decided to schedule a trip to the Sioux City, Iowa stockyards and to Vermillion, South Dakota. He invited both Frank Denholm, our newly elected First District congressman, and me on the trip. We flew out of Andrews Air Force Base on a propeller-driven Convair, a flight that took over three hours. During the flight I asked Hubert if he would mind giving me some advice on running for the Senate. I hadn't realized how much electoral magic would be contained in my request. I spent most of the three-and-a-half-hour flight listening to him hold forth on running, raising money, and every other aspect of politics that came to mind.

When we arrived at the Sioux City stockyards, Humphrey's original entourage had grown exponentially, now including not only those of us who had flown with him from Washington, but the entire Iowa press corps, local politicians, and assorted hangers-on. Like the Pied Piper, Hubert led this regiment up and down the reaches of the stockyards, commenting on the livestock, shaking hands with onlookers, hugging baby pigs, and generally practicing politics like it should be practiced. The only slip-ups Hubert made dealt with Denholm and me. As he raced through the stockyards, he would periodically do an about-face, causing collisions throughout the crowd that was following close on his heels. Each time he reversed his direction, he would encounter Denholm and me, introducing himself to us as though he had never met us before. I told Denholm that I thought it was a function of the large crowd and his frenetic pace. But I was wrong. The next morning, following a breakfast in the University of South Dakota's student union, Humphrey stood up to make a speech. We were sitting one table away from him when he told the audience of mostly university officials that their two fine Democratic congressmen, Denholm and Abourezk, had come out with him on the flight, but that he was sorry they couldn't join him at the breakfast.

Although I disagreed with Hubert's position on the Vietnam War and his slavish dedication to the Israeli lobby, I thought that he was one of the most colorful politicians ever to work in America. I think everyone who knew him was better off for his presence. Talking was his favorite game, and he was the world's best at it. If a senator chanced to walk onto the Senate floor in the middle of one of his speeches, Humphrey would simply stop and start all over again, wanting to make certain the senator heard every word of it. Hubert was such a political animal that one wag commented during the 1974 midterm Democratic Convention in Kansas City that in order to stop him from running for president, you would have to drive a wooden stake through his heart.

In the spring of 1972, the Republicans chose as their candidate for the U.S. Senate a Yankton lawyer by the name of Robert Hirsch.

Then Republican majority leader of the South Dakota Senate, Hirsch was a powerful public speaker, and, I thought, a downright mean politician. I began a number of my own speeches by saying that he was the only man I knew who looked like Richard Nixon and sounded like Karl Mundt. Hirsch towed the straight Republican party line on most issues, saying, in his own way, that the country ought to spend lots on defense and let the poor and working classes go to hell. During our single television debate, I planned in advance to take advantage of Hirsch's aggressive nature. I had voted in the House against virtually every defense spending bill, including one just a few weeks before the election. In the debate, Hirsch couldn't resist saying that Congressman Abourezk was selling America down the river to the Soviets, a charge that I knew he would get around to making at some point. So when he did, I smiled—no, I grinned—at the camera and said, "Now Bob, you know better than that." He could not contain his rage, and it showed on the tube, which was precisely what I was aiming for.

As campaigns go, my Senate race was much easier than the House race two years earlier. We were much better financed and better organized. I was better known, and also I was now taken seriously by the opposition. When I announced for the Senate seat in early 1972, I was challenged in the primary by George Blue, who was once chairman of the state Democratic party. Blue's entire campaign was based on his opposition to abortion and my support for legalizing abortion on demand. The anti-abortion groups had not yet come into their full strength, as they did in later South Dakota elections, but there were a few around the state that dogged my footsteps. Despite Blue's best efforts, however, he received only 20 percent of the primary vote, which meant that I had no serious problem in uniting the Democratic party for the general election in the fall.

In the general election, Robert Hirsch never came close. My campaign organization did weekly tracking polls by telephone, using a polling system originally set up by the Cambridge, Massachusetts poll taker, Pat Caddell, but executed by our volunteers. The polling came in handy as a way to follow voter sympathies, or animosities, down to election day. When the poll showed that my own aggressive campaign style was becoming too scary for women and the elderly, we did a quick mailing to women with recipes from my wife and a statement on social security for the elderly. It was, and is, a most distasteful system, much like market research for commercial products, but incredibly, it worked. It is a system that has been used by a great many candidates, but in recent years it was refined to extreme sophistication by Ronald Reagan's handlers.

Dick Shadyac, a lawyer in Washington, who is of Lebanese descent, was helping me raise money for the election. Dick served on the board of St. Jude's Hospital, the famed children's hospital in Memphis, Tennessee that researched cures and offered treatment for certain forms of cancer in children, free of charge. During the primary I asked Dick if he could convince Danny Thomas, the well-known comedian and St. Jude's founder, to make some campaign appearances for me. Dick said he would ask, and to everyone's surprise, Danny agreed to do it. We scheduled five Danny Thomas shows around the state, flew him to South Dakota at night from the Kentucky Derby in a small plane (he barely recovered from the fright of that stormy flight), and hauled him around the state for his appearances.

Later, in the general election, I convinced Arkansas Congressman Wilbur Mills, who was then the all-powerful chairman of the House Ways and Means Committee, to come to South Dakota for a couple of appearances. He flew out from Washington in a small, private jet, landing at Sioux Falls. When I picked him up, I asked him where had he gotten the jet. "Don't ask," Wilbur admonished me.

During the campaign I had occasion to visit with Earl Brockelsby, whom I had never forgotten since he saved the day back in 1970. Earl mentioned that someone from my home area, Mellette County, had offered to bet him a substantial sum of money that Hirsch would beat me. I told Earl to hold off betting until I could give him a fairly accurate polling figure. Within a couple of weeks of the election the tracking poll showed that Hirsch was unable to close the gap, although he had tried everything. John Thorne had already purchased in advance some of the best television time available, decreasing our worry about a last minute blitz by Hirsch. I then called Earl and told him to go ahead and make the bet. It must have been a shattering experience for the fellow who wanted so badly to see me lose.

My youngest son, Paul, who was twelve years old during the campaign got into a scrape at the Sioux Falls Republican headquarters. While chasing a girl his age down the street and into the headquarters, he kicked out the glass door when he tried to follow her into the office. I offered to pay for the window, but it was not enough. Incredibly, Hirsch's campaign wrote a newsletter in which Paul's errant behavior was featured. Someone showed me a copy of the article a few days before the election. The combination of exhaustion from the campaign and my building anger at Hirsch's tactics triggered an emotional explosion. On the Friday before election day, as I was campaigning on the street in Huron, I caught myself telling a stranger, a voter, how nasty I thought Hirsch was. Suddenly my error dawned on me. I then said to the stranger, "Why am I telling you all this?" Realizing that my judgment was impaired, I immediately canceled the rest of my appearances and drove directly to the apartment that we had rented in Sioux Falls, staying there until election day. I had enough presence of mind—just enough—to understand that in my exhausted condition I was acting like a fool and could only do damage to myself and to the campaign.

Well rested after my enforced seclusion, I spent election night in Sioux Falls at the home of a friend making phone calls to supporters around the country, thanking them for their help. What I really wanted to do was to watch the returns on television, but Pete convinced me that making the calls was more important. I saw just enough of the NBC coverage to hear John Chancellor telling his audience that James Abourezk, a part-Lebanese and part-Sioux Indian candidate from South Dakota had been elected. He got that, I presumed, from an article that Larry L. King had written a year or so earlier in *Harper's Magazine* on Mo Udall's race for majority leader. I was described this way in a one-sentence exposition as one of Udall's supporters.

The win was tempered, however, by George McGovern's defeat in the presidential race. Mary and I went down to the McGovern hotel headquarters—also Abourezk campaign headquarters—to offer our best wishes, but it was a place full of sadness, as one might expect. It was extremely difficult for me to address the group, but I was hoisted up on a chair in the middle of McGovern's campaign workers from which I shouted that we now had to start McGovern's campaign for reelection to the Senate. Although my words lightened their burden some and they began cheering, there was nothing that really could be said to compensate for McGovern's loss of the presidency.

We had to press on, however. George McGovern had to run for reelection to the Senate in 1974, and I had to move over to the Senate, after saying goodbye to friends in the House of Representatives. During the traditional round of farewell speeches for House members who were leaving their posts for one reason or another, one of my friends, Minnesota Congressman Bob Bergland (who later became Jimmy Carter's secretary of agriculture), took the floor to say that, "Jim Abourezk's election to the U.S. Senate has raised the intellectual level of both houses of Congress."

7

Advise and
Dissent

I had always thought being a U.S. senator would be the greatest job in the world. Lord knows it looked glamorous before I got there. It was a chance to have a great many people listen to me, to my ideas about how the world ought to be changed for the better. I was convinced that I could do the job in a different manner from all the others. I soon discovered, to my chagrin, that most people had no interest in ideas, or in changing the world, except for that part of it that might narrowly benefit them. When anyone did listen to me, it was only long enough to be able to put in a request for a pet project, to get an edge on their competitors, or to ask me to get something for them from the government. Perhaps there are still a few people in the country who are interested in ways to advance civilization, but they were not, I'm afraid, very visible when I was in office.

Although two years in the U.S. House should be enough time to disabuse anyone of the idea of political glamour, it was not enough for me. The first Senate Democratic Conference (actually, the caucus of Senate Democrats) after I was sworn in as a senator in 1973 was nearly overwhelming for a country boy from South Dakota. I was sitting in the same room with men I had watched on television for years—Arkansas Senator J. William Fulbright, Minnesota Senator Hubert Humphrey, Iowa Senator Harold Hughes, my own Senator George McGovern, Massachusetts Senator Ted Kennedy, among others.

Montana Senator Mike Mansfield, the majority leader, opened the conference with a statement welcoming all the new senators, giving his standard speech about how all senators were considered equals, that no senator was considered superior to any other simply because he or she had been there longer. I know that I should have held my tongue, but I couldn't resist. I raised my hand at the end of his statement and said that, if all senators were equal, I would like to be majority leader for a time. Mike took it with good humor, but the conference had more serious business at hand.

It was just after Nixon and Kissinger had ordered successive layers of bombs on North Vietnam over the congressional Christmas recess, aptly termed the "carpet bombing" of Hanoi, because it was so devastating in its power and so chillingly destructive against the civilian population. The bombing was the focus of the Democratic Conference, with speaker after speaker rising to denounce it. Clearly those senators who spoke against it were deeply affected by it, while those who still supported the Vietnam War sat in silence. Hawaii Senator Daniel Inouye, who was visibly shaking as he spoke, made one of the most telling points when he denounced the bombing as motivated by anti-Asian racism. "Had they bombed Germany, or Norway, or some European country," Inouye said, his deep baritone voice quivering with anger, "there would be a great outcry in this room and throughout the country, but the weak response tells me that to Nixon and to the press it's O.K. to bomb Vietnamese because they are nothing more than a bunch of 'gooks.' " He had struck a nerve. As he spoke I noticed a number of senators looking down at the floor. Wisconsin Senator Gaylord Nelson inveighed against both the bombing and the war by chiding one of the pro-war senators who had advocated all-out war against the Vietnamese, slapping him on the shoulder as he spoke, saying, "Had we listened to my friend here, I'm afraid we'd be in much worse condition today than we are."

But the speech that most strongly clings to my memory was delivered by Missouri Senator Stewart Symington. Symington, tall and distinguished, with a shock of gray hair, was one of the few senators who actually looked like a senator. His wife had died during the previous year, an event that had deeply affected him. "I've had occasion," he began, his voice heavy with emotion, "to spend a great deal of time with my grandchildren over the recent holidays. As we watched the news of the bombing, one of the little ones asked me, 'Grandpa, why are we killing so many people with our airplanes?' I had to try to explain to him why some people thought killing was necessary. It was an effort that forced me into deep thought about the entire concept of the war in Vietnam. I've decided that I am unable any longer to explain to my grandchildren the fact that my country has now become the bully of the world."

At that, Symington abruptly ended his speech and sat down, his emotions eluding his self-control. He put his head in his hands and, in front of the entire gathering of U.S. senators, sobbed unashamedly.

For me, there could be no encore to that meeting, and from then on my life in the Senate went downhill.

Being a senator does not include great intellectual discussions, research, sophisticated dialogue with other senators, or any of the other images that come to mind. Being a senator involves simply making decisions: Do I accept an invitation to make a speech in Sioux Falls, Rapid City, or Chicago this weekend? Which space should I choose for my Senate office when my turn comes? Whom do I hire for my staff? Do I agree to see this or that lobbyist? Do I accept dinner invitations in Washington for purely social reasons, or do I calculate whether attending a dinner is politically worthwhile? Will I raise any money or pick up a new political ally if I attend? Do I vote yes or no on any given political issue? How do I vote on issues that come up that I haven't studied, haven't been briefed on, or haven't been interested in? Should I try to squeeze in one more phone call from the seven or eight flashing phone lines before running to the Senate floor to vote? The ultimate decision is: is it all worth it? Should one deprive oneself of a normal family life in order to stay in office?

The most important decision of all, however, creeps up without warning, involving what kind of politician you want to be. You must decide whether your Senate office will be conducted within some sort of moral framework, or whether it will be used merely to advance your own ambitions. There are any number of politicians who run and serve only to gratify their own egos, ignoring the rapid decline of public responsibility on the part of both business and political leaders. A perfect example is the South Dakota senator who replaced me, Larry Pressler, who has become notorious over the years for his efforts to grab headlines. When he was a member of the House of Representatives, we had lunch together during a time when I was extremely active and constantly in the news. Pressler's only concern was how I got so much press. "Can I hire your press secretary?" he asked, not concerned with the substance of my activity, but only with the amount of press coverage it generated. After I stepped down and Pressler began serving in the Senate I recalled his naked hunger for publicity as I watched him scramble to get his name in the papers and on television. He ran for president—briefly—not expecting to win, but solely for the publicity. He went to Poland seeking the spotlight when Lech Walesa and the Solidarity labor union were in the news.

Pressler has of late developed a new technique for trying to get into the news—that of taking unexpected positions, then at the last minute, shifting his stance. He used this political "bait and switch" routine during the nomination battle over John Tower. Pressler let it be known that he was leaning against Tower's nomination, a position that under the circumstances gave him the press coverage he craved. Meanwhile President Bush was saying, most emphatically, that it was critical that all Republican senators hold the line for Tower. At the last minute Pressler, predictably, switched sides and voted for Tower's confirmation. Sadly, his career has been consistently one of "showboating," of seeking publicity for himself with little or no benefit for either the people of his state or for the country. Although Pressler is an extreme example of the self-serving type of politician, what he does is enough to give even opportunism a bad name.

Whatever power one has as a senator can be used either for oneself or for others, a fact that required me to decide early on whether to do something on behalf of the unorganized and the powerless—the Indians, consumers, Palestinians, the poor—or to avoid the controversial position of the advocate, to play it safe, and to try to stay in office forever. I do not believe, however, that the choices are mutually exclusive. I believe that one can take up temporarily unpopular causes and still be reelected, if reelection is indeed the objective.

My transition from the House of Representatives to the U.S. Senate was not too difficult for me. It was more like a seamless membrane—after the election my life did not really change much. There is, however, a difference between members of the House and members of the Senate. The ability to influence legislation and events is greater in the Senate. This stems, I believe, from the fact that there are fewer senators, and so the media pays more attention to them, and the public in turn perceives the Senate as more influential. It takes a House member years and years to achieve the fame, or the notoriety, of senators. Representatives toil outside the glow of the spotlight for most of their careers. They remain relative unknowns, and are perceived as such by the media, although they tend to be more knowledgeable and to have a better grasp of the issues than senators do.

Senators tend to be generalists in their approach to the issues, relying heavily on their larger staffs to keep them apprised of what's happening in the world around them. Senators rarely spend time on the Senate floor unless there's a vote, or unless they have an interest in particular legislation. For this reason Secretary to the Majority Stan Kimmit always stationed himself by the center doors when the Senate vote bell rang. When surprise amendments were offered to legislation being considered on the Senate floor, Stan was there to advise Democrats on the amendment, and, at times, on how to vote on it. When I was caught unaware of a vote, I would ask Stan, "What do you think about this one?"

"You would vote 'no' on this one, Senator," was often his reply. Or, he would sometimes say, "The good guys are voting yes on this one."

One more thing about House and Senate members. House members usually resent senators, or at least the attention paid to them. The resentment, or envy, is so great that whenever a House member gets a chance, he or she runs for the Senate.

After moving over from the House to the Senate, I continued to travel, to raise money, to campaign, and to be absent from home on weekends and in the evenings. Committee hearings gave the word "boredom" new meaning. Witnesses with their one big chance to speak before Congress would drone on and on, reading prepared testimony. I eventually became so impatient with them that I would open committee hearings with the admonition that, contrary to popular theory, U.S. senators *could* read, and that, if the witness would simply summarize his or her statement, I vouched that the full text would be read either by me or by someone in authority. It almost never worked, and I soon became aware of the reason. Most witnesses brought statements prepared by someone else, and if their lives depended on it, they could not *ad lib* the contents.

The rest of the time was spent talking and listening, in person and on the telephone, to constituents, to people who raised money, to contributors, and to the few lobbyists who came by. In order to do their work, members of my office staff needed decisions from me virtually every day. This involved hearing them outline the options that I had on the projects they were pushing or on positions I should take on upcoming legislation. Most conversations were interrupted by floor votes and had to be completed either while running to the floor or after my return.

I learned in a hurry that only those citizens who already had money, or advantages, were the ones who knew how to get into a Senate office. The poor and disadvantaged never came by, probably for a host of reasons, but mostly because they had no money and no hope of succeeding even if they could come in. My office eventually became known as the last resort for lost causes, which brought on a flood of those who couldn't get a hearing anywhere else. Insofar as the poor were concerned, I had hoped that my continuation of town meetings in South Dakota would afford them an opportunity to get a piece of the pie. I'm afraid, however, that hopelessness was so rampant among a large segment of the disadvantaged that even that kind of outreach failed to activate them.

But there were good times as well. Well, some of them were good.

Campaigning and raising money for other candidates was, for me, great fun. It was totally different from asking for money or votes for myself. In addition, it was a way to build up favors with other individuals and groups that would hopefully be returned when they were needed.

When, for example, Congressman Wayne Owens of Utah wanted to run for the U.S. Senate in 1974, he asked me to organize a fundraiser for him in Washington. At that time I still had the best list of contributors in the Senate, one that I developed during my 1972 race for the Senate, with the help of Chuck Fishman, who worked full time raising money for my campaign. In fact it was so good that Jay Rockefeller asked for, and received, my New York list when he ran for governor of West Virginia.

The Wayne Owens party was to be held at Averell Harriman's Georgetown house, with not only Averell and Pamela Harriman as hosts, but with Robert Redford and his wife, Lola, as guests of honor. With this all-star cast, how could I miss? It was going to be the easiest fundraiser that I'd ever done in my life.

On the day of the big event, when the crowds started coming to the party, Wayne, believing he was rewarding me for my work, asked me to join the dignitaries in the receiving line. Having suffered enough crowds in political life, I tried to beg off, but he kept insisting, so I finally agreed, posting myself at the end of the line.

By the time the guests reached me at the end of the line, they had already wended their way through fashionable Georgetown, entered the Harrimans' plush, antique-filled foyer, tiptoed through the ground floor of the Harrimans' exquisitely furnished salon, expensive carpets softening their footfalls and expensive art easing whatever eyestrain might have burdened them. From the house they emerged into the spectacular rear garden, planted and manicured to near perfection, a space that in South Dakota we used to call "the back yard."

Once the guests reached the receiving line, here is what they heard as they began shaking hands with the hosts.

"Hello, I'm Averell Harriman."

"How do you do, I'm Pam Harriman."

"I'm Robert Redford."

"I'm Lola Redford."

"I'm Wayne Owens."

"I'm Marlene Owens."

"I'm Jim Abourezk."

According to the *Washington Star* story the next day, two women who had just gone through the line, tittering over meeting Robert Redford, went off to the side where one asked the other, "Say, who's Jim Abourezk?"

"I'm not sure," the other one answered, "but I think he's the caterer."

When I first won nomination to run for the House in 1970, I got a letter from Congressman Mo Udall of Arizona. Mo wanted to run for House majority leader at the beginning of the next session and was hustling votes from all potential new members. He closed his letter with the routine "if-there's-anything-I-can-ever-do-for-you-let-me-know" line. I immediately wrote back and told him that he could come to South Dakota and make a speech or two in support of my candidacy. To my great surprise, he agreed to do so, and showed up during the campaign, giving rousing speeches on my behalf both in Rapid City and in Winner.

As everyone now knows, Mo lost the race for majority leader, but when he wanted to run for president in the 1976 Democratic primaries, I offered to help him in South Dakota. "Come on out for several days and I'll go around with you," I told him, confident that I could help him win the June primary. We spent five days flying all over South Dakota in his chartered propeller plane, appearing before big crowds at every stop. Jimmy Carter had not yet bothered to make an appearance in the state, but we were pleased when he scheduled a stop in the Black Hills at the last minute, making us believe that he was really worried about South Dakota. I would have bet my nonexistent fortune on Mo winning, but I would have lost it. He needed South Dakota to give him an added push, but Carter won.

I should have learned then that few presidential candidates are strong enough to carry my endorsement, because I had the same experience in 1974, when I was virtually the only supporter Walter Mondale had in the Senate when he first ran, briefly, for president. I was the photographer for the photo that he used in his presidential campaign newsletter. We made a few appearances together in South Dakota, but he gave up the campaign before it really got under way, telling the press that he was tired of sitting in Holiday Inns and airport waiting rooms. When, in 1977, I was preparing to announce my intention not to run for a second term, I went to see Mondale, who had just been elected vice-president, to tell him about my decision in advance of the announcement. He argued strenuously that I should run again, giving me the same rationale that I had heard before—that public-spirited people were hard to come by, and that I sort of owed it to the country to stay in, even though I was unhappy. I was ready for him. "Fritz," I said, "I'm tired of waiting in airport lobbies and cheap hotels." Naturally, he was unable to argue further.

A freshman senator's maiden speech was, at least in 1973, an occasion when presumably a senator would be able to reach oratorical heights never before attained. When my turn came, I decided to launch an attack on Richard Nixon and his behavior, not only in terms of his decision to keep the Vietnam War going, but also with respect to his domestic policies. Nixon was riding high following his big landslide in 1972, and he was on the verge of making the entire government bend to his distorted idea of governance. His overwhelming victory made him reach for more power than any one person should have. In my speech I called for the establishment of a Congressional Office of Management and Budget, so that we wouldn't have to rely on his budget figures. I suggested that we block appointments of his cabinet nominees, and, heresy of heresies, I called for cutting off funds for the salaries of his White House staff until he began obeying the law.

I viewed the Congress as a willing participant in Nixon's follies, because it had given up its tremendous powers of appropriation. The Congress, for example, could have ended the Vietnam War at any time it wanted just by deciding to stop its funding. Similarly, years later Ronald Reagan could not have supported the contras in Central America, nor could he have instituted Reaganomics, cutting taxes for the rich, had the Congress simply refused to go along with him. But I learned early on that there is a deliberate avoidance of responsibility on the part of the Congress. There is a collective cowardice at work that prevents the Congress from ever challenging a strong president, although the country would be much better off if it would. While members will individually grouse about the president and his programs, in most cases they vote to support the president's initiatives, avoiding blame if they go wrong, but accepting responsibility if they go right. Over time I've come to believe that this kind of avoidance is calculated. It allows the president to take the blame—or the credit—while members keep themselves free of controversy.

What is not too well understood by the general public is that presidents, and their handlers, have an urge for power that seems to feed on itself. That is, the more they get, the more they want, their appetites growing exponentially. Shrewd politicians, such as Richard Nixon and Ronald Reagan, know precisely how to buffalo the Congress. They fully understand the congressional penchant for cowardice in the face of a strong and popular president, and are able to exploit it to the hilt. But the presidential tendency toward abuse of power has, in most instances, also served to curb presidential power. Their overreaching eventually brings about a public backlash. The two most recent examples are Nixon's Watergate scandal and Reagan's Iran-contra scandal. But we should make no mistake about it: Congress does not lay back and plan on a hard presidential fall. Its timidity is ever present, with or without presidential transgressions.

One principle that I established early on was: when voting on the confirmation of a presidential appointee, always vote no, because if he or she is confirmed, it won't be long before your vote is proved politically correct. This approached worked most of the time, with one major exception—the confirmation of Elliot Richardson. Other than Bobby Kilberg, who ran the Indian desk in the White House, Elliot turned out to be about the only good major appointment that Richard Nixon made, and he proved it when he defied Nixon during the Watergate scandal. He resigned rather than follow Nixon's order to fire the special prosecutor.

My first encounter with Elliot Richardson was a positive one. I was a new member of the House of Representatives in 1971, when I learned that the Indian Health Service had actually refused to drill a water well for a group of Indian families on the Pine Ridge Reservation, although they had promised to do so two years earlier. The Indians living there were reduced to collecting their drinking water from potholes at the edge of the White River. I placed a phone call directly to Elliot, who was then Nixon's secretary of health, education, and welfare, and asked for his help. He listened to my story about the Indians, acted immediately, and within a few days the wells were being drilled. This amazed me, because ordinary run-of-the-mill cabinet secretaries show little or no concern for anyone below the level of millionaire.

In order to continue with Elliot Richardson's story, it's necessary to have an understanding of the similarities between the U.S. Senate and the system of tribal government that the Sioux Indians used before the white man came along and changed it. The Sioux pretty much did what they wanted, despite their recognition of various leaders within each tribe. Although there is a majority leader and a minority leader in the Senate, most senators do what they please, often ignoring the wishes of the leadership, yet still acting within the political constraints of their own situations. The concept of one overall Indian chief, as far as the Sioux Indians were concerned, was an invention of the white man. The Sioux neither recognized nor agreed with the notion of one person telling the entire tribe what to do. Like senators, each Sioux made personal decisions, within the social limitations imposed by the entire tribe. There existed holy men, men with strong medicine, war leaders, hunting leaders, but no tribal chief. So, in the last century, when the U.S. government tried to make Sioux culture assimilate to white culture, it had great difficulty. When the army would appoint a chief to distribute rations, or to make a treaty in exchange for promises to give up Indian lands, or to stop making war on the whites, the rest of the Sioux would ignore both the appointment of the tribal leader as well as the promises that he had made.

But around the turn of the eighteenth century, the Sioux developed a system, patterned after that used by other tribes, where respected elders would sit in council and make decisions on the tribe's behalf. These elders were called "Big Bellies." The younger warriors responsible for carrying out the Big Bellies' decisions were called "Shirt Wearers." This leadership system fell into disuse for a time, then was revived in the 1860s, at a time when the Sioux were under heavy attack from the U.S. Army. It was a time when the government was trying to move the Indians out of the way to make room for the wave of white settlers moving westward.

Shortly after I was sworn into the Senate in 1973, I was sitting in the Democratic cloakroom listening to the Senate's Big Bellies complaining about Nixon. Harold Hughes, Hubert Humphrey, and others were taking turns grunting and figuratively shaking their fists at him, threatening political vengeance in return for the myriad sins he was committing each and every day. Nixon and Kissinger had been telling the country that the carpet bombing of Hanoi was necessary in order to force the North Vietnamese into accepting a deal more favorable to the United States. Nixon also had decided to pick and choose where he would or would not spend money already appropriated by Congress for domestic projects, a practice that was then called "impounding." I pitched in, reminding everyone that I had recommended we cut appropriations for salaries for the White House staff as a way of bringing Nixon to his knees. I again suggested that we refuse to confirm all of Nixon's cabinet appointees, a proposal that received unanimous agreement from everyone in the cloakroom, Big Bellies and Shirt Wearers alike.

The first Nixon nominee to come up for confirmation was Elliot Richardson, who was at that moment secretary of health, education and welfare, but whom Nixon had nominated for secretary of defense. When the clerk began calling the roll for the confirmation vote—Abourezk was first—I winced because I liked Elliot, but in the interest of principle, of not going back on my word to the Big Bellies in the cloakroom, and of saving the republic, I shouted a strong NO, and went back to my office in the Dirksen building.

A few minutes later, a reporter called to ask why I had voted against Richardson.

"Why don't you ask some of the others?" I responded. "Why are you calling me?"

"Because yours was the only vote against him," the reporter told me.

It was my first lesson in the politics of courage as practiced by the U.S. Senate, and I've been apologizing to Elliot Richardson ever since.

The Richardson vote was an omen of what it would be like in the world's greatest deliberative body. There are some individual acts of political courage now and then, but hardly ever enough to mount a majority vote. The Vietnam War was a perfect example. Although public opinion was moving rapidly against continued

American involvement, and, in fact, a majority favored withdrawal in the late 1960s, Congress refused to cut off funding totally until 1975. The reason? As a body, Congress was afraid of criticism, of the "who lost Vietnam?" syndrome, so the war dragged on, expending both lives and money beyond any logic.

The same syndrome operated during the Reagan years. Reagan extracted virtually every legislative concession he wanted from the Congress. He succeeded not because his programs were so popular or so wise, but because he intimidated the Congress. Reagan, who could read a script as well as anyone, posed a public relations threat to members of Congress, who otherwise might have voted against his economic program, against aid to the contras, and so forth. But when it came time, later in his Administration, to criticize Reagan on his economic program and on his terrorist war in Nicaragua, there were very few members of Congress who had not voted with him and against their own beliefs, mostly out of fear, discrediting them as critics of Administration policy. Perhaps it will always be this way in a democracy, but the syndrome is also an excellent reason to sharply limit congressional terms. If a member of Congress is not worried about getting reelected, he or she will more often than not vote in the public interest rather than in his or her own electoral interest, which is now what happens.

I learned other political lessons in the Senate as well, such as the one hammered home by Senator Jacob Javits near the end of the 94th Congress, the essence of it contained in the Congressional Record of October 14, 1978, which I reread periodically as a reminder of the gruesome reality of politics. Javits spoke on the Senate floor late in the night as I was making a last-ditch effort to try to stop the natural gas deregulation bill from passing.

Senator Javits had grown both emotionally and physically tired of the debate. I am reproducing here his comments precisely as they appear in the Congressional Record:

> Mr. President, it has been said here a hundred thousand times that politics is the art of the possible. We know there are those here that are insisting—I will put it in absolutely the worst case that I know how—there are those here that are insisting on making the public pay, even though it will go to special interests.
>
> Even though that be true, the question that we have to ask ourselves, if what I say in my judgment is true internationally, is how much?
>
> How much? And if the price is not out of the ballpark, considering

the issue, we may have to pay it. That is why we are a democracy. We have to learn to function somehow.

Mr. President, I think we have arrived at that point, I simply believe that whatever we have to pay in this bill, for whatever these special interests demand as their price, we have to pay. I think we have gotten to that point. We have brought it to the point where now it has simply got to be done.

I guess I was not so surprised at the sentiment expressed by Javits. But I was surprised that he had vented it publicly on the Senate floor, and that he allowed it to remain in the Congressional Record when he could have just as easily stricken it later. I attribute the latter to exhaustion as well.

The principal reason that "special interests" can extract their price from the government is money. Possession of money itself generates power if it is used cleverly, that is, if it is used to impress members of Congress or to raise money from other wealthy persons. The ability of the rich to put their private jets at the disposal of members of Congress, to make available their beach houses, their condominiums, and all the other things that money can buy makes access to congressional and administration offices somewhat easier for them than most citizens. But it is campaign money that calls the tune, a fact recognized by every politician within a few minutes after getting into politics.

There seems to be a rule of inverse proportion in national politics: Members of Congress will scrutinize with exquisite precision appropriations of a thousand dollars or less, but will ram through those of a billion or more without much deliberation at all. Thus, poor welfare recipients become the focus of great congressional attention, the subject of a thousand speeches, while very little is said or done about the gigantic corporate "carry-out" specialists. Strangely, $700 toilet seats draw more press coverage than $20 billion arms boondoggles. Similarly, Texas Congressman Jim Wright was brought down by a nickel and dime book deal that allowed him to circumvent the limit on honoraria that he could receive. Very little was said, however, about his role in preventing the proper regulation of the savings and loan industry. This bit of influence peddling will cost the taxpayers in excess of $100 billion. What this country needs—desperately—is genuine campaign reform that will take all private money out of politics, allowing members of Congress to respond to the genuine demands of their constituents.

In 1973, not long after I began serving in the Senate, I introduced a resolution in the Senate Democratic Caucus initiating public financing of all federal elections—presidential as well as congressional. Actually, the resolution required the appropriate Democratic committee chairmen to begin hearings with the objective of ultimately passing public financing legislation. The resolution was not unique—public financing had been tried before—but in 1973 the timing was important. The Watergate scandal, which revealed the pumping of big sums of illegal money into Nixon's campaign, was just beginning to bubble over, and members of Congress were beginning to feel the sting of public reaction to it. The resolution eventually passed the caucus unanimously, because no one wanted to be caught voting against it, but not before it was subjected to a most interesting debate.

One of those in opposition to the idea itself, Senator Warren Magnuson, a crusty old northern committee chairman, voiced strong objection to any change in financing campaigns. "I don't have any real opposition against me in my state because the Republicans can't raise enough money to run a decent race. Why should I vote for something that will finance an opponent who would not be running against me except for public financing?" Magnuson argued.

Beyond my own arguments in favor of the resolution, augmented by Senator Adlai Stevenson III, the most powerful and moving voices came from two senators known for their less parochial view of politics and power—Senators Hubert Humphrey and Harold Hughes. Hughes confided to the members of the caucus that he would soon be leaving the Senate to become a Christian lay worker. His conscience, he said, would no longer allow him to continue in politics because of the way that he was required to raise money in order to run.

When Hubert Humphrey spoke, it was obvious that he was driven by his conscience as well. Of all his years in politics, he said, he had never done anything as demeaning and degrading as raising money. He spoke of how badly politicians are treated by those who give money, of how one literally had to sell his soul in order to raise the amounts necessary to run.

In obedience to the Democratic Conference, the Senate Rules Committee began work on public financing. The Congress finally passed a bill that session financing presidential elections with public money. But, as we later discovered, the bill omitted the most critical reform. Not only did we not include congressional elections in the bill, but we unwittingly created one of the most corrupting financing systems in American history—the PAC, the political action committee, a form of legalized corruption.

When I ran for the Senate in 1972, I spent about $425,000 for the general election, of which about $50,000 was spent on mailing out fundraising appeals. Although South Dakota has not increased in population since then, Tom Daschle, who ran and won in 1986, spent $3.4 million and Jim Abdnor, who lost the race, spent $3.2 million. The 1984 race in North Carolina between incumbent Senator Jesse Helms and his challenger, Governor Jim Hunt, absorbed nearly $40 million, a figure which, unless something is done about campaign financing, eventually will become the norm.

In talking both to candidates and to contributors, one learns that nobody really likes the system, but each one is abiding by a kind of regulated law of the jungle. You dare not let the other person outspend you, either as a candidate or as a contributor. As long as the system exists, those participating will continue to try to outraise and outspend the opposition. When you think about it, a candidate who runs for office without using all of the weapons available would be considered a fool by his supporters. Those who do not accept money from PACs are those who have other sources.

In the end, candidates will do whatever is necessary to win, and special interest contributors know this. The mere existence of single issue PACs should put members of the public on notice that they exist solely to influence a politician's vote in a specific direction. If, for example, an oil company PAC continues to feed money into a senator's campaign account, we can safely assume that the senator is voting just the way the oil company wants him to vote. Any betrayal of these short-lived principles would soon stop the flow of special interest money.

Although it has been in place for only a few years, the PAC system threatens to create the most narrow kind of politics—a government built from a special interest patchwork. Very little benefit for the general public can ever result from such a parochial structure. Unless the press, and in particular the television networks, are willing to spend a great deal of time and resources convincing the public of the need for change, conditions will only get worse. I hope that the PAC system can be changed before a major scandal mandates it, and before our government is totally revised in the direction of the special interests that are now financing most congressional elections.

What makes progressive change difficult is the tendency of the press, and the public, to focus on trivial matters rather than on the larger policy issues. Whether the subject is leveraged buyouts, corporate greenmail, oil spills in the Alaskan ecosystem, undue influence brought to bear on politicians by well-heeled lobbyists, or any other issue of the day, the press and the public tend to lose sight of who or what is the real culprit. When the Iran-contra scandal broke into public view, for example, about the only sane voice coming out of the Congress was that of Michigan Representative George Crockett, who said over and over, "It's the policies we should be concerned about, not the individuals." Although no one seemed to be listening, he correctly pinned the blame for the scandal on the system that allowed a loose cannon like Oliver North to charge around the deck of the ship of state.

The basis of most of our current foreign policies is the national security system, and yet it gets very little attention from the press, and hence very little from the public. Set up shortly after World War II, the system has been responsible for more death, destruction, and waste than any other single entity. It formalized the cold war, then succeeding hot wars in Asia in order to "contain Communism," as the policy was phrased. Tens of thousands of Americans and untold numbers of Asians have been killed and maimed as a result of the mindset that created and maintained the national security system. It was this covert system that allowed Reagan and his henchmen to repeatedly break the law by giving arms to Iran and money to the contras. In Oliver North's criminal trial he repeatedly offered as a defense his "belief" that he was doing what was best for the country, although he had lied time and again to the Congress. Additionally, we place the blame on the CIA for a great many sins, when we should be putting the responsibility where it belongs: on the president, who gives the orders to the CIA, and on the system of secrecy that permits him to subvert the legal limits of his office.

When, in March 1989, an Exxon oil tanker ran aground in Alaska, destroying the fishing industry there, along with a great deal of wildlife, the press zeroed in on charges that the ship's captain had been drinking. But responsibility really lies with the policy of drilling and transporting oil in an area whose ecology is as delicate as Alaska's. In much the same way that defense spending is given priority at the expense of social programs, oil drilling in Alaska is not conducted for the good of the United States, but to enhance the profit of the companies involved. Instead of adopting policies that reduce our dependence on the overall use of oil, such as a deliberate slowdown in high volume manufacturing, we support the drilling of oil reserves wherever the oil companies can profit from it.

The same is true with respect to the destructive system of leveraged buyouts and merger greenmail. Until the government takes seriously its responsibility to prevent the kind of high finance piracy that it now encourages, the abuses will continue, unhampered by the few highly publicized cases of insider trading that have put prominent Wall Street high rollers in jail.

One of the more pleasant duties I had in the Senate was representing small farmers. One could not ask for a better class of constituents, as opposed, say, to representing the rich or the arms merchants. Small farmers actually provided a wonderful political base for my brand of progressive politics. They were never overly prosperous, never content with the status quo, and were mostly willing to challenge the establishment. And they were happy, I believe, to see me take on the corporate and political elite.

But trying to obtain some sort of economic equity for them proved to be a formidable task. Small farmers are totally at the mercy of the marketplace, which is controlled by giant grain companies. Neither farmers nor ranchers, at least those in South Dakota, are in a position to set the price for their products. They take their grain or their livestock to market and receive the price set that day by the buyers. For whatever reason, they have never been adequately organized, and so they have no ability to control the flow of their product in order to regulate the price.

To prevent the total destruction of grain farmers, the government has, over the years, instituted various payment programs designed to give small farmers some sort of regular income. But the effort has neither been steady nor adequate, and it has been corrupted by the larger farmers, who have found ways to take advantage of the payment system. As the farm population ages, and as more and more small farmers are selling their land to larger ones, the country is losing a class of people who contribute tremendously to the nation's character. High land prices prevent would-be farmers from getting into the business, which in turn speeds up the disappearance of the small farmer.

At one point I made a vain effort to try to reverse this trend with legislation that would award a limited amount of land to small farmers, to be used by them as long as they lived on the land and farmed it. By preventing the sale of the land to large landowners, I believed that we would prevent young people without land from being forced to live and work in already overpopulated cities.

When I first ran for the House, I came out in strong support of the Oahe Irrigation Project, which was designed to take water from the Missouri River and transport it by canal to farmland dozens of miles north and east of the river. The project seemed to me to be the answer to a lot of problems. It would mean prosperity for the towns near the construction sites and for the farmers, who would be able to use the river's water to keep their crops growing in a climate where drought is not unique.

Although the area's newspapers and businessmen were hot for the project, there was a growing opposition to it by the farmers themselves that I initially failed to see. But opposed to the project they were. Led by George Piper and John Sieh, both farmers, the movement to kill the irrigation plan steadily grew into a sizable organized force. Called the United Family Farmers, the UFF, they objected to the kind of irrigation proposed, partly because of its exorbitant cost and partly because long-distance irrigation eventually ruins the soil at the end of the pipeline, where salts collect and leech into the topsoil. But the people who had early on been elected to the Oahe Conservancy Subdistrict board of directors were in favor of the project, and they were the only people that I saw and talked to for a number of years. The UFF kept plugging away, however, coming to Washington at their own expense, grabbing me on my visits to South Dakota, making their case to me whenever they could. I ultimately changed my position on the irrigation project, coming out in support of a bill that President Carter proposed to reject the Oahe, as well as many other irrigation projects.

My first involuntary committee assignment was on the Space and Aeronautics Committee. I had little interest in the committee's work, but I decided to make the best of it. The committee's duty simply was to oversee NASA. Oversight is too strong a word for what the committee actually did. Rather it ratified NASA's budget, which, I came to learn, was too large and far too unnecessary. Way back when, I had cheered when Alan Shepard and John Glenn went into space. I was proud when Neil Armstrong walked on the moon. But I came to realize how dramatic was the difference between the unmanned program, which actually does facilitate scientific progress, and the manned space program, which yields nothing but hype, and spends money—lots of it. The manned program at times seems to exist only to titillate the nerve ends of the national and local television anchormen and women, who in turn provide all the publicity that NASA needs to keep its budget swollen to a hundred times its proper size.

The shuttle program was just being considered by the committee when I first joined it in 1973. Somehow I came to suspect the wonderful things everyone was saying about the shuttle, so I asked Utah Senator Ted Moss, chairman of the committee, if I could get a second opinion on the efficacy of the shuttle. He agreed, which prompted me to bring as witnesses to the authorization hearings a number of prominent scientists, some of them Nobel Prize winners, who offered their views of the shuttle program. It was an impressive line-up, including Dr. James Van Allen, who discovered the Van Allen radiation belt, and George Rathjens, among others. Their testimony—that the manned program was simply an inefficient waste of money and other resources—was unfortunately ignored by most members of the committee, who couldn't wait to vote for its authorization. I've never counted the dollars that have been wasted since then, but had a fraction of the money gone to the unmanned program, America would be the beneficiary of a great deal more scientific information. As it now stands, we are reduced to cheering when a shuttle does not crash, or is merely able to get off the ground.

There is no better example than the space program of how thinking can become entrenched in official Washington, unless one includes the funding of the Pentagon. In basic terms, the Pentagon asks for, and Congress provides, hundreds of billions of dollars for military spending that is wasteful. I'm not speaking here of $700 toilet seats, which are, of course, an outrage. But such purchases are misdemeanors compared to the felonies that go unreformed and unpunished. I'm speaking of how hundreds of billions of dollars are authorized and appropriated for weapons programs, based not on how well they will provide for the nation's defense, but only on what they will do for the economy of a congressional district or of a particular defense company. As a result, the taxpayers are burdened with so-called defense spending that is used not for defense, but to create or hold jobs in someone's congressional district, or to continue to pile up profits for an arms manufacturer.

* * *

Perhaps the closest thing in the Senate to a club is situated in the bowels of the U. S. Capitol—a small, very private senators only dining room. It is open only for lunch. By agreement, no staff member, visitor, or Senate spouse may invade this inner sanctum, which contains two long oval tables, each of which seats about twelve people. Also by agreement, the Democrats sit at one table and the Republicans sit at the other, and there is no encroachment.

While the food is good, it is what one can learn there that makes the place interesting. During the Watergate hearings in 1973, Senator Sam Ervin of North Carolina, the Watergate Committee's chairman, sat at the head of the Democrats' table and provided us with his daily analysis of the morning's witnesses. Each day he would regale us, shouting, "Maurice Stans is a liar." Or, "I was raised a Scotch Presbyterian. You all know about that religion. They don't prevent you from sinning, they just prevent you from enjoying it."

When the Watergate hearings came to an end, most political junkies felt a tremendous letdown. They had become so attached to the daily drama that a sudden emptiness came over them when television reverted to other pursuits. I had the same feeling, but for me it was compounded by the fact that Sam Ervin no longer held forth at lunch time in the private dining room.

But in politics if there is a role to be filled, there will always be someone to fill it. Russell Long, son of Huey Long, began coming to lunch almost immediately after the Watergate hearings ended, telling stories about his Uncle Earl, who was, at one time, governor of Louisiana. By our request, he must have told each story seven or eight times, and without any perceptible dip on the laugh meter.

We would ask Russell, for example, to tell us one more time about "socks on a rooster," a story that arose out of one of Uncle Earl's campaigns for governor. Richard De Lesseps "Shep" Morrison, his opponent, had challenged Uncle Earl to a television debate. Uncle Earl declined, and continued to do so despite repeated requests. One day a reporter asked him why he refused to debate.

"You know what would happen if Uncle Earl agreed to debate 'Delasoups' on TV, boy?" Uncle Earl asked the reporter, referring to himself by name, as was his custom.

"Why, Delasoups would pull up in front of that TV studio in his long black limousine, pull down the shades, and have that long legged girl in there with him put makeup on his face to make him look better than he really is. Then he'd step out of that limousine wearing one of his $500 suits and go up to the studio in front of those TV cameras, and just the sight of him would make mince-meat out of Uncle Earl.

"You know what a $500 suit would look like on Uncle Earl? Why, just like socks on a rooster."

When Russell was a student at Louisiana State University he was a member of the debate squad. Because his father had been dead for some time, Russell sometimes looked to Uncle Earl for advice and counsel, and in this particular instance he asked him for advice on how to approach a debate topic.

"What's the topic?" Uncle Earl asked.

"Should ideals be used in politics?"

"What side do you have, boy?"

"Affirmative, Uncle Earl."

"Well, you've got the best side, boy." Uncle Earl said gleefully. "Just tell 'em 'hell yes,' you oughta use ideals or any other goddamn thing you can get your hands on."

It was a lesson that, I believe, Russell never forgot. During the debate on the natural gas bill in 1977, the oil and gas industry was accused by some senators of holding back reserves of natural gas to wait for the higher prices that would come with deregulation. To prevent the industry from withholding information on gas reserves, an amendment was offered that would permit the federal government to gather its own information, so that it wouldn't have to trust an untrustworthy industry.

Well, Russell was of the opinion that the government already knew too much about gas reserves. So when the newly elected senator from Nebraska, Ed Zorinsky, voted in favor of the amendment, Long rushed over to him and shouted excitedly, "You may not have any oil and gas in Nebraska, but by God you've got Mutual of Omaha, and one of these days you're gonna want a tax break for it. I'm chairman of the Finance Committee, so I'm the one you will have to come to for tax breaks." Zorinsky refused to change his vote, and most likely never asked Long for any tax breaks for Mutual of Omaha.

Although we seldom agreed on matters of policy, I always liked Russell, mostly because he was entertaining, but also because he never denied being what he was and for what purpose he was in office. He seemed to revel in the image that he was in the Senate to uphold the honor of the oil and gas industry and other large corporations in search of tax breaks. Almost any special interest could get a tax loophole installed in the tax code when Russell was chairman of the Senate Finance Committee. On the rare occasion that he rose to defend the poor and the vulnerable, I blamed it on an aberrant populist gene inherited from his father.

In 1973, at the urging of some consumer advocates, in particular Marty Lobell and John Lamont, I began an effort to focus attention on the role that the multinational oil companies played in controlling national energy policy. In essence, there was no policy, which is just the way the oil companies wanted it. The oil companies used the Arab oil embargo of 1973 as a rationale for drastically increasing the price of the oil they produced. The United States was importing only 6 percent of its oil from Arab producers at the time of the embargo, yet the oil companies pointed the finger of guilt at the "Ay-rabs," in order to obscure their own responsibility. They were joined, of course, by American politicians and by the Israeli lobby, both groups being more than happy to scapegoat Arabs. The politicians could have stopped the oil companies from raising prices, but evaded responsibility by blaming the Arab oil embargo. The Israeli lobby, fearful that the new power of Arab oil money would undermine its heretofore untrammeled transfer of tax money from the U.S. Treasury to Israel, wanted to destroy the credibility of the Arab countries by blaming them for all of America's economic woes.

I was generally avoided by the oil lobby during my time in politics, but I had one or two narrow scrapes with them. I suppose that at first the industry didn't feel it had to concern itself with an obscure senator from South Dakota, but following the gas shortage of 1973, when I started introducing legislation designed to break up the oil companies, I quickly became the object of their disaffection. The industry apparently took a dim view of my public contention that the gas shortage was contrived by the oil companies in order to increase their prices—and their profits.

One day in 1973, the American Petroleum Institute sent its South Dakota lobbyist, Gene Stearns, to visit me in Washington, apparently to find out what would quiet me down.

Stearns sat down in my office, gave me a big smile and began his conversation with, "Now, Jim, I know you don't really mean what you've been saying lately."

"About what?" I asked.

"About the oil industry," he answered, still smiling.

"But I do mean it," I said. "What makes you think I don't?"

It went right over his head. I judged from his attitude that oil lobbyists are used to getting their way with politicians.

"Well, I just *know* you don't mean it." Stearns repeated.

"Bullshit!" I said, much more firmly this time. "I mean every word of it."

Stearns looked stunned. After a few stuttering minutes, he excused himself and left. I heard him muttering to himself as he walked out.

For some reason, whenever I attended a dinner at one of the Arab embassies, I was inevitably seated near an oil or gas executive, or the spouse of one. This seemed to reflect a kinky sense of humor on the part of the Arab ambassadors, who were well aware of my politics. But as uncomfortable as I felt at being thrown into the midst of that crowd, I learned that the oil people were even more distressed about it than I was.

My first contact with an honest-to-goodness oil tycoon came in September 1975, during a dinner honoring Saudi Arabian Foreign Minister Prince Saud al Faisal.

As I stood talking to Fred and Nancy Dutton, a large man came toward me, drink in hand and wife in tow. His Texas drawl was so heavy that I thought for a minute he was putting me on.

"Sentah Abourezk, mah name is Maurice Granville and this heah is Missus Granville."

"Happy to know you," I said. The name meant nothing to me. "Where are you folks from?" I asked.

"Well, Sentah, you may not know who I am, but I know who you are. I'm chairman of the board of Texaco."

I felt a *klong* coming on. (A klong is a medical term that denotes a sudden rush of shit to the heart.) I had no idea what to do or say next. My bill to break up the oil companies had just been offered on the Senate floor as an amendment to the 1975 Natural Gas Deregulation Bill. I was the sworn enemy of this man and all he stood for. But he solved my problem with his next utterance.

"What are y'all in the government gonna do to get awl out of the ground when y'all get done puttin' us outa business?"

He was referring, I assumed, to my amendment, which had nearly been passed by the Senate not long before. While this divestiture amendment would force the oil industry to give up control of its vertical operations, it would by no means put anybody out of business. In fact, it would put new people into business, while taking away the big companies' power to withhold oil in order to raise prices.

I thought to myself, *you sonofabitch*, but aloud I said, "Well, if we put you out of business, I assume you'll be looking for work. So we can hire you, right?"

For a dedicated capitalist baron, he took that fairly well. He didn't blanch. He didn't vomit. He didn't run. He merely said there was "no way" he was "gonna work for the government."

Then he began looking at the cigar I was smoking. It was a Cohiba that I had picked up during my visit to Cuba a month earlier.

"You know, I'm a cigar man myself," Granville said, showing great resilience. "Why don't I just send you along a box of good cigars—the kind I get on special order?"

Taunting him had been fun, so I thought I'd try it again.

"No, thanks," I said, holding up my Havana cigar. "I have a lot of Havanas, so you needn't bother. As a matter of fact, I just came back from Cuba last month, and I saw one of your old refineries down there."

It wasn't true. I hadn't really seen any refineries at all, and, in fact, I didn't know whether Castro had actually expropriated any Texaco property, but the opportunity was too good to pass up.

"They're taking good care of it," I went on. "They're keeping the fittings shined up and the whole place painted."

I knew that I had scored when I saw his lips turn white. "Yeah. Those sons of bitches cost us more'n sixty-two million dollars," he lamented. Granville spent the next fifteen minutes or so following me around, trying to convert me to his point of view, and even offering to come to my office to educate me on the tremendous problems of the "awl" companies.

His complaints centered on two separate pieces of legislation that I introduced early in my term affecting oil policy. One was a horizontal divestiture bill. It would have required the multinational oil companies to give up their ownership of alternative energy sources, such as coal and solar power. (Mobil Oil, among others, had always argued that higher prices and other benefits were needed in order to "search for oil," but during its "search" Mobil purchased Montgomery Ward, a company that produced lots of profits but no oil.) The idea behind the bill was that an oil company, if given the chance, would raise the price of alternative energy sources it owned to the level of oil prices, hence the call for divestiture.

The second bill would have required oil producers to break up their vertical control of the oil industry; that is, they would not be allowed, at the same time, to own the oil wells, to refine what their wells produced, to transport what they refined, and to market what they transported. This was called, of course, vertical divestiture. There is much too much leeway for shenanigans in the current setup, giving the oil industry the opportunity, which I'm certain it rarely passes up, to adjust their prices, their profits, and their taxable income in a way that is beneficial to them and harmful to the rest of us.

One day in a committee hearing I was in the process of eliciting testimony from Howard Hardesty, then an executive of Continental Oil Company. Howard was, unfortunately for him, too honest for his own good. I asked him if he, as an executive of Conoco, would ever permit the coal marketing subdivision of his company to undersell, on a BTU equivalent basis, the oil marketing subdivision. He said, "no," which was precisely the point I had tried to make to support my argument for horizontal divestiture. Unfortunately, Hardesty's confession provided little help with respect to changing policy on horizontal ownership.

By 1975, I had gained some new allies for the vertical divestiture legislation. Phil Hart of Michigan, Gary Hart of Colorado, and Gaylord Nelson of Wisconsin joined me in a major effort to pass the vertical divestiture amendment. At the press conference we held to announce it, the smart money was scoffing at us, but to the surprise of everyone, the amendment drew forty-six votes, sending the oil industry into deep shock over such a close call. Texaco subsequently spent tens of millions of dollars on advertising, believing, perhaps accurately, that its problem had nothing to do with its pirate-like behavior, but merely with its public image.

During my time in the Senate I struggled to advance the cause of alternate sources of energy—wind power, solar power—to no avail. I learned that if corporations could not find a way to profit from alternatives to fossil fuels, the government would not touch them. I wondered aloud during the deregulation filibuster whether 20 oil companies or 200 million Americans ran the country. Now I know. There was very little support for advancing the technology to create such alternate sources of energy. Nuclear power, on which corporations can make a profit, was popular, as were oil and coal.

* * *

Halfway between downtown Detroit and Detroit's airport there is a huge tire that figured prominently in George McGovern's 1972 presidential campaign. Five or six stories high, its purpose is to advertise tires made by the Uniroyal Tire Company. In 1973, I went to Detroit to make a speech to the Arab-American community. I was driven into the city from the airport by a Wayne County deputy sheriff who couldn't resist telling me what had happened there the year before.

Near the end of the 1972 campaign George McGovern was scheduled to speak in Detroit. The deputy sheriff had been assigned to assist the Secret Service. Just before McGovern's plane was to land, the lawmen made one final sweep of the route into the city from the airport.

Suddenly, behind the huge tire they discovered a parked car— one that had not been there a few minutes earlier. Several patrol cars surrounded the intruder. The police crouched, drew their guns and approached. They drew closer and closer, still unable to discern the car's purpose. When they looked inside the car they saw a man and a woman in fierce copulation.

Relieved that there was no security risk, but nevertheless impatient with the intrusion, the officer in charge pulled open the door and shouted, "Will you get the hell out of here? Senator McGovern is coming through this way any minute now."

Without the slightest slowing of his passion the man croaked, "Goddamn it, let us finish. He's gonna lose anyway."

Few people in politics can match George McGovern's sense of humor. When he was told about the Uniroyal tire incident, he laughed for a long time. As a general rule, I'm wary of politicians who have no sense of humor. Its lack is an indication that they take themselves too seriously, and when someone in a position of power does that, look out. Richard Nixon was totally humorless. So was Jimmy Carter. Kissinger is an exception to the rule. He has an excellent sense of humor, but it was of no help to the Cambodians, the Chileans, and others when he decided to play world power politics with their lives.

George McGovern is, without doubt, one of the most decent people in politics. He was seen by many in 1972 as the "anti-war" candidate, but he was much more than that. He was the spear carrier for the American liberal movement. A man of wide learning, of great intellect, and of tremendous civility, he was viciously pilloried by the media during his run for the presidency. What I find most amazing is that virtually every issue McGovern raised in the 1972 campaign is now commonly accepted dogma—from his reasons for opposing the Vietnam War to his proposals on poverty and the national economy. He spoke of Nixon's corruption throughout the campaign, all of it falling on deaf ears in the media's rush to ingratiate itself with the president. Yet today, after knowing a great deal of what Nixon did and was trying to do to the country,

McGovern is still vilified by some editorial writers and columnists who, at the same time, are busy rehabilitating Nixon, the famous unindicted coconspirator. What I find interesting is that, while the mainstream press and many Democratic party leaders cannot bring themselves to admit that McGovern was correct and Nixon was wrong, members of the public have recovered from the poison pumped into their political systems by these opinion makers. Ordinary people have themselves rehabilitated McGovern, not much caring what the establishment says about him.

In much the same way, we were misled by the establishment press on the Vietnam War. Initially advertised as a war to contain Communism, to prevent the falling of all the Southeast Asian "dominoes," it became a war of near total destruction of two societies—Vietnam and America. The war had precious little to do with Communism or its containment, but it had a great deal to do with manifestations of machismo on the part of Presidents Kennedy, Johnson, and Nixon, and their top handlers. Someone once wrote that our staying in the war was meant to prove the staying power of the men running our country. But beyond proving how tough Lyndon Johnson, the Rostow brothers, Henry Kissinger, and Richard Nixon were, the war totally polarized American society and allowed the escalation of violence to become routine and habit-forming. In Southeast Asia the results were more devastating. Fully one million people were killed by American firepower in Vietnam and Cambodia. The upshot of Nixon's and Kissinger's use of Cambodia as a killing ground was the murderous takeover of that country by the Khmer Rouge, who slaughtered untold millions in their madness.

Beyond the destruction of human life and character caused by the Vietnam War, the American economy has yet to recover from the bottomless pit of armament spending undertaken by successive Administrations since the 1960s. The lesson of Vietnam is one that each successive Administration has yet to learn, because there is a presidential urge to prove American might by plunging U.S. troops and firepower into little Third World countries that do not conform to our idea of how they should behave in our empire. Again, it is the public that remembers much more than the politicians. It is the public that prevented Ronald Reagan from sending troops to Nicaragua, raising an outcry each time he rattled his saber. He got in and out of Grenada too quickly and managed the news (read "he lied") too well to catch the criticism he deserved. But public pressure kept him from the many invasions that he yearned for.

Stopping U.S. military intervention became more difficult, however, after the passage of the War Powers Resolution Act in 1974. I had originally supported the bill when it was first introduced, but by the time it reached the Senate floor, I had changed my position and strongly opposed it. My first impression of the Act was that it would prevent Richard Nixon from remaining in Vietnam, but I eventually became convinced that the Act would give a president— any president—more power than he is accorded by the Constitution, and certainly more than he ought to have in any event. Ronald Reagan proved both in Lebanon and in Grenada how correct my analysis was.

Unless there is a direct attack on U.S. territory, the Constitution requires a declaration of war by Congress before the president can commit troops outside the United States. The War Powers Act changes the Constitution in a backdoor sort of way. It allows the president to decide on his own to inject American troops into a conflict on foreign soil. Then he must get congressional approval in order to continue the intervention. But as Reagan demonstrated in Lebanon, and LBJ and Nixon in Vietnam, when a president commits troops, then calls forth all the cheap, petty jingoism he can muster, it is politically difficult—even seen as unpatriotic—for Congress to vote to "cut and run." It is a dangerous law, and I'm convinced that the country will eventually regret its enactment.

I came out strongly against the Act after studying its implications, and with the help of Mark Raskin and Bob Borosage of the Institute for Policy Studies wrote what I thought was a powerful speech in opposition, delivering it to an unusually crowded Senate during debate on the bill. Within a few seconds after I finished haranguing the Senate by pointing out in exquisite detail all the defects and flaws of the Act, Edmund Muskie, who obviously had not heard one word of my magnificent speech, walked over to me and thanked me profusely for supporting it.

In 1974, I also tried to change the way that the CIA is allowed to operate. I had heard stories about its clandestine operations for a long time. In Chile, under orders from Kissinger and Nixon, the CIA helped General Augusto Pinochet and his generals overthrow the government of Salvador Allende, resulting in his assassination. The agency had assassinated African leaders that it didn't like, and had attempted, on a number of occasions, to murder Fidel Castro.

While its agents were presumably having great fun implementing the president's notion of hegemony over other, smaller countries, it seemed to me that there must be a better way for a great country such as ours to operate. Unlike a lot of critics of the CIA's covert activities, I believe that the agency is actually nothing more than the president's private hit squad, available to rub out anybody who makes the president politically uncomfortable. I could never accept that Salvador Allende's democratically elected Socialist regime was in any way a threat to the security of the United States. Allende threatened the political security of Richard Nixon and Henry Kissinger, however, simply by coming to power. But why, in the name of democracy itself, should a president be allowed to unleash a band of hired killers to overthrow someone whose only danger is that he might offer a comparison between socialism and capitalism? If we are confident enough in our system, why should we worry when a Third World country wants to experiment with something different?

The various attempts to kill and depose Fidel Castro by the CIA, actually on the order of more than one president, were made legitimate by the same reasoning as the more recent efforts to overthrow the Sandinistas in Nicaragua—that they are dictatorships. This reasoning is just so much hogwash. Chile under Allende was a democracy, yet it was targeted for overthrow; under Pinochet it is a dictatorship, yet we've sent no hit squads to topple his government.

In 1974, even before the Church Committee disclosed all the CIA's outrageous conduct, I introduced an amendment on the Senate floor that would have outlawed all covert operations, assassinations, bribery of foreign politicians, and other dubious activities, while allowing the CIA to continue to collect intelligence. I believed then and I believe now that we have a right to try to determine the intentions of other countries toward us.

The amendment lost. It received seventeen votes, and I doubt that, even after the disclosures of the Church Committee, it would have gotten many more. The result of the committee's exposé was the formation of permanent intelligence oversight committees in the Senate and the House, both of which are virtually toothless. The committees, as the children of the sixties used to say, have been "co-opted" by the CIA. I discovered this when I called a colleague who served on the Senate Intelligence Oversight Committee, asking him to lodge a protest against some CIA action that I had heard was in the works. "I can't do that, Jim," he said, "it would ruin the good working relationship we have with the Agency."

The members of the Intelligence Committee are in a most untenable position. They are sworn to secrecy. And although the CIA is obliged to notify the committees of a planned covert action, the committees cannot stop an action even if they disagree with it. They can only try to persuade the Administration not to undertake it. It would be impossible for the committees to follow every detail of a covert plan in any event. In a recent example, if we assume that the oversight committees approved of Reagan's efforts to overthrow the Sandinistas, which I do not think they did, they would not have been informed of the methods to be used to overthrow them. The result was the mining of Nicaragua's harbors, the production of an assassination manual written by the CIA for the contras, among other outrages committed in the name of the founding fathers. Members of the intelligence oversight committees, are, therefore, effectively prevented from conducting their prime responsibility of oversight, and worse, are silenced by the very system that the Congress established to rein in the CIA.

The argument that I used to support my amendment in 1974 is still valid. If there is, somewhere in the world, an enemy of the United States that poses a danger to us, the proper, and, I believe, the most effective—and constitutional—solution is for the Congress to declare war and openly send our military out to do the dirty work. At least the American public would then have an opportunity to debate both the costs and the benefits of such undertakings.

Americans should be made to understand why people in some countries, who ordinarily would be pro-American, intensely hate us. Our government has conducted enough covert attacks on Third World countries to create enemies everywhere. We are blissfully unaware of most of the attacks by those in our government's pay. As it now stands, when America and Americans come under attack by some Third World country, we are left to question why anyone could be angry at us. When Americans are kidnapped in Lebanon, or when U.S. airplanes are hijacked and Americans are tragically killed, neither the press nor our leaders provide us with the underlying reasons why violence is directed against our nationals. We are left, therefore, to believe that the killers and the kidnappers are merely mad terrorists, who kill randomly for no apparent reason. Each incident is simply another occasion for jingoistic politicians, including our president, to beat the drums of hatred against countries or people who respond to our covert violence with violence of their own.

Not long after I moved into my Senate office in 1973, I was

visited by Brady Tyson, now a professor at American University in Washington. Accompanying Tyson was a member of the Brazilian Parliament who opposed the dictatorship and wanted to talk to me about what was happening in Brazil. He explained that he was permitted to side with the opposition only if the press did not print his statements for public consumption. There were, he said, thousands of people opposed to the dictatorship, but they were mostly in prison. Of those who were not killed outright by the government, the rest were either tortured or simply left to languish behind bars.

I was shocked by what I heard. It was something totally new to me, so I asked what I could do. The Brazilian then said that continued American support of the dictatorship made it appear as though no one cared what happened. If someone in authority could make periodic public statements denouncing the dictatorship's actions, he said, at least those in prison and dissidents still at large could hold out some hope that things would improve. I could not underestimate, he said, the importance of offering just a little hope to them.

I subsequently prepared and offered an amendment to the Foreign Aid Bill that would deny U.S. foreign aid to any country that violated the human rights of its own citizens. Of all people, Hubert Humphrey, who was managing the bill for the Foreign Relations Committee, strenuously opposed me, and I lost the amendment. Although Humphrey's public image was one of rebellious outsider, he was really the quintessential insider, a zealous patriot, obedient to the Administration's—any Administration's—foreign policy. I attributed Hubert's support of the Nixon Administration's position to this peculiar trait. But there were some senators who voiced support for the idea, so the following year I tried again, only this time I offered an additional amendment to deny funding for the police training program. To my surprise, Humphrey accepted the police training amendment, and shortly afterward the Office of Public Safety (OPS), the parent organization of the police training program, began shutting down. OPS was a hybrid organization ostensibly run by the Agency for International Development (AID), but in reality it was a CIA program for training foreign police. I had gotten word that most of the police they trained went back to their countries and used advanced torture techniques to suppress domestic dissent. Strangely, Americans were helping foreign dictators remain in power. But this has been the hallmark of our foreign policy, not only under Nixon, but under each president since then.

As long as a foreign country is under U.S. control, its dictatorship is of no concern to us.

I knew the cause of human rights legislation was becoming popular when, during the following year, I reintroduced the same human rights amendment and Senator Alan Cranston introduced an identical one approximately thirty minutes after mine was defeated. Cranston used virtually identical wording, as well as the same arguments, so I could only assume that he was going through the exercise to please some human rights constituency. Although he lost as well, more and more people both in the House and in the Senate began to focus attention on the issue of human rights. In the House, Congressman Tom Harkin of Iowa was able to pass, for the first time, an amendment denying U.S. aid to countries that did not extend basic human rights to their own citizens. His legislation ultimately became law.

The author's maternal grandmother,
Sadie Mickel

The author's maternal grandfather,
Peter Mickel

The author's mother,
Lena Abourezk

The author's father,
Charlie Abourezk

*Jim Abourezk in front of his
parents' house in Wood, circa 1938.*

The entire Wood High School Student Body, 1946–47. Abourezk is in the first row on the right.

*Lena & Charlie Abourezk,
the author's parents.*

C. Abourezk Mercantile, Wood, South Dakota, circa 1935. From left, Eli Abourezk, the author, Virginia Abourezk, and Josephine Abourezk.

Wood High School's baseball team. The author is the third from the left.

Boot camp, San Diego Naval Training Center, 1948. The author is in the third row from the top, third from right.

The author accompanies Roy Acuff.

Tex Fletcher

Election night, 1970. Abourezk volunteers cheer the news of his upset victory.

Abourezk for Senate rally, 1972, Webster, South Dakota. Hubert Humphrey, the author, and an undecided voter. Photo by Jim Mackay.

Negotiations at Wounded Knee, March 1973. From left to right: the author, Senator George McGovern, Sievert Young Bear, Leonard Crow Dog, and Russell Means. United Press International photo.

The author with Fidel Castro at his farm near Havana, August 1975. Photo by Saul Landau.

Congressman Mo Udall, the author, and Buddy Meredith performing at a Udall for President rally, Rapid City, South Dakota, 1976.

At the Barrages (a presidential palace), Cairo, Egypt, 1976. From left to right: Anwar Sadat, the author, Judy Miller, and CBS correspondent John Sheahan.

Washington, D.C., April 19, 1977. Senator James Abourezk presents two Cuban cigars to President Jimmy Carter in the Oval Office as Senator George McGovern looks on. Abourezk and McGovern had just returned from a trip to Cuba.

"One thing about Abourezk, he sure livens up a dinner."
Rocky Mountain News, 1977.

Schorr cartoon, The Kansas City Star

*Senator Ted Kennedy and the author at a Judiciary Committee
hearing. Kennedy is saying: "Abourezk, if your enemies see this picture
of us together, I'm in big trouble."*
Photo by George Thames,
The New York Times.

The author being frisked after his arrest in front of the South African embassy, Washington, D.C., 1984.

The author with Yasir Arafat, Baghdad, 1988.
Photo by Harold Samhat.

8

Filibuster

After all the years of filibustering by Southern senators in an effort to stop the passage of civil rights legislation, and after all the filibustering by Alabama Senator Jim Allen against progressive anti-trust bills, I found it interesting that no one ever tried to change the rules on filibustering until after I began using the filibuster to take the side of the consumer. The new rules, passed by the Senate after I left in January 1979, make it virtually impossible to conduct the kind of filibuster that I staged in 1977.

It all started in 1976, when Senator Phil Hart of Michigan brought up on the Senate floor a bill to improve the anti-trust laws—a bill strenuously opposed by the Business Roundtable and their minions in the Congress. Now the Business Roundtable was not what you'd call a pussycat lobby. It was, and is, a lobbying group made up of at least 400 of the Fortune 500 companies, with all the power that their money can bring to bear on America's politicians. Actively opposing the bill on their behalf was Senator James Allen of Alabama, the undisputed master of the Senate rules, outside of Majority Leader Robert Byrd and the Senate

133

parliamentarian, of course. In particular, Allen was most creative with respect to what is known as the post-cloture filibuster.

Permit me to explain what a post-cloture filibuster is. Unlike the House of Representatives, the Senate allows unlimited talking time on legislation, that is, unless all the senators agree to limit the duration of a debate. When such an agreement is reached, the amount of time set for debate depends on the number of senators who want to take part and how long each wishes to speak. But when no time limit is set, the debate can go on as long as there is a U.S. senator left standing and still able to draw a breath. Apart from an agreement to limit debate time, the only way to prevent a talk-a-thon, or a filibuster, is for the Senate to vote on a cloture motion. Simply stated, cloture is the Senate's way of telling verbose senators to shut up. If a cloture motion passes, each senator is then limited to a maximum of one hour of debate on the bill in question. In 1976, however, a loophole existed in the rules that provided a way for senators, after cloture was voted, to circumvent the one-hour time limit. If any amendments were introduced before the cloture vote, each one could be called up and voted on *after* cloture without being counted against the allotted one hour of time. This dizzying phenomenon is called the post-cloture filibuster.

Jim Allen was smart. He would introduce a lot of amendments just before the cloture vote, and then he would spend the rest of the session forcing the Senate to vote on each and every one of them. Not only did we vote on each amendment, which alone took fifteen minutes, but then we would vote on a motion to reconsider the vote, which took another fifteen minutes. If too many senators left the floor after the vote, Jim Allen would demand a quorum call. It would take another half hour or more to get the minimum of fifty-one senators back on the floor to fulfill the quorum requirement. If the required number of senators failed to reappear, Jim would make a motion for the sergeant-at-arms to bring them by force to the floor. This motion would require another vote. Because neither the motions nor the votes were charged against Jim Allen's time, if he had enough amendments and could physically stand it, he could go on all year.

The rules also specified that once cloture was voted there must be unanimous agreement of the senators on the floor in order to raise any other issue. This meant, of course, that a senator could, simply by objecting, prevent anything other than the bill under debate from being acted upon. All this, I soon found out, was what the textbooks defined as power.

Phil Hart was sick with cancer in 1976. He grew progressively weaker during the filibuster over the anti-trust bill, but he wanted to see it through. It was a bill that he had wanted to pass all during his career. Because I was on the Judiciary Committee, and just as importantly, because I wasn't campaigning for reelection, I was available to help Phil oppose Allen's filibuster.

Hart's doctors wanted him to rest either at home or in a hospital, but he refused to obey them. He stayed on the Senate floor, retreating to the sofas against the back wall whenever he became too exhausted to sit at his desk. Meanwhile Jim Allen was convinced that, if he could delay the final vote long enough with his post-cloture filibuster, he could force a compromise that would weaken the legislation enough to please his Business Roundtable friends.

So the filibuster dragged on, first on the bill, then on the conference report after the bill had passed. At one point during the filibuster I asked Senator John Durkin of New Hampshire to watch the floor for me while I went to relieve myself. To play it safe, I told Durkin, who was a newcomer to the Senate, to object to anything that came up, without exception. Because I would be gone only a short time, this instruction seemed easier than trying to explain to him whose requests would be safe and whose might be dangerous.

That's when Tom Eagleton came on the floor. He had indicated to me earlier that he wanted to call up a couple of amendments on something entirely unrelated to the bill—and I had promised him that I wouldn't object.

But John Durkin knew nothing of our agreement, so he objected.

"I cleared this with Senator Abourezk," Eagleton shouted.

"I continue to object," Durkin said.

"Will you ask Abourezk?" Eagleton screamed.

"I object." Durkin said, faithful to my request, at which point Eagleton lifted the handful of documents he had wanted to offer, threw them at Durkin, and stomped out of the Senate.

That filibuster was a piece of cake, however, compared to the one I took on in 1977.

Senator Howard Metzenbaum of Ohio asked me to help him filibuster the natural gas deregulation bill that year. I imagine that he had a couple of different reasons for asking me. I was against deregulation, as he was, but unlike him, I was familiar with the Senate rules, knowledge of which is absolutely essential to keeping a filibuster going. Unwittingly I had been preparing for something like this for a long time. My training as a civil engineer, my total immersion in litigation as a trial lawyer, and the experience I had acquired fighting against three separate Jim Allen filibusters gave me, so to speak, a triple whammy of expertise and discipline, suitable for manipulating the Senate rules into a heavyweight delaying strategy.

The effort to deregulate gas prices has an interesting history. The federal government instituted regulation of natural gas prices in the 1930s to prevent price gouging by an industry that had a near monopoly both on the supply and the transmission of natural gas. Deregulation, long sought after by the natural gas industry in an effort to increase their profits, ultimately passed both houses of Congress in 1956, and, but for a major scandal that year, it would have been signed into law by President Eisenhower. During the debate on final passage, Republican Senator Francis Case of South Dakota rose on the Senate floor and disclosed to the world that the Superior Oil Company had offered him a $2,500 bribe in exchange for his support of the legislation. Incredibly, despite the scandal created by Case's disclosure, the bill passed the Senate. But President Eisenhower correctly decided that the smell of foul play was too overpowering, so he vetoed it.

Deregulation was never mentioned again until 1973, when oil shortages gave the oil and gas industry the courage to renew their campaign. Deregulation almost passed then, and it came close again in 1975. By 1977, the industry had picked up so much support that when the Energy Committee split on a nine-to-nine tie vote on the deregulation amendment, it retaliated by manufacturing an artificial fuel shortage. The natural gas industry understood that deregulation would pass if they could frighten the public and the Congress. Ordinarily a tie vote means defeat, but Senator Henry M. "Scoop" Jackson, chairman of the Energy Committee, announced that he would send the bill to the floor anyway. Our informal count indicated that it would pass if the entire Senate were to vote on it. This made a filibuster necessary to delay the final vote until either the pro-gas senators grew tired, or until we could change enough votes to defeat it.

I knew that the whole affair would not be easy. It would be a major undertaking, and I wasn't overly anxious to begin, knowing that I couldn't quit until it was over. The filibuster would require my total concentration to the exclusion of everything else—specifically other legislation and family life. I talked it over with Pete Stavrianos, whose opinion I valued more than any other person's. What Pete said finally convinced me that I should go through with it: "If you can succeed in stopping the deregulation of natural gas, you will have done more in this one short stroke than in all your years of public service." He left me with no other choice but to join the effort.

I told Metzenbaum that both of us had to be ready for the immense peer pressure that would be placed on us during the filibuster. I knew all too well what Senator Byrd would do to try to stop us. The constant roll calls and late night sessions would cause most senators to complain about missing dinner engagements, evenings with their families, speaking trips outside of Washington, and so forth. They would exert heavy pressure on us to abandon it, but I told Metzenbaum that we had to resolve from the beginning to resist the efforts to stop us. A half-hearted filibuster, I told him, was worse than none at all.

Howard and I knew there would be a cloture motion, and we knew that we would not be able to defeat it. So I asked Bethany Weidener, the energy expert on my staff, to work with Metzenbaum's staff to prepare amendments to be introduced. Bethany had worked in the field of energy for only a few years since I recruited her from the Institute for Policy Studies, but she learned so quickly and so well that her advice was much sought after on Capitol Hill. In addition to the storehouse of knowledge that she had accumulated, she was quite brilliant in formulating public energy policy. Metzenbaum and I introduced exactly 508 amendments prior to the cloture vote, giving us the right to call them up and have them voted on after cloture was voted. Cloture was voted after the second day, and the dance began. We called up amendments, demanded a roll call vote on each one, demanded a vote on either a motion to reconsider the original vote or a motion to table, and demanded a quorum call each time the floor was emptied of senators. Everyone was harassed by this process, but it was our only weapon.

As I had predicted to Metzenbaum, the pressure to stop the post-cloture filibuster started coming in hot and heavy. Senator Warren Magnuson of Washington complained that, at least, in a regular filibuster, you were able to learn something. But in this one, he said, all you could do was sleep. After a few days into the filibuster, Texas Senator John Tower sat down beside me and said, "Abourezk, someday when I decide not to run again, I think I'll start acting like a prick, too." I responded with a great big knowing smile.

I assigned Maine Senator Bill Hathaway the job of "chaser,"

making certain that there was never a quorum of senators on the floor. If I could keep enough senators off the floor, I would be able to demand a quorum call, then a vote on requiring the sergeant-at-arms to round up senators, then a vote to table this motion, then a vote to reconsider the motion to table. Because I was not debating, and because the votes were not charged against the one hour of time allotted to me, under the post-cloture rules, chasing a quorum off the floor was a valuable tool. To this end, Bill Hathaway read from a tome in the most boring voice he could muster each time there were too many senators on the floor. It would not take him more than thirty seconds of reading to literally empty the Senate. And each time he did, I would call for another quorum count.

Before the filibuster began, George McGovern had introduced a lengthy amendment proposing the creation of a government energy corporation. It was a piece of legislation that I supported, but it also presented, for me, a wonderful opportunity to advance the filibuster. Using an obscure parliamentary technique, I called up McGovern's amendment, then asked for a roll call vote on it. Once the senate agreed to the vote, I demanded that the chair divide the amendment into separate parts, which, under the rules, was considered divisible. The parliamentarian looked at the amendment, then groaned as he advised the presiding officer that it had to be divided into over twenty sections. Because a roll call vote had been ordered on the entire amendment, *each section would now require a separate roll call vote.*

McGovern was at first furious with me, but as he began to realize that the forces for deregulation outnumbered those against it, his attitude changed. In a move typical of McGovern's honesty, he later rose to speak about how wrong he had been about my manipulation of his amendment. He spoke of how important it was to stop deregulation by any means, even if it meant ruining his proposal for a government energy corporation.

We were in control of the Senate floor for thirteen days, during which time President Jimmy Carter, who started out on our side, switched positions to oppose us and to favor deregulation. For me it was a lesson in duplicity at the highest levels of government.

Early in the filibuster, I had asked Frank Moore, Carter's congressional liaison, if the president would make a statement opposing deregulation. He agreed to propose the idea. We never received a direct confirmation from Moore, but a couple of days later Carter made the statement that we had asked for during a speech that he made in Virginia on behalf of Henry Howell, the Democratic candidate for governor.

Subsequently we gave Frank Moore a list of senators whose support for deregulation was soft, and asked that Carter trundle them up to the White House to convince them to vote with us. The White House staff kept hauling these senators in, but Carter changed not one vote. I later learned from one of the senators that he never really tried. Instead of applying heat to the wavering politicians, Carter made each visit into a social event. But I didn't know this then, and I was perplexed by Carter's failure to get results.

There was no question, however, that all of Carter's people—Frank Moore, Dan Tate, and Fritz Mondale—were against deregulation. On the tenth day of the filibuster, Metzenbaum and I met with Mondale late in the evening in the Capitol office of the Senate's sergeant-at-arms, Nordy Hoffman. We explained to Mondale that Carter was not having much luck switching votes and that we needed his advice and assistance. Metzenbaum suggested that, because we seemed to be getting nowhere, the Administration ought to help us find a way to end the filibuster without making it look as though we had caved in. Mondale told us that Schlesinger was the expert on the matter, and that he would ask him to come to the Hill to talk to us.

The next morning, Saturday, Secretary of Energy James Schlesinger came up to the Senate. We met in the vice-president's office just off the Senate floor. Schlesinger, a Republican carryover from the Nixon Administration in which he had been secretary of defense, was brought in by Carter to fulfill two objectives: to throw a bone to the Republicans and to keep an eye on nuclear affairs for the military, because money for nuclear weapons is the largest part of the Department of Energy's budget.

Metzenbaum told Schlesinger that there was not much use in continuing the filibuster, because nobody was changing his vote. I agreed that we would probably have to give up the struggle, but I thought that we should hang in a bit longer. A test vote taken the night before showed that we needed to switch only a couple of votes to defeat deregulation. I told Schlesinger that I was convinced he and Carter could swing the votes if they made one more big push. We ended the meeting and returned to the Senate floor.

A few minutes later, Les Goldman, Schlesinger's aide, pulled me off to the side and told me that Schlesinger was impressed with my arguments in favor of continuing, and that he, Schlesinger, agreed to make one more effort.

On Sunday, as I later learned, Majority Leader Byrd and Senator Russell Long met privately to devise a plan to crush the filibuster. As the meeting was described to me by a staffer who sat in, both were violently angry, and Russell Long spent part of the time mimicking me objecting to the parliamentary maneuvers that they were planning. The two apparently called President Carter at the White House to demand his cooperation. Although no one witnessed the call, it must have taken place, because that was the point when Carter totally switched positions, coming out against the filibuster virtually overnight, and without notifying those of us trying to stop deregulation.

On Monday morning, as we prepared for the Senate session to start, Metzenbaum told me that he had heard a rumor that Carter was sending Mondale to the Senate to help crush the filibuster. Mondale and I had been good friends all through my time in the Senate. I had helped him out in his brief presidential campaign in 1974, and we had been political allies on a number of issues when he was in the Senate. I was unable to imagine that Mondale would be willing to do anything adverse to our cause, because I knew that he agreed with our position on natural gas. My optimism—or naivete, depending on your point of view—did not last long.

Earlier that morning, I had bumped into Schlesinger and his entourage coming out of Byrd's office, but I had smelled nothing fishy then. When Mondale entered the Senate chamber and took the presiding officer's chair, I approached him and said, "Fritz, someone told me that you're up here to stick the knife into us. Would you do that?"

Mondale instantly tightened up. "Jim, you can depend on me to do the right thing," he blurted out as his face turned a bright red.

There was no mistaking his reaction. A deal had been made and he was part of it. Then Bob Byrd rose and began calling up my amendments, one by one, and, one by one Mondale ruled them out of order.

I was on my feet, shouting objections to the procedure and asking for a parliamentary ruling on Mondale's actions. When my requests were ignored, I asked for a vote of the Senate to appeal his rulings. Each time I made a request it was arbitrarily denied by Mondale, or worse, he would refuse to recognize me at all.

Pandemonium broke loose on the Senate floor. Everyone began shouting in protest against Mondale's heavy-handed rulings. Even senators who opposed both the filibuster and my position on natural gas were angered, rising to denounce the actions of Byrd and Mondale. To them it was a question of principle. They saw a threat to the system of fairness on which Senate procedure is based. Then, in the midst of the pandemonium something both strange and funny happened.

Majority Leader Byrd asked for recognition from the chair, and was advised that he had already used the hour allotted to him. In order to speak further he had to get the unanimous consent of the Senate, a request that was ordinarily granted. But when he made the request, Senator John Culver objected. Suddenly Byrd spun around and loosed all of his pent-up anger directly at Culver. He said nothing about either Metzenbaum or me, who had been the burrs under his saddle for the thirteen-day filibuster, but, looking straight at Culver, he spoke passionately about all the times he had "carried the spear" for the liberals, expressing total resentment at the mistreatment now being meted out to him by those he had helped. Then he broke into tears, a spontaneous act that succeeded, unwittingly, in bringing temporary quiet to the Senate floor.

After a time, I rose, got recognition, and called Jimmy Carter a liar. What I actually said was that during my entire adult life I knew that governments lied, but I had never thought that Jimmy Carter would lie. I was playing on one of the themes of Carter's campaign for the presidency in 1976, when he repeatedly vowed that he would never tell a lie to the American people. Senator Jim Allen walked over to me, and demanded—privately—that I apologize to the president. I told him that I refused to do so until the president first apologized for stabbing me in the back. Then Allen returned to his own desk in order to try to get everyone to calm down. He got recognition, and then began addressing the tactics used by Mondale and Byrd, in response to those senators who were complaining about them. "The steamroller you complain of," he said, "is nothing like the steamrollers in the past. I can bear witness to this from my flattened out body."

Then he pointed in my direction and said, "I observe the distinguished senator and note that his body has not yet been flattened by the steamroller."

Everyone then began shouting for recognition, including me. Somehow I was recognized. It seemed to me a perfect opening to continue Allen's effort to break the tension that hung over the Senate like an unwanted cloud of Los Angeles smog. Not only were the senators emotionally tired from thirteen days of virtually nonstop filibustering by amendment, but they were physically exhausted, making them more grouchy than usual. So I said, "I rise on a point of personal privilege because the shape of my body has been impugned."

No one expected to hear any levity at that point, which I guess made it all the more effective in breaking the tension. "I cannot help it if I'm fat, and I wish that the senator from Alabama would somehow recognize that fact."

More from relief than from a line that was not all that funny, the entire Senate broke out in sustained laughter.

A few minutes later I called together the small band of Democratic senators who had supported the filibuster, asking for advice on our next move. Surprisingly, we still had at our disposal more than 300 of the original 508 amendments that we had introduced at the beginning of the filibuster. With that many amendments it was possible to keep the filibuster going for the rest of the year, but because Carter was no longer even pretending to switch votes, there seemed to be no advantage in doing so.

Ted Kennedy pulled me off to the side and suggested that we end the filibuster, but that we put the blame for the whole affair at Carter's feet. (Kennedy was undoubtedly laying the groundwork for his primary challenge against Carter in 1980.) Given our anger at Carter and Mondale for what we saw as their treachery, it seemed like a reasonable thing to do. So Metzenbaum and I called a quick press conference at which we described what had happened.

A week or so later, after tempers had cooled, Carter invited Metzenbaum and me to the White House for what he called a "discussion." The only reference that he made to the filibuster was a brief, casual comment to the effect that we had handled the whole matter rather well. I took that as the only way he knew how to apologize for his double-dealing. The only comment that he would give the press after the affair ended was that he was not responsible for the filibuster.

Our filibuster ended in late 1977. At the beginning of 1978, the House-Senate Conference Committee was unable to iron out the differences between the two gas deregulation bills they were working on. Metzenbaum and I were members of the Conference Committee and we compounded the difficulty by using every opportunity to prevent agreement by the committee members. The Carter-Schlesinger response to the committee's failure to produce a unified bill was to cut a deal with Republicans on the committee and those Democrats who supported deregulation. To that end they invited committee members to the White House for secret meetings in an effort to build a consensus. Of course, Metzenbaum and I were excluded from the meetings. We were outraged, but we were unable to stop the meetings, which I was convinced were illegal.

But I soon discovered another lever I could pull—my vote on the Panama Canal Treaty. Getting the treaty ratified by the Senate was a major centerpiece of Carter's foreign policy. Although I had previously announced my support for the treaty, I decided to use my vote, which at that point happened to be the crucial 67th, as a bargaining chip to stop Carter and Schlesinger from completing their effort to deregulate natural gas.

During the days leading up to the canal treaty vote, I told Dan Tate, Carter's man in the Senate, that I intended to withhold my vote until Schlesinger stopped holding the secret Conference Committee meetings in the White House. What Schlesinger and Carter were trying to do was to get an agreement from a majority of conferees, then present it as a *fait accompli* to the rest of us, preventing a public debate on the question. I knew that if the meetings were held in public, those in opposition (which included even some pro-oil senators who believed that the bill deregulated gas too slowly) could probably defeat the bill.

At a few minutes after six on the day that I informed Dan Tate of my decision to vote against the treaty, Jimmy Carter called. His voice was soft, betraying none of the tension that he must have felt, knowing that his greatest potential foreign policy achievement could go down the tubes if he failed to convince me to vote with him.

"Jim, I hear you're upset with me," he said.

Carter had always encouraged people to use his first name, but I was angry enough to be fiercely formal. "I am *Mr. President*," I said. "In fact, I'm so upset that when I woke up at three-thirty this morning to take a piss, I couldn't get back to sleep. And the longer I lay there, the madder I got about the secret meetings that you and Schlesinger are sponsoring at the White House. Finally, at five this morning, I got up and wrote a speech denouncing the meetings and announcing my intention to vote against the treaty next Tuesday."

I was totally unprepared for Carter's response. "Now Jim," he said, "if you ever have trouble sleeping at night like that again, just call me up. You can always talk to me if something like this is bothering you."

Suddenly my anger dissipated and I heard myself laughing, almost uncontrollably.

"No, no, I'm serious," Carter shouted over my laughter.

"That's a great line," I said, while he protested again that he was not joking. I suddenly realized that he was genuinely sincere about it.

The events that followed resembled fraternity rush week. Carter phoned me a great deal, pleading with me to vote yes. He called everyone I knew in politics asking them to try to get me to change my vote—Ted Kennedy, John Culver, Fred and LaDonna Harris, Saudi Arabian Prince Bandar, among others.

I had always intended to vote for the treaty. To do otherwise would have violated a lifetime of principle and belief. To me, the United States was an occupying power in the Panama Canal Zone. It was my conviction that sovereignty over the canal belonged to the Panamanians. But I also felt strongly about stopping the deregulation of natural gas and the astronomical price increases that I knew would come with it.

I couldn't express my true feelings about the canal treaty publicly, at least not until I had wrung out the concessions on the natural gas legislation that I wanted from the Administration. When everything else failed, Carter tried another tack. I had told Carter at one point that I wanted his commitment that he would stop holding secret meetings. He had indicated that stopping them was no problem for him, and that he would send Energy Secretary Schlesinger to me to discuss the matter.

Schlesinger appeared in my office in all his arrogant splendor, reminding me of a prisoner of war about to make a statement with a guard's gun in his back. He told me that the president had ordered him to come to see me. "That's all he told you?" I asked. "Nothing about the meetings in the White House?"

"That's all," Schlesinger replied.

"Goodbye, Mr. Secretary," I said, absolutely flabbergasted.

It was clear that Carter intended to do nothing about the Conference Committee, and that he probably perceived, correctly, that I would be unable to vote against the treaty. At the time of the vote, I supported it, it passed, and the Conference Committee reached agreement on a deregulation bill later in the year. The only satisfaction that Metzenbaum and I derived was the knowledge that the filibuster delayed deregulation and the increase in gas prices for over a year.

Looking back on Carter's presidency, one can see many reasons why Jimmy Carter was a one-term president. He was softened up by Ted Kennedy in the 1980 primary. He was saddled with American hostages held in Iran for the last year and a half of his Administration, including the crucial election campaign period. And equally important he was viewed by the public as a vacillator, someone who didn't really believe in what he was doing.

There was good reason for the public's reaction to Carter. His entire national career was based on sniffing the wind to see what was momentarily popular, a technique that he tempered with a pious attitude that he thought would carry him past the political rough spots. To him, this was the way smart politics was done. But to the public he appeared weak, an image that presidents cannot convey and remain popular. The best comparison I can offer is that of Ronald Reagan. Although his policies were highly unpopular, he was able to keep his head above the slime in which his Administration wallowed because he appeared to believe in what he was saying and doing. He looked sincere, an attribute developed from years of acting in bad movies in Hollywood. But Carter never knew how to pull it off.

* * *

Senator James O. Eastland was the last of his kind. When he retired from the Senate I felt a certain sadness, even though he had voted against civil rights legislation, in favor of corporate interests, against every issue I was for, and in favor of every issue I was against. He was a classic racist, who once commented to a colleague after Egyptian President Anwar Sadat spoke to a joint session of Congress, "Ah believe that fella's a nigger."

When Chilean dictator Augusto Pinochet visited Washington, Eastland told me, as we sat in the cloakroom one day, that he had hosted the general at a luncheon. "Ah told Pee-no-shet that I thought he ought to jail all the leftists and hang all the Communists. And he said that was exactly what he was doing."

But Eastland had one quality that very few in politics possess— at least today. He never tried to fool anyone about himself or his positions. He knew where he stood, and so did everyone else. Eastland was able to get along with liberals such as Ted Kennedy, mostly, I think, because he recognized that each member of the Senate ultimately had to answer to his or her constituency. As long as others recognized that he, too, was responsible to his constituency, they would get along just fine.

As chairman of the Judiciary Committee, Eastland had one rule—every senator in the Democratic majority could chair a sub-committee, even if this meant creating a new one. Thus, John

Tunney chaired one called Constitutional Rights. I chaired a couple of different subcommittees, moving from Separation of Powers to Administrative Practices and Procedures. The important thing about subcommittee chairmanships was that a substantial amount of money for hiring staff came with them.

When I was first appointed to the Judiciary Committee in 1975, I went to Eastland's office to talk about appointments to various subcommittees. Some of my liberal colleagues had advised me with respect to "Eastland protocol," so when Eastland offered me a drink, I accepted. We talked and drank, and several toddies later I was appointed chairman of one subcommittee and a member of several others.

One of Eastland's staff had interrupted a time or two during our drinking bout to tell him that the chief executive officer of TransAmerica Corporation was in the waiting room. "Let him wait," Eastland growled, "We'ah talkin'." Eventually we ended our conversation, and as I lurched out of his office, I stopped in front of a photograph of Eastland standing beside an old man wearing bibbed overalls, a pointed hat, and a beard cut straight across at the bottom, a perfect stereotype of a Southern mountain man.

Admiring the photo, I asked who it was.

"That's old E.C. Clark of Clark County, Mississippi," Eastland replied. "In Clark County, you either get all the votes, or none, depending on what E.C. says." Then he said with a grin, "Ah get all the votes."

"When that picture was being taken," he went on, "E.C. was telling me how he had just got done fixin' a jury."

Eastland used the English language sparingly. He rarely made a speech on the Senate floor, and when he did, it was only to read a short, written statement. He generally limited his conversation to asking his guests what they wanted to drink, and he avoided issue discussions at all costs.

On the third floor of the Capitol just above the Senate floor there is a small office occupied by the secretary of the Senate. It must seem to anyone in the corridors that a great deal of important business is conducted there because of the steady flow of U.S. senators in and out of the office. The core of the office is an inner room that holds a sofa a few chairs, and, of course, a portable bar. It was one of the better watering holes around, a preferred meeting place where Jim Eastland used to preside in characteristic silence.

Whenever I showed up at the office, the conversation would

inevitably turn to the subject of Indians. Because few people in the Senate had ever bothered with American Indians—except to try to take away their land and water—I was looked upon as an eccentric because I was an advocate for Indian rights.

One day in the third floor office I was sitting with several other senators when Senator John Pastore of Rhode Island began talking about Indians. Everyone took their turn telling what they knew about Indians, when suddenly, in a burst of loquacity Jim Eastland sat forward, lifted his glass, and in his best back country Mississippian accent announced, "Ah nevah saw an Indian woman who wasn't virtuous."

Then he settled back into his corner of the sofa, reverting to total silence once again. It was a silence broken only when he would order his car to be brought around, or when he would direct the Cotton Council, the cotton industry's lobbying group, to deliver another case of Chivas Regal to the Senate secretary's office.

Some committee chairman actually would prevent hearings on issues they didn't agree with. Eastland's loose management style encouraged legislative efforts by even the most liberal members of the Judiciary Committee, however. For example, although I was never able to pass a bill on "uniform standards," I was allowed to hold enough hearings on the issue to at least focus attention on it. Uniform standards is a technical term that applies to the operations of such private laboratories as Underwriters Lab. The impetus for reform of the standards system came from a staff person on the committee, John Ray, who later went into city politics, and is currently a city councilman in Washington, D.C. What we tried to do was to require uniform standards for testing commercial products, preventing any one heavyweight in a given industry from buying standards that were favorable to it. The standards industry was totally unregulated, allowing any one private standards lab, such as Underwriters Lab, to dominate testing of consumer products and to control the approval process.

The best example of the need for some kind of regulation concerned the natural gas industry. John Ray found a fellow who had invented a simple device that would have saved tremendous amounts of natural gas each year. It was a flue damper that, when attached to the chimney of a natural gas furnace, prevented cold air from entering a home via the chimney when the furnace was not running. The inventor could not get clearance from the private lab that approved such devices. I accused the gas industry of blocking approval, and presented ample evidence to support my claim.

Unfortunately, the issue was too exotic to attract interest from other senators. John Ray and I plugged away at it for a couple of years until I left the Senate, never, however, getting enough support to pass legislation on it.

Because uniform standards was not considered a "sexy" issue, I was usually the only senator present at committee hearings. So occasionally I resorted to one of my old tricks to try to bring other committee members out for the hearings. I would ask John Thorne to set up TV lights and an inoperative TV camera in the hearing room. Notified by their staffs that the media were present, other senators would begin drifting into the hearings to make an appearance before leaving again.

Another issue that met with little sympathy from the Senate was grand jury reform, an issue that I was also able to air as a member of the Judiciary Committee. I was convinced that federal prosecutors had been using the grand jury system too often as a weapon aimed at people innocent of any crime, but who were political opponents of either the prosecutor or the Administration in power. The grand jury, a panel of citizens drafted to review prosecutorial actions by the State, was originally intended to prevent false prosecution of the innocent. Presumably, the grand jury would be able to protect innocent people from a malicious prosecutor. I became interested in this issue during the Nixon Administration when the Justice Department was overly active in going after Nixon's political opponents. I was never able to get legislation passed that would reform the grand jury system, but the hearings exposed the issue, keeping it alive for a time.

I had much better luck, however, with an amendment to the Watergate Reform Act, which came from the Government Operations Committee to the Judiciary Committee. While the bill was in Judiciary, I offered an amendment, drafted by staffer Chuck Ludlam, to establish the Office of Special Prosecutor. Such an office seemed necessary to me after watching Nixon order his attorney general not to prosecute members of his Administration. No one on the committee really wanted the amendment, so I literally had to force it on them by threatening a filibuster in committee. It was eventually accepted, under threat of course, and became law. Under the Reagan Administration, the Office of Independent Counsel, as it is now called, has become one of the most active offices in Washington.

Perhaps the most important and the most powerful lobby of all is one's home state constituency, reflecting the politician's primary yearning to get elected. When one's constituency gets turned onto an issue and gets organized, it is a pressure group that has no equal anywhere. Senator J. William Fulbright always took heavy criticism for his distasteful votes on civil rights legislation during the turbulent years of the civil rights movement. His response was that he never voted against his constituency on an issue that they knew as much about as he did, which in Arkansas at the time included civil rights.

Something akin to Fulbright's dilemma once faced one of my Democratic colleagues who joined the Judiciary Committee after I did. Senator Joe Biden of Delaware, known as a liberal nationally, was anxiously trying to push through the committee a bill on school busing that he and Senator William Roth, the Delaware Republican, had coauthored. The federal court in Delaware had ordered a busing plan to desegregate the schools there, a decision which was, needless to say, highly controversial in Delaware, generating support from blacks and great outrage among whites. The purpose of the Biden-Roth bill was to overrule the court decision and thereby cancel the busing plan.

Clarence Mitchell of the NAACP approached me to ask if I would lead the fight against the bill in the Judiciary Committee. If I could hold up passage of the bill until the court's ruling went into effect, the legislation would be nullified. As a member of the committee, Biden was expected to push hard to get it passed there and moved onto the Senate floor. I wondered aloud why the noted civil rights liberals on the committee, such as Ted Kennedy and Birch Bayh, had not been asked to help. Mitchell said that they couldn't, for one reason or another, so I agreed to try.

When Eastland gaveled the committee to order on the appointed day, Biden called up the anti-busing bill for consideration. Eastland recognized me and I told the committee members to make themselves comfortable, because I intended to speak at length. Everyone immediately understood what was coming, and when I began reading a long, boring tract of some sort, they began drifting out of the committee room. When enough members had vanished, I reminded the chairman that a quorum was not present. He had no choice but to adjourn the meeting.

Biden leaned over to me, fire coming out of his eyes, "Abourezk, you sonofabitch, if I ever vote for another one of your bills, it'll be a cold day in hell."

"Calm down, Joe," I told him, "You're eventually gonna thank me for doing this."

"Like hell I will you dirty bastard." Biden snorted, stomping out of the room.

I suppose it was because Eastland rather liked Biden's anti-busing bill that he called a committee meeting the next day to continue consideration of it. The Judiciary Committee members dutifully trooped in, and I began reading from the same tract. Once again Eastland had to adjourn the meeting for lack of a quorum and Joe Biden grew even angrier. For the next couple of days, we went through the same routine. Because the bill was important only to Biden, no one else could stand to sit through a boring reading by Abourezk, and so Eastland was unable to keep a quorum.

A few days later, Biden came into the scheduled committee meeting, this time with a broad, friendly grin aimed directly at me. "Jesus, Abourezk, you were right," he said. "I *am* gonna thank you. You should see the Delaware newspapers—big front-page headlines saying, 'Biden Battles Liberals in Washington.' " He was unabashedly elated. "They love me back home. How did you know this would happen?"

I knew, but I didn't tell Biden how I knew, about the politics of self-perpetuation. Congressman Phil Burton had once told me how it was done in the California State Assembly. Burton was known as the ultimate wheeler-dealer, liberal in his politics but pragmatic in his approach to the profession. When he was a California state assemblyman, he watched, over a period of years, another assemblyman, representing San Francisco's Chinatown, introduce a bill in Sacramento designed to benefit Chinese immigrants. Each year the bill would lose in the state assembly, and each year he would return to Chinatown, promising that he would reintroduce the bill and fight hard for its passage. He was consistently reelected with comfortable margins.

Frustrated merely from watching, Phil Burton told his colleague that he could help him get the bill passed and made into law.

"Mind your own business," he told Phil.

Although Eastland established a friendship with Ted Kennedy, he eventually grew irritated with me, more because of my aggressive style than because of my politics. During meetings of the Judiciary Committee, like most chairmen when a motion or an amendment is proposed, he would ask if there was any discussion. I knew the game was up for me when I offered an amendment to a piece of legislation under consideration, and Eastland asked, "Is there a motion to table?"

* * *

Jim Eastland made the Senate an interesting place before he left. But gone as well from the Senate are even more interesting senators, such as Gaylord Nelson, Jim Pearson, Fred Harris, George McGovern, John Culver, and, of course, Tom Eagleton, all of whom took their work seriously, but not themselves, and especially not their colleagues. Remaining are such humorless people as Jesse Helms, in addition to a gaggle of new, sanforized, pre-shrunk, blow-dried senators whose convictions are as deep-seated as today's public opinion polls. Which is why there is a feeling that the Senate has lost both its character and its sense of humor.

I think John Culver would win first prize for humor in any setting and in any year. He has a wit so quick that I suspect there's a miniature gag writer positioned inside his head, spewing out lines. When a group of us were talking in the Democratic cloak room one day, eighty-year-old Senator John McClellan was lying on a leather sofa sound asleep, his mouth open and his hands clasped across his chest. Culver came in, looked at McClellan, turned to the rest of us and said, "Why don't we move the chairman out to the Capitol rotunda, put some lilies in his hand, and announce that he's lying in state?"

When Howard Metzenbaum and I were filibustering on the natural gas bill, Majority Leader Robert Byrd decided that he would break the filibuster by holding an all night session. Around 3:00 A.M. Culver came into the cloakroom and saw Senator Jennings Randolph of West Virginia asleep, actually on the John McLellan memorial sofa. Jennings had been in the Congress since 1932, with some interruption, and even at the age of seventy-five showed surprising physical energy.

Culver surveyed the cloakroom for a brief moment, then deciding on his course of action shouted, "Wake up, Jennings, there's a high school class from West Virginia out in the corridor. They want their picture taken with you."

Randolph's reaction was instantaneous. He sat straight up, ran his fingers through his thinning hair, adjusted his necktie, and asked Culver, "How do I look?"

It was not until he reached the corridor, devoid of high school students, that he realized it was another Culver prank. But it was what Jennings Randolph did next that earned him the admiration of politicians, both young and old. After walking out to the Senate floor, he looked around and saw other senators, all of whom were younger than he, hardly able to keep their heads up because of the late hour and the incessant roll calls. He asked for recognition from the presiding officer, and then began delivering what was to be a three-hour speech on the history of natural gas legislation. He did it to give, as he put it, "my younger colleagues a chance to get some sleep."

The prize for lack of humor would have to be shared with a number of senators, but South Carolina Senator Strom Thurmond is strongly in the running. In 1981, after I left the Senate, and just after the Republicans had won a majority of Senate seats, I ran into Strom and congratulated him on taking over the chairmanship of the Judiciary Committee from Ted Kennedy. "You know, Strom," I said, "I've taken down Ted's picture from my office wall and I've replaced it with yours."

Strom looked at me, clearly disturbed at what I'd said, and replied in all seriousness, "Now don't do that. You're gonna hurt Ted's feelings."

Humor was sometimes unintentional as well. King Hassan of Morocco, definitely a serious monarch, was responsible for one of the classier put-downs when he came to the United States for a visit in 1978, and was hosted for an afternoon tea by the Senate Foreign Relations Committee. During the question-and-answer session, Senator Clifford Case of New Jersey rose to challenge the king. It was clearly an effort by Case, a vocal supporter of Israel, to embarrass an Arab ruler. Case asked King Hassan to comment on a now-forgotten controversy in which President Jimmy Carter was embroiled with Republicans in the Senate. The King declined.

"I do not wish to become involved in the internal politics of America," he said through his interpreter.

Case would not leave it alone. He rose one more time and rephrased the question. This time there was no mistaking the royal outrage.

"I cannot answer your question because I am neither a Democrat nor a Republican. I am a constitutional monarchy," a declaration that quickly put an end to Case's efforts.

I thought that the Senate Foreign Relations Committee's practice of inviting foreign rulers to lunch, or to tea, was a fairly useful one. I was invited to several of these sessions, mostly when Middle Easterners came to town, and even once during a visit by Margaret Thatcher, but before she was Prime Minister, and still part of the opposition.

One lunch that I did not attend, but which was described to me by a senator who was present, was held for the prime minister of Botswana and hosted by Senator John Sparkman of Alabama, then chairman of the Foreign Relations Committee. Sparkman, if you recall, ran for vice-president with Adlai Stevenson in 1952. He was always a decent person, a good senator, both liked and respected by his colleagues. Senator Sparkman's advancing years had cursed him with narcolepsy, an affliction that caused him to drop off to sleep at the most embarrassing moments.

After the luncheon dishes were cleared, Chairman Sparkman, sitting just to the right of the prime minister, stumbled through a written introduction of his guest, then presented him to the senators gathered in the committee room.

"I'm terribly happy to be here," the prime minister opened, his clipped British accent betraying a disciplined English education.

"The last time I came to America," he continued, "the attention of the entire nation was focused on Vietnam, and especially on Watergate. I'm afraid the problems of Africa were placed on the rearmost burner."

He was warming up to his subject. "But now, things seem to be totally different. I'm happy to say the concerns of Africa appear to be getting the undivided attention of your government . . ."

At precisely that point in the prime minister's talk, Sparkman fell into a deep sleep, his head dropping onto the shoulder of the prime minister, who was forced to push it away.

As often happens in Congress, some of the best humor stems from the most serious matters. For example, no controversy has ever generated or sustained more animosity in the Western states than the one that has raged between environmentalists and sheep ranchers on the subject of coyotes. Out in the Great Plains of the United States—more specifically in the sheep country of South Dakota, Wyoming, and Montana—a huge fight has developed over the problem of controlling coyotes, beautiful wild animals which, to put it simply, kill sheep and eat them.

Without talking to a sheep rancher face to face, it is difficult to gauge the depth of bitter emotion inspired by the economic losses they suffer from the killing of their sheep by coyotes. Environmentalists, on the other hand, maintain that ranchers exaggerate their losses and that, in any event, the importance of a few dead sheep is far outweighed by the importance of maintaining the coyote as a living species. Of equal concern to environmentalists is the prob-

lem of the residual kill—the death of other animals and birds that
feed on poisoned coyote meat.

When Richard Nixon signed Executive Order 11613 banning
the use of the coyote poison called "1080," environmentalists
were delighted, and sheep ranchers, naturally, were outraged.
The burden of explaining the 1080 ban fell on Secretary of the
Interior Rogers Morton, a former Maryland Congressman. When
Wyoming Senator Cliff Hansen was deluged with constituent
demands for either reinstatement of 1080 or for some kind of
substitute weapon to control coyotes, he arranged a meeting in
Washington between a group of Western ranchers and Secretary
Morton. In an attempt to appease the ranchers, the secretary
brought along an Interior Department biologist to explain the
government's actions.

When Morton was asked by the angry constituents to provide
an explanation, he turned immediately to the biologist, who stood
up and began citing the reasons for the ban. "It was," he said, "the
residual effects of 1080 poison on eagles, as well as other birds and
animals, that forced the Administration to outlaw its usage. As an
alternative, however, we are now working on a chemical that will
sterilize the male coyote. This chemical will avoid the residual
damage to other wildlife, because it affects only the coyote. We
expect to be able to take care of the problem in this way."

Suddenly a frustrated, angry rancher stood up, interrupting the
biologist, and addressed himself to Morton. "Mr. Secretary, you've
got this thing all wrong. Sterilizin' 'em won't do a damn bit of
good. Those coyotes ain't *fuckin'* those sheep, they're *eatin'* em."

Some of the greatest contributions to congressional humor came
from the amusing crew of politicians that Chicago's Mayor Richard
Daley sent to Washington over the years. Daley rewarded loyal
supporters with various positions, sometimes allowing them to run
for the U.S. House of Representatives and the U.S. Senate.

I had heard many times the story about an old Chicago politician—part of the Daley machine—who won his first election to the
House when he was well over seventy years old. On the day after
his election, he was tottering about the House floor as a puzzled
Sam Rayburn looked on. Unable to stand it any longer, Rayburn
gave the gavel to another congressman and climbed down from the
Speaker's dais to satisfy his curiosity.

"I just want to know," Rayburn asked, "why you decided to run
for Congress at your age?"

Appearing stunned by the question, the old freshman replied, "Why, Mr. Speaker, it was my turn."

The year 1972 was also Congressman Roman Pucinski's "turn." Pucinski, affectionately known as "Poochie" by both friends and enemies, was something of a human dynamo. A congressman from Chicago, he was the nemesis of anyone who got in his way, shouting challenges to opponents during debate on the House floor. He was most famous, however, for his ability to instantly shift his political position whenever it suited him, sometimes even within the same speech if he thought it would help his cause. This tactic, of course, totally baffled his opponents.

As a loyal member of the Daley machine, Poochie was offered up by Daley as a sacrifice against Senator Charles Percy in the 1972 Senate race. Everyone assumed it was a lost cause because of Percy's popularity and Poochie's reputation as a Daley man.

Congressman Mo Udall of Arizona and I were eating lunch in the House members' dining room one day when we were approached by Chicago Congressman Frank Annunzio. Udall said, "Frank, I see that Poochie's been slated by Daley to run against Percy. Is he gonna be to Percy's left or to his right in this race?"

"You guys." Annunzio said with great exasperation. "You guys worry about where the left is and where the right is. But Poochie he don't give a shit."

I always liked Frank Annunzio, but I was absolutely endeared to him when I heard the story that journalist Nina Totenberg told about him.

It was 1973, a time when beef prices were rapidly rising. Annunzio introduced an amendment in the House Banking and Currency Committee that froze the price of beef. It passed. Immediately after the vote, he was approached by *Wall Street Journal* reporter Al Hunt who asked for his comment on the amendment.

"This is a victory for the American people," Annunzio said.

But overnight the beef lobby cranked up, and the next day a move was made to reconsider Annunzio's amendment in the committee. The freeze on beef prices was defeated.

Al Hunt went up to Annunzio immediately after the reconsideration vote and asked for his response.

"The American people got fucked," Annunzio said.

"I can't put that quote in," Hunt told him. "This is a family newspaper."

"Then tell 'em," he said, "the American family got fucked."

* * *

Pressure on politicians comes in all shapes and sizes, and from virtually every direction. No matter the source of the pressure, the objective is the same—to try to influence congressional legislation.

Joe Floyd owns the largest television station in South Dakota—KELO in Sioux Falls. Joe has always been a booster of South Dakota and of politicians he likes. He called me one day to tell me that Arthur Taylor, then president of the CBS television network, was to appear before Phil Hart's Antitrust Subcommittee of the Judiciary Committee. When he asked me if I would attend the hearings and be nice to Taylor, I balked. Joe had never asked me for anything, and this was not too big a favor. All I had to do was show up at a hearing to impress one of his business colleagues with his political clout. "I've got an awful lot of work to do, Joe," I told him, "and I'd really rather not go." But Joe insisted, and so, not wanting to lose his goodwill, I agreed. "And call me when the hearings are finished, will you Jim?" Joe said.

The hearings, I learned, were on the subject of pay television versus "free" television, meaning the commercial kind from which Arthur Taylor made his living. I sat through the testimony of three or four witnesses who represented the networks and cable TV, doodling, daydreaming, essentially passing the time until Arthur Taylor would appear. Suddenly, Phil Hart passed me a note asking me to chair the hearing because he had been called to the Senate floor. I agreed. The next witness was Arthur Taylor, who came on, obviously with full assurance from Joe Floyd that Abourezk would be a friendly questioner. Actually, I had intended only to say nice things about his testimony.

But he overreached. He talked at length about the advantages of the wonderful benefits of "free" television over the evils of pay cable television, which, he said would penalize the poor people of America. Somehow, I couldn't envision either Arthur Taylor or CBS worrying very much about the poor. As he continued his harangue, I looked up from my doodling, anger percolating upward through my veins. Suddenly I heard myself saying to Taylor, "What do you mean, 'free' television? Free until you're forced to buy toilet paper or toothpaste, then we pay through the nose, don't we?"

It was Taylor's turn to get angry. Network presidents, I suppose, are unaccustomed to dealing with uppity senators. He argued. I argued back, until finally and mercifully the hearings came to an end. I returned to my office and called Joe Floyd. "How did the hearings go, Jim?" Joe asked in anticipation of a good report.

"I'm afraid I didn't behave myself too well, Joe," I told him. "I think that I raked Arthur Taylor over the coals."

"Oh, my God," Joe Floyd was nearly apoplectic over the phone, "I told him you'd be his best friend on the committee."

Politicians can overcome pressure by choosing either simply to ignore it or by meeting it head on. I chose the latter course in dealing with one of the great pressure groups in the country—the American Bar Association, which has somehow become virtually the sole arbiter of people selected for federal judgeships. The ABA has taken it upon itself to approve, or disapprove, Congress's judicial nominees, and Congress has, in a way, gone along with it. The ABA's pressure, it turns out, is a bit more stylized than most, appearing in the form of a sophisticated committee with, as they say, only the public interest in mind. Although I was never a member of the American Bar Association (ABA), I had always thought highly of the organization, comprising as it did the elite of the law profession. That is, until I actually saw the group in action in front of the Judiciary Committee.

Don O'Brien, an attorney from Sioux City, Iowa, had been nominated by President Carter to be the federal judge in his district. I had known Don for years. He had worked in the Kennedy campaigns and for McGovern in his presidential campaign, and I knew him to be a decent person and a competent lawyer. John Culver, who had recommended him to the Administration, asked if I would chair the Judiciary Committee hearing on his confirmation. I agreed, and Culver and I opened the hearing. The three members of the ABA Committee on Judicial Selection testified first, telling us that O'Brien was not qualified to be a federal judge. I was momentarily stunned. Then I asked the witnesses why they thought the way they did. I was told that O'Brien had failed, while he was a county prosecutor over twenty years earlier, to notify a prosecutor in another county about a piece of evidence in a criminal case. After pursuing this case further, it appeared to me that the ABA committee was vastly overreaching, that O'Brien was in no way obliged to know about a case in another county, and that he certainly was not required to notify the prosecutor. I said so to the ABA committee witnesses, and asked if they had anything else to justify their charge that he was unqualified.

One of the ABA lawyers then said the most amazing thing. He told me that it appeared to him that O'Brien was a sloppy office manager.

"Based on what?" I asked. Based on a letter that O'Brien had received from someone for which no file was created until several months later, the ABA lawyer said.

What? I shouted. That's your evidence that he's a sloppy office manager? Like most lawyers, O'Brien undoubtedly kept a loose correspondence file where letters were kept until a need arose to open a specific file on a case. Even if the letter had been floating in mid-air for several months, I couldn't believe that the ABA would base their opposition on this.

I flatly and vehemently stated that they had no grounds that would persuade the Judiciary Committee, then leaned over to tell John Culver that I intended to go to lunch. If he wanted to continue chairing the hearing for a few minutes, he could do so, then adjourn until I returned.

Culver had originally asked me to chair the hearing because he had gotten wind of the ABA's opposition, and wanted to, as he said, "lay low." He thought that I could take the edge off the ABA's criticism without his getting embroiled in an Iowa controversy. It made perfect sense to me. Why should John unnecessarily get in the middle of a brouhaha, when I could just as well handle it for him? So I was unprepared for Culver's next move. As I left for lunch, he was just beginning to harangue the ABA witnesses about their extremely partisan behavior. John and I had both earlier agreed that the ABA was against O'Brien for two basic reasons. He had been a partisan Democrat and he was what attorneys call a plaintiff's lawyer, that is, someone who represents little people who sue the establishment, the insurance companies, and other corporate interests. It was obvious to both of us that the ABA wanted judges in place who sympathized with the establishment, rather than someone who might decide against it if the facts warranted it. When I returned to the hearing nearly an hour later, Culver was still reading the riot act to the fuming ABA witnesses, who obviously were accustomed to delivering harangues, but not to receiving them.

When I finally adjourned the hearings, I told Culver that the ABA would surely re-group and try to defeat O'Brien's nomination. My strategy was to get a quick vote of the Judiciary Committee before they could round up opposition and then run the nomination over to the Senate floor for full Senate approval. We were able to do just that. Before the afternoon was over, Don O'Brien had been confirmed as a federal district judge, throwing the ABA judicial selection committee into a tizzy. They bitterly complained to the Senate leadership about the speedy confirmation, but to no avail. Judge O'Brien, incidentally, has since chalked up an outstanding record as a judge, impressing everyone with his ability and his fairness.

I had to face a different kind of lobby pressure after I became chairman of the National Parks and Recreation Subcommittee of the Energy Committee. Phil Burton was my counterpart in the House. It was our intention, in 1977, to expand the Redwoods Forest National Park in Northern California. To do so would, of course, require that the government condemn and pay for the forests owned by the timber companies. Word had come to us that the timber companies were in the process of clear-cutting that part of the Redwood Forest still in private ownership. Instead of selectively cutting the redwoods, they were clear-cutting a massive 160-acre area.

Phil held some tumultuous hearings in San Francisco, instead of in Eureka where the redwoods were located. He did so for safety's sake, because the timber companies had organized a gigantic protest by the loggers and others dependent on the redwood industry. The demonstration, however, moved from Eureka to San Francisco, with truckers hauling gigantic redwood logs, some of them several feet in diameter, on flatbed trucks and parking them in front of the San Francisco Federal Building.

When the time came for my subcommittee to move on the legislation, I traveled north to Eureka, and, instead of holding hearings, I called a town meeting. Virtually everyone interested in the industry attended. I had been out to the redwoods earlier that day, where I was shown a large area that one of the timber companies had clear-cut a few days earlier. To me there was just one reason the company would have done so, because they knew that I was coming to look at the site.

At the town meeting, I accused the timber companies of deliberately trying to provoke me and the entire Congress by creating what could only be described as a moonscape in the center of the redwoods. It was my suspicion that the companies saw redwood timbering petering out in a few years, leaving them with land of greatly diminished value. They saw, I believed, more profit in government condemnation and payment for their timber holdings than in a slow death of the industry. I said so, emphatically, at the town meeting.

Then Burton and I drafted a bill to expand the park, introduced it, and when its turn came for consideration on the Senate floor, the timber companies made a maximum push to increase their compensation for the land that the government wanted to condemn. California Senator S. I. Hayakawa became the point man for the timber companies and offered their amendments, all of which would have increased the price paid to the timber companies. His amendments failed.

I lined up more than enough votes to pass the expansion, but nearly lost them when I grew overconfident and began to taunt Hayakawa and the small core of Republicans supporting him. The timber people had programmed a series of speeches for Hayakawa to give in support of his amendments, and had gotten various senators to read them as each amendment was introduced. Remembering a similar gimmick that Jack Kennedy had used in his 1960 presidential campaign, I noted in one of my rebuttals to Hayakawa that he and his Republican cadres were like circus elephants, marching in order, with the tail of the one in front held by the trunk of the one behind. It was too much for the Republicans, a number of whom later came pouring out of their cloakroom, challenging me and nearly upsetting my previously smooth-sailing strategy.

In 1978, Phil Burton and I worked together to create what came to be called the Omnibus Parks Bill. It was a huge piece of legislation that created a number of new parks and expanded a number of existing ones. Included in the bill was a park that had been proposed by a senator, whom I will call Louie. Ostensibly, he wanted to establish a park for the benefit of the Indians in his state, because it would be set aside specifically for them. However, he passed the word around the Senate that he didn't really want the park established, but had introduced the bill only to curry favor with the Indians. Phil Burton told me that he knew that the site was a choice one upon which certain developers had cast their eyes, and Louie, he said, wanted to save it for them. At the hearings for this particular park, Louie sat beside me on the dais hoping to take credit for the proceedings. I announced to his constituents, who had traveled to Washington to testify, that they had no stronger supporter in the Senate for their park than Louie. He was beaming when I finished, and the Indians went away feeling good.

When mark-up time for the Omnibus Park Bill came around—the time to amend the bill and write it into final form—I was negotiating on the phone with Interior Secretary Cecil Andrus. The Office of Management and Budget had given him a dollar limit beyond which we could not go, and we were trying to agree on which parks to cut out of the bill in order not to exceed the limit.

"Now, we can take out this park, can't we?" Andrus said, referring to Louie's park, "because I'm told that Louie doesn't really want it."

"No way, Cecil," I told him. "You'll face a filibuster from Louie if you try that. I heard him with my own ears telling his constituents that he would fight to the very end for the park."

That convinced Andrus, who left the Indians' park in the bill, and we went on to the next item. Of course, Louie was outraged, but powerless to protest. Burton and I chuckled about it for days.

We also tried to expand the Manassas Battlefield Park, located not too far from Washington, but the bill died in the Senate Energy Committee. Again, the expansion would have required condemning and purchasing private land that is part of the battlefield. Virginia Senators Bill Scott and Harry Byrd, Jr. had notified the members of the committee that they were opposed to it, and, as a tip of the hat to senatorial courtesy, most of the committee bowed to their wishes. The expansion was dead for the rest of the session, as far as the committee was concerned, until the last night of the 1978 Senate session.

The last night of each Senate session, before final adjournment and the fall elections, has always been a time of great confusion. The majority leader, whoever he is, tries to pass as many bills as possible, and of necessity they are passed by unanimous consent. There is no time for extended debate. If any senator threatens a filibuster, the majority leader will, in most cases, abandon the piece of legislation in question. Occasionally, as at the end of the 1978 session, when both Senator Bob Byrd and President Carter wanted the natural gas deregulation bill passed in the worst way, the leader will push hard to overcome a filibuster.

I made a practice of sitting up all night at the final Senate sessions, beginning at the end of the 1974 session, keeping an eye out for legislation that might not be in the public interest, or, to put it another way, that might allow some special interest to carry off the Capitol dome. The end of the 1978 Senate session—my last one—droned on into the night. At some point in the wee hours, Phil Burton, who recognized no one's courtesy, sent over for Senate action the House version of the Omnibus Parks Bill. The bill made no mention whatever of the Manassas Battlefield Park expansion. What it did, however, was to expand the park by simply redrawing its boundaries on the map. It was a clever move, I have to admit, and Burton would have succeeded had it not been for some unknown staff person who finked to Harry Byrd, Jr.

Upon learning of Burton's scheme, Harry rose and denounced the practice, and because there was a long night ahead of him, he propped himself up against the clerk's desk and personally read every bill sent over from the House, even before they were given to the clerk. Phil tried one more time that night, but Harry caught him. Harry grew more tired, but also more determined. At one point during the night, Burton came in from the House side, walked over to my desk snorting with laughter at Senator Harry Byrd, Jr., who was nodding as he stood guard at the clerk's desk, every few minutes dropping off to sleep while standing up.

I noted that in 1988 the Congress finally succumbed to the demands of preservationists to expand the Manassas Battlefield Park by purchasing the area from a developer who had intended, among other outrages, to erect a large shopping center there. Of course, the ten-year interim had driven the price of the land up astronomically, which must have unsettled both Bill Scott and Harry Byrd, Jr., two of the nation's more celebrated fiscal conservatives.

Speaking of lobbies and of political pressure, 1976 was the year the Israeli lobby decided to flex its muscle on the Arab boycott issue. Ever since Israel created itself by taking over Palestine and chasing out the Palestinians who lived there, the Arab countries have conducted a boycott of Israel. Israel's lobby in Washington drafted legislation intended to prevent American companies from cooperating with the Arab countries in their enforcement of the boycott. In 1976, both the House and the Senate had worked up a bill that was totally oppressive for Americans to follow. It was a bill developed by congressional "crazies," virtually preventing any contact at all between American companies and the Arab world.

The bill was being called up during the last days of the 1976 session as I was struggling against another of Jim Allen's post-cloture filibusters. Senator John Tunney of California had called up the Civil Rights Attorney's Fee Bill on the floor, which prompted Jim Allen to begin filibustering in an effort to defeat it, or, at worst, to water it down. This prompted Tunney to leave almost immediately for California to campaign for reelection. (It was his toughest campaign and his last—he lost the election.) At first, Majority Leader Byrd carried the ball, managing the legislation for Tunney for a while, but it began to interfere with his work as leader. Jane Frank of Tunney's staff asked me a few days later if I would care to manage the bill against Allen's filibuster. Because I had no election to run in, I agreed, and began trying my best to wear down Allen. Because it was toward the end of the session, and because we were in a post-cloture condition, having the opportunity to manage the bill would also allow me to prevent other undesirable legislation from being called up, including the anti-boycott bill.

Senator Bill Proxmire of Wisconsin asked to be recognized. He

made a motion to appoint Senate members of the Conference Committee to settle differences on both versions of the anti-boycott bills.
When Proxmire moved to appoint the conferees, I objected. He
waited a for a time to see how serious I was about it, then he renewed
the motion for conferees. I objected again.

A day or so later, he tried it again, and I objected again. This time
he came over to me and told me that it was embarrassing for the
Democrats to have a Democrat objecting to his motion, because the
plan was to have Carter "beat Gerry Ford over the head" with the
issue in their upcoming television debate. It was the Administration's
position that the anti-boycott legislation was harmful to U.S. business interests.

I told Proxmire that I didn't care who objected, as long as the
bill was stopped. I suggested that he find a Republican to do the
objecting. A few minutes later, he walked over to me with Senator
John Tower of Texas in tow. "John will do the objecting," Proxmire
told me.

"Is it true?" I asked Tower.

"Yes, it is," he grinned. I then made Tower give me his word that he
wouldn't let the bill go through, and turned it over to him. Proxmire
renewed his motion, and good to his word, Tower objected, again
and again, until the session was concluded.

The bill died at the end of the session, but over the holidays at
year's end, the Business Roundtable, represented by Irving Shapiro
of the Du Pont Company, began negotiations with the Israeli lobby.
Eventually they agreed to a compromise that the Roundtable
thought their members could live with.

Then, at the beginning of the session in January 1977, it fell upon
Senator Adlai Stevenson of Illinois to mark up the bill in the Senate
Commerce Committee. I was in the Democratic cloakroom when
Stevenson called me. In a hushed voice he told me that he needed my
help. "I'm in here (the Commerce Committee room) offering the
amendments on that anti-boycott bill, and Bookbinder and Brody
are operating as though they own this place." Hyman Bookbinder
and Dave Brody were lobbyists for the American Jewish Committee
and B'Nai B'rith, respectively. "They're in and out of the committee's
office," Stevenson continued, "you know, the one behind the hearing
room. They've pushed some kind of button, and I've received hundreds of telegrams telling me not to sell out Israel with my amendments. For God's sake, Jim, these are the amendments that the Israeli
lobby agreed to. They're breaking their agreement."

"What do you want me to do?" I asked.

"Get a hold of some press and try to get a story written about what they're doing. That might stop them."

I called a reporter at *The Washington Post*, told him about it, then said that if he found the story interesting, he should interview Stevenson. He did, and a small story appeared the next day, giving Stevenson enough breathing space to finish the mark-up.

*   *   *

There is one bit of senatorial courtesy—known as the "hold"—that is occasionally used as leverage. A "hold" is a request by a senator that the majority leader notify him if anyone should try to bring up the legislation placed on hold. Its purpose is to allow a senator to come to the Senate floor to debate the legislation, without having to wait for the bill to be called up. At the end of a session a hold is usually enough to kill a bill, unless the majority leader believes the legislation is so important that he will allow it to be brought up despite the threat of a filibuster. I had earlier convinced the Senate Rules Committee, and ultimately the whole Senate, to establish the Senate Select Committee on Indian Affairs, replacing the Indian Affairs Subcommittee of the Energy Committee. The select committee was due to expire at the beginning of 1979, after I was to leave office, and I was desperately trying to get it renewed during the last days of the 1978 session. What was stopping me was Nevada Senator Howard Cannon, who had placed a hold on the renewal legislation.

Cannon put a hold on renewal of the Indian Affairs Committee because I had earlier placed a hold on a bill that he reported out of his committee. In 1977, I had heard from a Budget Committee staff member that at the end of the session Cannon would try to ram through a bill that would, among other things, provide a $3 billion giveaway to the airline industry. The money would subsidize the airlines that were being required to introduce quieter aircraft. The acquisition of subsidized aircraft would allow the industry to sell its older, noisier planes to foreign airlines, recouping a substantial amount of money. In short, it was a huge windfall, a boondoggle for the airlines. I placed a hold on Cannon's airline bill early on, and on the last night of the 1978 session, he was trying to make a trade with me—he would release the Indian Affairs Committee renewal in return for my release of his airline bill. I told him that I refused to allow the airline subsidy bill to go through.

It was a standoff, but I was fairly confident of winning. I pretended that I didn't care whether the Indian Committee was extended, which put Cannon into a panic. What he was most concerned about was section two of the airline bill that provided for additional safety requirements desired by the Federal Aviation Administration. He came back to me, this time resigned to give up on the subsidy, offering to allow the Indian Committee extension if I would allow section two of his bill to pass. "All right," I said, "but you'll kill section one?" He agreed. In a rare, happy ending, the Indians had their committee extended and the airlines had to find money elsewhere, most likely from the many tickets I've purchased since then.

The game of "reciprocal holds"—legislatively emulative, I thought, of the system of checks and balances built into the Constitution—was played more than once that year. I had introduced an amendment that would force the removal of J. Edgar Hoover's name from the FBI building. The conservative Republicans were in deep shock over the move, but they laid low, thinking that I would never be allowed to call it up. But I used another parliamentary technique to have the amendment brought up for a straight up or down vote on the Senate floor. The minute that I had it put on the floor calendar, the Republicans clamped a hold on it. I then found a bill that the Republicans wanted, one that would name a federal building in one of the Northeastern states after one of their conservative heroes, actually a conservative Democrat. When I did that, the Republicans then put a hold on a bill sponsored by Tom Eagleton that would have named a monument after Supreme Court Justice William O. Douglas. The Republicans' strategy worked. Eagleton complained bitterly to me for days, until I finally relented and released the hold on the naming of the federal building, and like dominoes, holds on all the other bills fell away.

The same year, 1978, I offered an amendment to the White House appropriations legislation to cut off funds for Richard Nixon's pension, his government-funded staff, and his other federally provided perquisites. I did this after reading about the outrageous amount of money that he was getting for being the first president to resign in disgrace. When I called up the amendment, only two senators voted for it—Kaneaster Hodges of Arkansas and I. I expected a few more votes, but the best part came when *The Washington Post* ran an article about the vote. "Senate Rejects Move to Cut Off Nixon's Penison," the headline read. Bob Thomson, from Jimmy Carter's White House lobbying staff, sent me a photocopy of the headline, but covered up the "on" on the word

"Penison," making the headline read, "Senate Rejects Move to Cut Off Nixon's Penis." Thomson's accompanying note suggested that I was beginning to play rough. I wrote back, telling him I'd do the same to both him and Carter if they didn't stop trying to deregulate natural gas.

9

Somebody
Out There
Hates Me

Most lobbies, no matter how good they are, fade into insignificance beside the most effective—and vicious—of them all. Israel's lobby in Washington, known simply as "the Israeli lobby," or, "the Lobby," has refined to a high art form the techniques of putting pressure on members of Congress and on the Administration.

Although the Israeli lobby is a familiar institution around Washington, D.C., its work is not too well known around the country. It consists of a number of support groups both in Washington and throughout America that work to further Israel's interests. Its most visible component on Capitol Hill is AIPAC, or the American Israel Public Affairs Committee, which should be distinguished from a political action committee (PAC) that collects money for candidates. Now headed by Thomas Dine, a former staffer for Senators Frank Church and Ted Kennedy, its founder and most famous head was I. L. "Sy" Kenen, now deceased. He was followed by Morrie Amitay, who now runs a PAC.

AIPAC is joined, however, by such major Jewish organizations as the American Jewish Committee, the American Jewish Congress, and B'nai B'rith, all of whom have lobbyists working the halls of Congress. These organizations are buttressed by the "synagogue circuit," a group of rabbis who participate in the haranguing of their congregations with the Israeli party line.

Although sentiment in the American Jewish community is changing as a result of the uprising in the West Bank and the Gaza Strip, over the years the Lobby has been a formidable force, doing Israel's work in the nation's capital. The way the Lobby works is perhaps best described by its effort to override President Ford's threat against Israel in 1975. Ford and Kissinger were insisting on a change in Israel's policy toward negotiation with the Arab countries following the 1973 war, and Israel was resisting. Ford then announced a "reassessment" of America's policy toward Israel, meaning that our arms shipments to Israel would be stopped until it came around to our way of thinking.

The Lobby drafted a letter to Ford with the intention of having a great many senators sign it, essentially threatening to override Ford's arms blockade. Lobby operatives took the letter to Senator George McGovern's staff, telling them that Senator Ted Kennedy had already signed it, and that McGovern shouldn't be the only prospective presidential candidate left off the list. Then producing McGovern's signature, they confronted Kennedy's staff with the same ultimatum.

One senator, who shall remain nameless, told me on the night before the letter was released to the press that he had refused to sign it, understanding full well that it was to be used to prevent a U.S. government initiative in the Middle East. When his name appeared on the list of signatories the next day, I asked him what had happened.

"Jim," he said, "after I refused the Lobby, I received phone calls from four or five Jews in my state who had worked to get me elected last time around. These weren't guys who had simply written checks. They were professionals, men who actually left their offices and their businesses to work in my election. How could I refuse them?"

The Lobby reached its high point that year, obtaining seventy-six senators' signatures on the letter, which forced President Ford to back down and to drop his reassessment of our policy toward Israel.

I came to learn early on in the Senate that any manifestation of support for a Palestinian State, or conversely, any sign of dissension from U.S. Middle East policy makes one a pariah of sorts. Senators who criticize Israel do so at their political peril. The Lobby hurls the charge of "anti-Semitism" against those who dare to voice opposition to Israel's occupation of contested territories, to the bombing of Arab refugee camps, and to other ghastly practices which, when undertaken by any other country, bring great cries of protest from the same people who will not allow criticism of Israel.

Some of America's most brilliant people have been elevated to pariah status by the Lobby. Noam Chomsky, the MIT linguist, has become a target of more vitriol than non-Jewish pariahs. His principled stand on the rights of the weak and the vulnerable, which, unfortunately for him include Lebanese and Palestinians singled out for destruction by Israel's government, has made him a special target of the Lobby and its minions. Chomsky writes prolifically about the Middle East in a way that displeases those whom Gore Vidal calls "Israel Firsters," the cadres of men and women whose primary goal in life is to insure a continuous flow of money from the American treasury to Israel. Similarly, Edward Said, Edward Parr Professor of Comparative Literature at Columbia University, has struggled mightily and successfully to overcome designation as a pariah by the Israeli lobby. Said's first sin is that he was born a Palestinian. Second, he is a member of the Palestine National Council, the Palestinian diaspora's legislative body. But his greatest transgression has been to write and speak articulately about Palestine and Palestinians in a way that makes Israel look like the aggressor nation that it is.

Author Gore Vidal has come in for unfavorable recognition by the Lobby. He wrote an essay for *The Nation* magazine a couple of years ago in which he undertook a political mugging of Norman Podhoretz, editor of *Commentary*, and his wife, the neo-conservative activist, Midge Decter, describing them, among other things, as the "Lunts of the right wing." His most damaging attack came when he linked Podhoretz and his wife to what he called "the Israeli Fifth Column," those who seek to ensure a continuous flow of American money to Israel, no matter what. His *Nation* essay was only the first shot in the literary war that followed, but it was the most public. Later, Podhoretz used the pages of *The Washington Post* to respond to Vidal's assault on him in *The Nation*.

Vidal's essay, and the responses it generated, became one of the longest running shows that *The Nation* had ever hosted. For each letter that *The Nation* printed castigating him, it ran a brief response by Vidal, so biting that the letter writers must have regretted ever becoming involved in the controversy. I was delighted by

Vidal's sustained attack on these two symbols of the Israeli lobby, compelling me to invite him to speak to the 1988 Annual Convention of the American-Arab Anti-Discrimination Committee (ADC).

His speech to the ADC, in March 1988, dealt primarily with the course of the American empire. Both Vidal in his speech, and I in my introduction, noted the presence in the audience that day of Leon Wieseltier, *The New Republic's* literary editor. I introduced him as a representative of the Israeli lobby's in-house journal. Wieseltier, unable to contain his rage, wrote a column in the next issue of *The New Republic* describing Vidal as "grotesque" and Abourezk as "puerile." But Vidal returned the insult in his new book of essays, *At Home*. He included his ADC speech in the appendix, adding to it an introduction in which he mentioned the presence in the audience of *The New Republic's* "dreaded secret agent, code name *Weasel*," whom he easily recognized by his "shoulder length gray fright wig" and his "rabid, ruby-red eyes."

All the efforts to suppress Vidal have been unsuccessful, however. His books and essays continue to sell at record rates, disproving the theory generally held in publishing that you can't disagree with Israel and get away with it.

I became even more aware of the Israeli lobby's influence and the need to resist it during the 1982 Israeli invasion of Lebanon. The first few weeks of reportage by the U.S. media following the Begin-Sharon invasion in June 1982, gave the impression that not much was happening of import in Lebanon. There was ample reason for this misperception. The media *here* were reporting only what the Israeli government was handing out to the reporters *there*—military communiqués they were called. But what was really happening was best described by the word "blitzkrieg." I was receiving firsthand reports from people and organizations in Lebanon that described the savage assault by the Israelis on Lebanese and Palestinian civilians, cities, and villages. The reports of the devastation were grotesque, but none of it was appearing in American newspapers.

The Lebanese-Israeli border had been relatively quiet for a year because of a cease-fire engineered by American diplomat Philip Habib. In fact the only breaks in the cease-fire were the dozens of attempts by the Israeli military to provoke the PLO by firing at them across the border. Suddenly, when Abu Nidal's terrorist group shot Shlomo Argov, Israel's ambassador to Great Britain on London's streets, General Ariel Sharon, then Israel's defense Minister, decided that this was sufficient provocation to send his armies across the Lebanese border in a full-scale invasion. Never mind that Abu Nidal had been at war with the PLO for a decade, or that he had been sentenced to death by a Fatah military tribunal, he was an Arab. Accusing the PLO of trying to assassinate Argov, Sharon retaliated by bombarding Palestinian targets inside Lebanon and by launching the invasion.

Sharon at first announced that he wanted only forty kilometers of Lebanese territory cleared of "terrorists." The press swallowed his story whole and said little or nothing about Israel's violation of the cease-fire and the atrocities that its army was committing on its way north. The Israeli military laid siege to Lebanese cities, cut off their supplies of water and electricity, bombarded the Arab civilians with awesome fire power, and refused to let medical supplies into the targeted areas. Tremendous suffering resulted. Instead of reporting what was happening, which might have helped stop the invasion, the press reported on Jane Fonda, Tom Hayden, and other brave celebrity souls who were trundled up to the front lines by Israel's public relations experts so that they could endorse the invasion.

Aside from the U.S. government sending money to Israel to pay for the invasion, nothing was happening in Washington. In Congress, where words are ordinarily more plentiful than stars in the Milky Way, there was total silence. Nothing. Senators and House members, who in most circumstances are great defenders of freedom, had totally lost their voices. Congressional human rights advocates were heard proclaiming the necessity of the Israeli invasion, their words urged on, of course, by the Israeli lobby, whose task it was to drum up American support for Israel's violence against the Palestinians.

In an effort to prick their consciences, and hopefully to silence the voices of support for Israel's onslaught, I wrote a letter condemning the invasion to every member of Congress, and raised enough money to reprint the letter in a full-page ad in The Washington Post. In it, I pleaded with the Congress to do something about the tragedy taking shape in Lebanon as a result of the Israeli invasion. Prior to my letter, I don't think that anyone in Washington was aware that Israel was shutting off water, food, and medical supplies to Lebanese cities and towns. I'm not sure how much immediate effect my letter had on members of Congress—the silence remained deafening. However, the atrocities in Lebanon were so outrageous that ultimately even the domesticated press began broadcasting and writing sanitized versions of what was actually happening.

There were some alarming exceptions, however. The most amazing response came, I thought, from a newsman, Gordon Peterson, who was the anchor for the local news hour on channel nine, the CBS affiliate in Washington. Watching the belated network coverage of Israel's brutal destruction of Beirut, Peterson came to believe, incredibly, that Israel was getting a bum rap, so he produced a ten-part series on Israel showing its positive aspects, which he ran during his news show each day. The series was an upbeat travelogue that, considering the circumstances, was shameful in its boosterism. But Peterson was the unabashed booster of Israel, even in the face of its documented brutality during the summer of 1982.

I would reserve the hottest corner of hell, however, for those commentators who wrote and spoke so gleefully about the comparative efficiency of American weapons as opposed to Soviet ones. The comparisons were made immediately after the siege of Beirut came to an end, when the butcher's tally of the dead and wounded was totaled up. It became a point of pride with these folk that American weapons furnished to Israel were clearly more efficient at killing than the Soviet weapons given to the PLO. These cold, ruthless discussions of the relative merits of various weapons systems reminded me of the Nazis. As though the arms merchants and their minions were not craven enough, the American media dutifully featured these discussions, reinforcing the notion that killing Arabs is of little concern to those of us living in the capital of the free world.

Early on I was terribly afraid that the record of the invasion and siege of Beirut would be lost altogether, so I decided to spend some of ADC's dwindling cash reserves to send a film crew to Beirut to record what it could, and from it, to make a documentary. Produced in 1982, it was called "Report From Beirut: Summer of 1982," a short, twenty-one minute documentary that sought to show the effects of the Israeli invasion of Lebanon and the siege of Beirut.

I found Don North, a former ABC newsman, who agreed to produce and direct the project. He took along Kip Durrin, a Washington-based cameraman, and his own son to handle the sound. They entered the war zone through Israel, intending to work their way north to Beirut. I marveled at North's gumption; at the time he was on crutches and wore a full-length cast on one leg.

When North and his crew arrived in Israel, the authorities put a hold on their filming, telling them that they would have to spend a week in briefings before they could go into Lebanon. Understanding that Israel had no interest in any Americans covering what it was doing, North embarked on a new strategy. Using great initiative, he turned around and flew to Nicosia, Cyprus, where he paid a small boat operator $500 to transport the crew to Junieh, the Lebanese port just north of Beirut. He and his crew then filmed the battle in Beirut for several days in July.

When North finished filming and took the crew from West Beirut into East Beirut on his way to Junieh, the Israeli soldiers at the border checkpoint began to search his luggage. Fearing they would confiscate his film, North protested with great vehemence that his leg had been shattered by Israeli weaponry and that he intended to tell the entire Western world about what Israel had done to him. The Israeli guards, anxious about Israel's public image, forewent the search and sent him on his way through the checkpoint.

North began editing the film in Kip & Ginny Durrin's studio in the Adams-Morgan district of Washington. When he showed me the first cut, I commended his filming and editing, but I registered my shock at the film's happy ending at a time when the siege was still on and Israel was still dropping tons of explosives on Beirut. I told him that I didn't think that the final image of two giggling children walking hand in hand accurately described the reality of the situation, and that I did not want to be associated with a misleading portrayal of the invasion. Shouting something about artistic freedom, North walked off the job, telling me that he would have no more to do with the film. So I prevailed upon Saul Landau to finish the editing. Saul had made a number of documentaries over the years, many of them prizewinners. He had done a film biography of Fidel Castro, and his film about Paul Jacobs and the Nuclear Gang had won the 1980 Emmy award for best television documentary, as well as the George Polk Award for Investigative Journalism.

Saul agreed to complete "Report from Beirut" on one condition: that he would take no money for the work. I agreed, and the result was the most heart-rending footage I've ever seen. The film focused on what happened to Beirut civilians during the siege—how they lived and how they died as the targets of the most dangerous weaponry that the United States had provided to Israel. It was, I decided, a testament to the insanity of the arms industry and of those who had unrestricted control of the weapons—phosphorous bombs, cluster bombs, and ordinary bombs used for carpet bombing. I was amazed that anyone in West Beirut had survived. As it was, 18,000 Lebanese and Palestinian civilians were killed, and

174 ADVISE & DISSENT

30,000 more were wounded, so devastating was the first-strike firepower that Israel had flung into Beirut.

We ordered dozens of home video copies of the film and distributed them to ADC chapters around the United States. Saul entered the film in three separate film festivals and it won an award in each of the three. But getting "Report from Beirut" shown on any television network, public or private, was another matter. I have special feelings—most of them negative—for public television after trying to get it aired there. PBS flatly refused, citing a policy against running films by advocacy groups. But at the same time it was running a series of pro-Israeli interviews paid for by a private foundation, which clearly was nothing more than pro-Israeli propaganda. WETA, the Washington public television station, finally agreed to run the film—long after Israel pulled out of Beirut, and at 11:30 P.M. on a Sunday night, when, I imagine, the audience must not have exceeded a few dozen.

The U.S. government has historically yielded to Israel's demands and to pressures from the Israeli lobby. Today U.S. policy in relation to the Middle East is in the throes of dramatic transformation, with American diplomats regularly meeting with PLO representatives. But this was not the case before 1988, when the Administration finally decided to accept Yasir Arafat's pledges that he was sincere in wanting to make peace.

For example, in 1976, I invited Shafiq al Hout, the PLO representative in Beirut, to be the guest of honor at a lunch that I wanted to host for him in the Senate. Because officials of the PLO are not allowed to travel outside a twenty-five mile radius from the United Nations, Shafiq had to get a special visa from the State Department to be able to come to Washington. Back then, the State Department did not refuse such requests from members of the Senate, so Shafiq was given the visa. But along with it came the restriction that he could not make any public statements during the trip, under threat of immediate deportation.

The State Department was never really worried about any security threat from Shafiq. He is a nonviolent Palestinian diplomat who sounds like Charles Boyer and looks like Douglas Fairbanks, Jr. The reason that he and other PLO officials are forbidden to travel and make speeches throughout the United States is because the Israeli lobby does not want them arguing their case here. Consequently, Henry Kissinger, a closet Zionist, made a promise to Israel in 1975, on behalf of all the people of the United States, without consulting any of us, of course, that the U.S. government would neither speak with nor recognize the PLO until the PLO recognized Israel. We hear, of course, that Israeli leaders refuse to discuss anything with the PLO out of concern for Israel's security. But the argument does not wash, because whenever Israel wants favors from the United States, it maintains that it is able to hold off the Soviet Union in the Mediterranean. Thus Israel's professed fear of a three thousand-man PLO army equipped only with small arms is a major contradiction. Israel does not want to talk to the PLO, because if it did, it might have to end its occupation of the West Bank and the Gaza Strip. But the United States? There seemed to be no rational reason why the United States would not want to talk to one of the major groups involved in the Middle East conflict. After all, in order to reach peace in South Africa, even the right-wing Reagan Administration declared that Pretoria should talk to the outlawed African National Congress, South Africa's equivalent of the PLO.

The reason for past U.S. refusal to negotiate with the PLO lies in what the press and some politicians euphemistically call "domestic political pressure." What they mean is that the Israeli lobby in the United States has found the political erogenous zone of most congressional candidates—money—and applies pressure on that zone very effectively. Because most politicians care very little for either Arabs or Jews, it becomes for them simply a matter of who can contribute the most money to their campaigns. American Jews give more campaign money than American Arabs, which is why the Israeli lobby has been able to force the State Department to prevent the PLO from arguing their case in the United States, where the ability to argue it really counts.

I invited a number of senators to the al Hout luncheon, which was held in one of the committee hearing rooms in the Dirksen Senate Office Building. Amazingly, almost all of them showed up. Earlier that morning, I ran into Abe Ribicoff on the Senate floor and asked if he would be interested in meeting Shafiq. Abe said that he was willing to listen to anyone and agreed to come. Shafiq spoke for about fifteen minutes before the vote bell rang, causing everyone at the lunch to jump up and go to the Senate floor to vote. Ribicoff did not return after the vote, although everyone else did.

Later that day, I was called by a reporter from *The Washington Post*, Spencer Rich, who asked what had happened at the meeting. I told him that I had no interest in pinning a target on those who had attended, and refused to talk to him about it. Because he already had the list of those who had been at the lunch, he informed me that he would just call them directly. The next day, not only did *The Washington Post* have a story on the luncheon, but the *Jerusalem Post* carried banner headlines trumpeting the fact that Abe Ribicoff, the only Jew at the meeting, had had lunch with a "PLO murderer."

I was not privy to what was being said in Ribicoff's office, but it was not long afterward that Abe had to pay the price for being uppity with the Israeli lobby. He eventually submitted to the lobby's pressure by introducing legislation assessing tax penalties against U.S. companies taking part in the ongoing anti-Israeli boycott. The legislation was passed and became law. I came to call the Al Hout lunch the "Shafiq al Hout Memorial Tax Penalty Lunch," perhaps one of the most expensive lunches ever served in the Senate.

* * *

Although all during my time in the Senate I was constantly visited by people from the Arab world, for some reason, my office also became the stopping off place for Israelis of various persuasions. Perhaps my most famous Israeli visitor was Nathan Yalin-Mor, who came by to introduce himself in late 1973. From 1944 to 1948, Nathan Yalin-Mor was one of the three leaders of the Stern Gang, a vicious group of Jewish terrorists operating in Palestine. (Yitzhak Shamir was also one of the Stern Gang's leaders). There was no terrorist act too violent for the Stern Gang to commit, from sending letter bombs to British politicians to slaughtering Arabs and Englishmen who were considered enemies of the Zionist movement. In fact, after having read J. Bowyer Bell's book, *Terror Out Of Zion*, which documents all the major terrorist acts committed by the Stern Gang and the Irgun, another Jewish terrorist organization, I concluded that the military wing of the PLO had been comparatively mild-mannered. The Stern Gang murdered Lord Moyne in Cairo in the 1940s, assassinated UN mediator Count Folke-Bernadotte in Jerusalem in 1948, and slaughtered countless British soldiers and Arab civilians. Lord Christopher Mayhew, back when he was a member of the British House of Commons, told me that the Stern Gang had sent a letter bomb to him. He escaped injury only because his secretary opened it, giving her the brunt of the blast. I asked Nathan outright if he had ever sent letter bombs to British politicians, to which he immediately answered, "Oh, yes, we sent lots of letter bombs."

By 1973, however, Nathan had become a dove. As he explained to me in his slow, heavily-accented voice, "Senator, I am here because I have traveled all over the world to try to bring peace to the Middle East. I have talked to everyone whom I think might be able to help. I have even talked to the PLO, and I have been criticized by people in Israel because the PLO is called a terrorist organization. But I don't mind, you see, because I was once a terrorist myself."

Nathan was overweight and moved about slowly, making him seem older than his years. There was no question in my mind that his conversion from terrorist to peacemaker was thorough and genuine. I was attracted to this avuncular figure, and we struck up an immediate friendship. Because suggesting peace between the Palestinians and Israel is unpopular with the Israelis and their lobby in Washington, the only way Nathan could get appointments with politicians was if I made the calls for him. He was not taken seriously by Washington politicos, because they largely danced to the tune of those Israeli supporters who could provide them with campaign money—something Nathan could not do.

When Nathan died a few years ago, his passing went almost unnoticed, which I thought was sad. It was another piece of evidence that more attention is paid to people who advocate murder than to those who try to prevent it.

Menachem Begin also came to Washington to visit, although he did not come to see me. After his surprise election as prime minister of Israel in 1977, he made a pilgrimage to Washington to meet those people with whom he would do business while in office. Before Israel declared itself a state in 1948, Begin was the head of the *Irgun*. Among other acts of violence committed at Begin's orders was the blowing up of the King David Hotel in Jerusalem while it contained dozens of Arabs and British soldiers and, together with the Stern Gang, the massacre of 230 civilians in Deir Yassin, a village in Palestine.

As was traditional, the Senate Foreign Relations Committee held a function for Begin to which all senators were invited. During the meeting, I tried to remain calm and silent, not wanting to disrupt the gathering with my dissenting views. But as I observed the nauseating display of senatorial servility, I could take it no longer. U.S. senators, representing the most powerful nation on earth, were almost prostrating themselves before the prime minister of a small country. I think the moment that really got to me was when Senator Harrison Schmidt, one of our former astronauts, asked obsequiously, "Mr. Prime Minister, do you think the Arabs really want peace?"

I suddenly found myself on my feet, first giving Begin my name so that there would be no mistake about my identity. Then I said, "I heard your press conference earlier today in which you said that you were willing to take part in peace talks with the Arabs. But you also said that you would never sit down with the PLO to negotiate peace. Because the PLO is a major party to the conflict, wouldn't your refusal deadlock the peace talks even before they began?"

There was a captive audience of seventy-five or so U.S. senators, so Begin held his finger in the air and asked, rhetorically, "Who is the PLO? . . ."

"The PLO," I said, interrupting him, "represents the Palestinian people, and it is at least as legitimate as the *Irgun* was."

Begin then earned his pay, not as a politician and not as a terrorist, but as an actor.

"Sacrilege!" he shouted. "It is a sacrilege to compare the PLO to the Irgun. The PLO kills children, joyfully, willingly. We were different. We were fighting for our freedom." Then he must have remembered that others in the room had read some of the history as well, so he quickly added in a quieter voice, "Of course, we sometimes made mistakes, and if an innocent person was killed accidentally, we always apologized."

I tried to interrupt him again, but, accustomed to outshouting other Knesset members, he refused to yield the floor. At the first break in Begin's oration, Senator Alan Cranston quickly moved to adjourn the meeting on the grounds that time had run out. As everyone filed out of the room, I overheard John Glenn telling another senator, "Abourezk could start a riot in an empty hall."

* * *

Until I arrived in Washington, I knew almost nothing about the Israeli lobby and the Middle East conflict, even though I grew up in a Lebanese-American household. My parents spoke about it sparingly, an omission that left me, like most Americans, vulnerable to opinion from the mainstream press, which glorified the Israeli position at the expense of the Palestinians and the Lebanese.

After I arrived in Washington in 1971 to begin serving my House term, I received a steady stream of visitors, many of them wanting to express themselves on the Palestinian-Israeli conflict, making me more and more interested in the issue. The B'Nai B'rith lobbyist, Dave Brody, was my most frequent visitor from the pro-Israeli side, bringing around statements for me to endorse and suggesting legislation that I could cosponsor. On the Arab side there was no organized lobby, but I found myself receiving Arabs and Arab Americans who wanted to see what a real live Arab-American congressman looked like. There had never been an Arab-American senator, and only two Arab Americans had previously been elected to the House of Representatives—George Kasem from California, who had served a term or two in the 1960s, and Abraham "Chick" Kazen from San Antonio, Texas, who was currently serving in the House. After my election Chick Kazen came to be called the leader of the "Lebanese Caucus."

I spent the next two years learning about the Middle East, but not saying much. In 1973, while returning from a junket to Moscow via Geneva, I was contacted by the Lebanese ambassador to Geneva. He passed on to me an invitation from the Lebanese government to visit Lebanon. "Why not?" I told him, and flew with my thirteen-year-old son, Paul, from Geneva to Beirut.

Visiting the Palestinian refugee camps in Beirut gave me the shock of my life. Amid the conspicuous affluence of Beirut sat huge rows of squalid tin huts with open sewers running down the middle of the narrow streets that separated them. Palestinian children were playing in those streets, climbing up and down on rubble that had been produced by shelling or bombing, I didn't know which, and in general placing their own health in danger from the unsanitary conditions.

A Palestinian doctor who worked in the camps took me on a tour, describing to me the miserable conditions of the refugees. We had long talks about how they got there—about the 1948 Arab-Israeli war, the wars since then, and Israel's intransigence since it had acquired its tremendous military power.

I left Lebanon feeling immensely betrayed. For most of my adult life I had believed that Israel had been picked on by the Arab countries. And, like most Americans, I clung to the image of Israel created by *Exodus* author, Leon Uris. His book, and the movie by the same name, glorified Israel's naked land grab. (Much later, I learned that, in 1985, an author named Art Stevens had written a book about the public relations business entitled *The Persuasion Explosion*, in which he reported that a New York public relations expert, Ed Gottlieb, who had been hired by the Israeli government after the creation of Israel in 1948, had commissioned writer Leon Uris to go to Israel and to write the novel *Exodus*.) To learn in Lebanon that the truth had been stood on its head was an emotional shock for me. That feeling, juxtaposed with the impression the squalor of the refugee camps had made on me, put me in an angry mood.

Less than six weeks after I returned home from that trip, the Egyptians crossed the Suez Canal and attacked the Israeli Army in the Sinai desert, beginning what the Arabs called the 1973 War and what the Israelis called the Yom Kippur War. Shortly after the war, Israel's supporters introduced on the Senate floor a $2.2 billion appropriation to pay for Israel's part in the conflict. I then saw more clearly the propaganda advantage that the Israelis had in the United States. The war was called an "invasion" by Israel's supporters and the American press; yet both Egypt and Syria had attacked only the territory taken from them by Israel in the 1967 war. In fact, Syria had announced that it would stop its advance once it recovered the Golan Heights.

Senator J. William Fulbright and I tried to defeat the appropriation, but we lost big. As the vote was rolling up in favor of the appropriation and against our position, Senator Stuart Symington of Missouri approached me and asked, "Jimmy, do you know why you're losing this vote?"

"Why?" I asked.

"Because the Jews vote and the Arabs don't," he said. This was the same statement that would get Billy Carter in deep trouble with a pro-Israeli American press corps years later.

In December 1973, I rounded up some of my staff members and my brother Chick and started out on an expanded tour of the Middle East. We started in Lebanon, went on to Syria, then to Iraq, Kuwait, the United Arab Emirates, Saudi Arabia, Egypt, Jordan, and Israel. I met with most of the Arab leaders, with the exception of Saddam Hussein of Iraq, because U.S.–Iraqi relations were strained and our welcome was not very cordial.

After visiting Lebanon, we spent four days in Syria. I came down with some sort of virus while in Damascus, which kept me in a hotel bed for most of our stay there. My second cousin, Samir Ouais, a Damascus physician who had trained at the University of Iowa, treated me for the illness, faithfully making house calls at the hotel a couple of times each day.

Before the virus struck, however, I had attended a meeting with Syrian President Hafez al-Asad. Henry Kissinger had just been to Syria not many days before I arrived, and had negotiated a renewal of diplomatic relations with Asad. The United States still had no ambassador in Damascus, but Tom Scotes was slated to serve as the first American diplomat since relations had broken between the two countries over the 1967 Arab-Israeli war. We talked in Asad's windowless reception room, interrupted every few minutes by power outages, which, Asad explained, were due to the Israeli bombing during the October war of the power station that furnished Damascus with its electricity. I had not remembered reading about any bombing of Arab civilian areas during the war, but the damage caused by Israel's bombs was evident all over Damascus.

In Saudi Arabia I met with King Faisal, who had, not long before my arrival, imposed an oil embargo against the United States. The embargo became a recurring focus of our discussion. I mentioned that there was some talk in upper echelon U.S. government circles that the United States might invade Saudi Arabia and take the oil fields by force. But I learned something about Faisal's determination that day. "If they invade," the King told me, "we will blow up the oil fields and we will go back to digging onions out of the desert, just like we used to do before we found oil."

If my reception was cool in Iraq, it was downright frosty in Israel. One of the big issues drummed up by the Israeli lobby in the United States was the concern that several Israeli pilots captured by Syria during the 1973 fighting were being tortured and killed. Fred Ward, a photographer friend who was also on the trip, wanted to interview the Israeli pilots. Syrian President Asad had arranged for me to see the pilots. While Fred photographed, I interviewed the pilots on tape. We took the tapes with us to Israel and contacted their families, who came to our hotel to pick them up, accompanied by someone who was obviously a member of Israeli intelligence.

Those were the last friendly faces we saw in Israel. Golda Meir refused to meet with me, on the grounds, I was told, that she was suffering from the shingles. But her affliction did not prevent her from seeing Henry Kissinger, who to her was both more important and more friendly than I. Shlomo Gazit, then in charge of the occupied territories, agreed to see me, as did Teddy Kolleck, the mayor of Jerusalem. I ate lunch with Ephraim Evron, then working in the Foreign Ministry, who later became Israel's ambassador to the United States. When I was in the hotel in Tel Aviv, a couple of West Bank Palestinian journalists came by to pay a visit, but for the most part, Palestinians kept, or were kept at, a distance.

My tour of the Middle East marked the beginning of a long battle with the Israeli lobby. In January 1974, not long after my return, I was invited by the Washington Press Club to make a presentation about the trip. Honestly stating what I believed, I told the audience that it appeared to me that the Arab confrontation states, Syria, Jordan, and Egypt in particular, were more interested in the economic development of their countries than in spending money on a military buildup. Each Arab leader, I told the audience, had assured me that they were willing to sign a peace treaty with Israel provided that Israel would withdraw to its pre-1967 borders and allow a Palestinian state to come into existence. Wolf Blitzer, then working for *The Near East Report*, the newsletter published by AIPAC, rose to ask a couple of hostile questions, then left.

The next issue of *The Near East Report* contained a major article on me, strongly implying that I had sold out to the Arabs. I was furious. The thought running through my mind was that if Israel's case had to depend on lies and personal attacks, there must be precious little substance to it. I. L. Kenen, then the director of AIPAC, sent copies of the article to people whose names were on my publicly-filed contribution list, telling the recipients that Abourezk did not deserve their contributions based on the contents of the article. The battle escalated from that point onward. At different times Kenen would send messages to me through various intermediaries, including Paul Jacobs and George McGovern, that he was going to "get Abourezk." I don't suppose that I would have ever become so deeply enmeshed in the Middle East conflict had I not been attacked so unfairly at the outset.

I did find a way to turn the Lobby's animosity to my advantage for a brief time. The Israeli lobby wanted to keep me out of Middle East affairs at all costs, if necessary by helping me do something else. In 1975, I decided to campaign for a seat on the Senate Judiciary Committee. In order to get the seat, it would be necessary to beat out Senator James Allen of Alabama, who was senior to me, and who had applied for membership on the committee long before I had. So I sought help from everyone I could. I contacted civil liberties groups and any other organization that had an interest in Judiciary Committee legislation. I knew that while most Jewish groups agreed with my position on civil rights and civil liberties, and opposed those of Senator Allen, my Middle East position would prevent members of the Israeli lobby from lifting even a finger to help me.

Nevertheless, on a whim, I approached Dave Brody, the B'Nai B'rith Anti-Defamation League lobbyist, to ask for his help. "Dave," I said, "if I fail in my fight to get on the Judiciary Committee, I intend to try for the Foreign Relations Committee. I suspect I won't be refused for that if I get turned down for Judiciary." Success was imminent. Brody immediately agreed to do what he could to help me win the Judiciary Committee seat. Although I had no real interest in the Foreign Relations Committee assignment, it was obvious that Brody and his colleagues were not taking any chances, so they pitched in to help me.

Despite that temporary aberration, the Israeli lobby has done what it could to embarrass me over the years and to try to ruin my credibility. One of their attempts involved my oldest son, Charlie. As soon as he had graduated from high school, Charlie left home and spent his time moving around from Colorado to South Dakota, working when he could find work and bumming around when he felt like it. His life-style upset me. I wanted him to get a college degree, and he wanted to show me that he could do what he damned well pleased. It was a normal father-son relationship.

He moved in with Celo Black Crow and his family on the Pine Ridge Indian Reservation in southwestern South Dakota, and after a time began drawing food stamps to live on. I knew nothing about it until a former Episcopalian minister-turned yellow journalist, Lester Kinsolving, wrote about it in a small suburban Washington newspaper. It was not Kinsolving's first attack on me. Years earlier, he had attacked me in the columns he wrote for *The Rapid City Daily Journal*. And, as was my custom, I ignored his latest broadside.

Then, sometime later, Spencer Rich from *The Washington Post* called and asked me to comment on the fact that my son was living on food stamps. I refused to talk to him about it. He continued to call, saying that he was going to write the story whether or not I talked to him. I responded by saying that he was asking me either to denounce my son for what he was doing or to approve of it, and that I would do neither, especially not for Spencer Rich and *The Washington Post*. He called me a number of times, mostly at home, and each time I refused comment. He ran the story anyway, headlining the fact that "the son of Senator Abourezk was on food stamps."

I was outraged. My wife, Mary, was mortified. She considered it the worst invasion of our family's privacy in all the time I had been in politics. George McGovern and Abe Ribicoff took to the Senate floor to denounce the *The Washington Post* for trying to discredit both me and the food stamp program. Larry Stern, one of the *Post*'s editors protested bitterly to Ben Bradlee, the executive editor. Tom Zito, then a *Post* reporter, also protested the unfairness of the story to Bradlee. Believing that he was offering a remedy,. Bradlee told Zito to do a story on other prominent people whose children were living on food stamps. Zito, who later called to tell me about it, said that when he discovered that Bradlee's daughter had been living on food stamps in Oregon, Bradlee killed the story altogether.

Mary stewed about the matter for a long time. She never got over it, and when one day she read a story in the *Washington Star* about the wife of another senator, reporting on her alcoholism, she called the woman, although they had never met. Identifying herself, Mary said, "I read that story about you in the *Washington Star* and I really sympathize with you. I know exactly how you feel."

"What story?" the woman asked, obviously surprised.

Mary realized the mistake she had made, but it was too late. "The one about your alcoholism problem," Mary croaked.

"Oh, do you have an alcoholism problem?" the woman asked.

"No," Mary said, desperately trying to bail out of the conversation, "I have a food stamp problem."

One of the objectives of the Israeli lobby is to control the flow of information from the Middle East to the United States. They seek to suppress information that will embarrass Israel and to emphasize news that is unfavorable to the Arab world. Fearing reprisals from the Lobby, American journalists often cooperate with them by censoring information critical of Israel.

For example, *Washington Post* journalist Bob Woodward, of Watergate fame, wrote several articles in February 1977, detailing a series of payments that the CIA had made to King Hussein of Jordan over a twenty-year period. The total was comparatively small, amounting to something less than $10 million over two decades, but the *Post* carried the story as its lead for nearly a week, giving it huge front-page headlines. It was played in such a way that it was highly embarrassing to Jordan. The day after the story broke, I read a small squib in the *Wall Street Journal* that discussed Woodward's story, casually mentioning that Israel had received money from the CIA as well. This aside did not appear elsewhere. It was not in the *The Washington Post*, and it was certainly not in any other U.S. newspaper.

After reading the *Wall Street Journal* article, I called Hal Saunders, who was then in the State Department, and asked him what he knew about Israel receiving CIA money. His response was, "I'd better come to your office and brief you on it." The next day Saunders showed up with two CIA officials in tow. They told me that Israel had received over ten times as much money—between $70 and $80 million—as Jordan had received from the CIA over the same time period. What was interesting about the disclosure was that Israel planned to give the money to black African countries in exchange for their voting in support of Israel in the United Nations. In return for the money, Israel was supposed to turn over to the United States intelligence gathered from Russian Jewish émigrés. What struck me as unusual was the fact that Israel's UN representative routinely made speeches at the United Nations denouncing the Arab oil countries for buying African votes with oil, or with oil money.

The first thing I did—naively, as it turned out—was to call Bob Woodward. "Did you know about the CIA money for Israel when you wrote the articles?" I asked him.

"Yes, I did," he responded.

"Why didn't you write about it?"

"I understand how you feel about the purported imbalance in press coverage of the Middle East, Senator," Woodward said, "but in my view, the payments were two entirely different matters. King Hussein used the money to give to Bedouin tribes in Jordan. The Israelis used it for something altogether different."

It was, in my opinion, an outrageous attempt to justify what he had done. I asked him if the difference wouldn't have been better discerned by the readers of the The Washington Post. I told him that he had deliberately spared Israel the same embarrassment he had heaped on Jordan, and rung off. That was the easy part. I tried with all my might, which turned out to be precious little, to get the mainstream media to print the story about Israel. No one wanted to touch it; they didn't want to risk embarrassing Israel. Ultimately Jack Anderson ran it, but much later, and without anyone picking it up nationally. This episode was a perfect example of how much and how long the American press has protected Israel from unfavorable publicity.

In 1973, Wolfe Charney was chairman of the annual Yeshiva University dinner in New York. Charney, a New York lawyer, invited me to be the main speaker at the event for an honorarium of $500. I accepted, and spent some time happily preparing my speech and deciding how to spend the honorarium. About two weeks before the dinner, Charney called to tell me that the students wanted me to issue a statement before coming to New York.

"What kind of statement?" I asked.

"You should say that you believe in face-to-face negotiations in the Middle East."

This conversation took place before the October 1973 war, when Israel was using the face-to-face argument as a propaganda weapon against the Arab countries. The Arabs, still reeling from their defeat in 1967, were so militarily and diplomatically weak that negotiations were out of the question until they could restore some of their strength. Sadat had not yet completed his military buildup, and was trying to get the United States to intervene diplomatically to settle the conflict. It was about then that Henry Kissinger deemed Sadat's peace initiatives unworthy of his time and was busy trying to undercut Sadat's standing with his chief sponsor, the Soviet Union.

"As a matter of fact," I told Charney, "I happen to believe that face-to-face negotiations are quite proper. But I do not intend to let Golda Meir use any of my public statements to beat Egypt, Jordan, and Syria over the head."

"It doesn't look good for the dinner," Charney said.

Within a few days, the president of Yeshiva, Rabbi Israel Miller, asked if he could come to Washington to see me. When he arrived he also pressed me for a statement, saying that the students were picketing against me, and that the matter could be resolved if I would just make the statement he was asking for. I again refused, and he left. The next day Charney called me again, telling me that the students were really upset.

"Would you feel better if I didn't make the speech?" I asked.

"Yes," was his answer. I didn't go to the dinner, prompting George Agree, a Democratic activist from New York, to swear under his breath when I told him the story.

"They're for face-to-face negotiations in the Middle East, but not in New York," he said angrily.

I can't say that the ongoing confrontation with the Israeli lobby has been all bad news however. It has had its interesting moments as well, such as the time late one Friday night in 1976, when a resolution of disapproval was reported out of the Senate Foreign Relations Committee (by Hubert Humphrey and Clifford Case) that would have killed a proposed sale of Maverick missiles to Saudi Arabia. John Sparkman of Alabama, then chairman of Foreign Relations, rose early Monday morning before an empty Senate, and moved to send the resolution back to committee. President Gerald Ford and Vice-President Nelson Rockefeller had worked over the weekend to convince Sparkman to make the motion. Their strategy was to get the resolution back in committee long enough to change one or two votes, which would effectively kill it because the deadline was rapidly approaching, after which the sale would be automatically approved.

I was on the Senate floor early on Monday morning, because I was fighting against a Jim Allen filibuster, then in the post-cloture stage. This meant that nothing could be introduced on the Senate floor without unanimous consent. One objection would defeat any motion brought up on the floor.

By prearrangement with Vice-President Nelson Rockefeller, Republican Minority Leader Bob Griffin looked the other way when Sparkman offered the motion to recommit. Bob Byrd, the Democratic leader, made no move to stop it, because the motion had been made by the committee chairman. I said nothing, because I was all for the recommittal. After Sparkman stumbled through the text that had been prepared for him to read, there was no objection by anyone, so the motion was granted by the presiding officer. Not more than a half hour later a steaming Clifford Case charged onto the Senate floor and sought recognition. He looked directly at Bob Griffin and denounced the procedure by which he, Clifford Case, the ranking Republican on the Foreign Relations Committee, had not been informed when Sparkman made the motion to recommit legislation in which he was interested. When he finished lecturing Griffin for failing to protect his rights, he asked unanimous consent that the resolution be brought back out to the floor.

I objected.

Case then turned all his fury against me, telling me how discourteous it was to object to his request, because of his status on the Foreign Relations Committee, and because he had not been on the floor when Sparkman made the original motion. When he finished, I suppose believing that he had convinced me, he again made a unanimous consent request to have the resolution reported back to the floor.

I looked him squarely in the eye and objected again. Case stormed out of the Senate, as hot as he was when he first came in. The bill stayed in the committee until the Administration found enough senators to change their vote, defeating it in committee. Whenever I saw Nelson Rockefeller after that, he never failed to remark, "Say fella, do you remember that deal we pulled off on those Maverick missiles?"

* * *

I received a call one day in 1974 from Martin Peretz, the owner of *The New Republic* magazine. He said he was calling to ask a few questions about the honoraria I had received from "Arabs." I had been misbehaving on the Senate floor with respect to some Middle East issue or other, he said, and he wanted to write about the money I had been getting for my speeches.

I told him that I had fully reported all of the honoraria for the speeches I had made in 1973, and that the sources and amounts were a matter of public record. But, I said, in spite of that I would be happy to answer his questions.

"But first," I said, " you have to answer one of my questions."

"Go ahead," Peretz said.

"Is it true that *The New Republic* is now the house organ for the Israeli lobby?" I asked.

He exploded, denying it with great vehemence, then toward the end of his tirade added that in many ways he thought I was a good senator in spite of my being wrong on the Middle East. I responded by saying, "You're goddammed right I'm a good senator because I'm independent of every special interest, whether Arab or Jew, including *your* special interest, and I intend to stay that way."

He wrote an article in *The New Republic* that made it look as though I was the world record holder for honoraria, implying that they were the source of my political views. I had earned some $49,000 in honoraria in 1973, largely because local Arab-American groups all over the country were anxious to listen to and look at the first U.S. senator of Arabic descent. What Peretz didn't report was the honoraria earned by other senators—Hubert Humphrey was one who came to mind—who had spoken before Jewish groups. Their totals made mine look minuscule.

But Israel's supporters never gave up. As I stated earlier, they have effectively used the charge of anti-Semitism to silence critics of Israel's policies, as well as critics of America's policies toward Israel. The accusation is enough to cow the average liberal, who has difficulty handling the allegation. It has never worked on me. I have always resented the accusation that I'm a racist simply because I disagree with Israel's policies. I was always amused by Joe Rauh, the noted civil rights attorney in Washington, who, for many years, would approach me with the greeting, "Jim. I don't let anybody call you anti-Semitic around me."

To which I would respond, "Gee, thanks, Joe."

Then there was the unique way that the Zionist Organization of America in Denver tried to ambush me. They objected to my speaking because I did not follow the Democratic platform, which called for support of Israel.

I was asked, in 1977, by the Colorado Democratic party to fill in as a speaker for Walter Mondale, who had been recently sworn in as vice-president. I was to appear at the annual Jefferson Jackson

Day Fund Raiser in Denver. At that point in my political career—I had already announced that I wouldn't run again—I was making a concerted effort to spend more time at home with my family. I protested—slightly—then agreed to go, saying that I would bring my wife with me.

But on Monday night, five days before the dinner was scheduled, the arrangements committee for the affair held a meeting to which the Denver press was invited. Apparently this committee had no authority over the choice of speaker, that being the province of the state Democratic party chairman, Monte Pascoe. But this little detail in no way deterred the arrangements committee, which proceeded to consider a motion to "disinvite Abourezk," on the grounds that he was not sufficiently pro-Israel.

Totally unsuspecting, I was called Tuesday morning by some of the Denver press, who obviously smelled a good story coming on, asking for my reaction to the committee meeting.

"My reaction . . . my reaction?" I repeated, trying to think of something to say. "Well, I can see that there are some supporters of Israel out there. Now let's see if anybody in Denver supports the right of free speech."

The press now had a certified controversy—one that bubbled along on the front pages for the rest of the week. Arnie Zaler, the head of the Denver chapter of the Zionist Organization of America, told a reporter that since the Democratic platform called for support of Israel, I should not be allowed to speak, because I did not obey the platform.

When I arrived in Denver on Friday, I announced to an airport press conference that, although I had taken an oath to uphold the Constitution of the United States, the Constitution did not require me to swear allegiance to the State of Israel.

By then the Denver newspapers and television stations were editorializing in my favor and against the efforts to cancel my appearance. But even though that was no longer the issue—Arnie Zaler apparently saw his position slipping and on Wednesday had told the press that he was in favor of ending the confrontation—I was angry enough that I continued to attack both the arrangements committee and the Zionist Organization of America, Denver chapter.

By the time Saturday rolled around, immense amounts of publicity had doubled the anticipated size of the crowd for the dinner, and "Abourezk" had become a household word in Denver. Most amusing was the total discomfort that the controversy was causing the politicians in Colorado. Only Senator Floyd Haskell felt secure enough to publicly acknowledge his friendship with me. During their brief speeches at the beginning of the program, Governor Dick Lamm, Senator Gary Hart, and Congresswoman Pat Schroeder all landed squarely on the fence, reflecting their fears of how relentless the Israeli lobby can be when officeholders get out of line. Although I originally had not intended to speak about the Middle East at the dinner, I rewrote my speech to include a blistering attack on the Israeli lobby for its efforts to stifle free speech. I also included my support for an independent Palestinian state.

The audience reacted wildly in favor of my call for a Palestinian state, as well as to my criticism of the Israeli lobby. There were several standing ovations both during and after the speech. A few days later someone sent me a copy of a Denver Jewish newspaper that contained a quote by Congresswoman Pat Schroeder, who at one time had been a friend, to the effect that it was terrible for Jim Abourezk to come to the dinner and say the things he did. I simply clipped the article and mailed it to her with a note saying, "Some demagogue has been giving interviews and using your name, Pat. I thought you'd better know about it." But I never received an answer.

The most interesting reaction, however, came from Arnie Zaler, who asked to meet with me on the night of the dinner. We sat down in a private room after the dinner to talk, and he asked why I insisted on continuing the fight. I explained that he tried to embarrass me, and that I could neither take it lightly nor let it pass without responding. Then I told him that I thought he should go through the same process that I had experienced with respect to the Middle East question, by taking a trip to some of the Arab countries and visiting the refugee camps. I said that if I could find the time to go with him, I would introduce him to Yasir Arafat so that he could talk to him directly. His reaction was, to me, a great surprise.

"Do you honestly think I could meet Arafat?" he asked, almost wide-eyed. When I told him that he most certainly could, he never lost his excitement, wanting only to talk about the prospect of meeting Arafat for the rest of our meeting.

After I returned to Washington, Zaler continued to call me over the next several months, asking when we would be able to make the trip. Unfortunately, I was not able to go back to the Middle

East for some time, and, to my knowledge, Arnie never got to meet Yasir Arafat.

* * *

Dr. Clovis Maksoud is currently the Arab League's permanent representative to the United Nations. He is also one of the great characters of the Middle East, a voluble, verbose, sixty-year-old Lebanese cherub who was born, of all places, in Oklahoma, but who moved to Lebanon with his parents at the age of three. Part of his education was completed in Lebanon, part in England, and part at George Washington University Law School in Washington, D.C.

His command of the English language is highly impressive. Once, when he was speaking to members of the House of Commons in London, he began regaling his audience, finger pointed in the air, with "the struggle in the Middle East is more than a struggle between Arab and Jew. It is a struggle between transcendental Zionism and Pan-Arab Nationalism. . . ."

He was interrupted by a member of the House of Commons, a supporter of Israel, who said, "Excuse me, sir. Would you kindly use the English language while speaking here."

Following the October 1973 war in the Middle East, in which the Arabs fared better than they had in the previous three wars, Maksoud was asked by a journalist to comment. "In every dimension," he began, "metaphysical, political, psychological, and existential, it was a magnificent victory . . . within the context of our defeat."

My favorite story about Clovis—he sometimes refers to himself as "My Excellency"—deals with his journey to Baghdad, Iraq in 1961. Known as a friend and adviser to President Gamal Abdel Nasser of Egypt, he was also an editor of *Al Ahram*, the major Egyptian newspaper. He had written a book about Nasser and his goals for the Middle East. He was lecturing in India when he was contacted by the Iraqi Ambassador, who told Maksoud that he was invited to stop over in Baghdad to speak at a dinner.

Clovis accepted with pleasure—after all it was a chance to make a speech—and took the propeller airplane to Baghdad, an all-night journey. When he landed at the Baghdad airport, he looked around for the welcoming party. Two men in uniform were at the gate asking the deplaning passengers, "Who is Clovis Maksoud?"

"I am." Clovis said, initially delighted at the honor being paid him.

"You're under arrest. Come with us," they said, putting him in a taxi. Because he had flown all night, he was unaware that overnight there had been a *coup d'état*. More importantly, the leader of the coup, Abdel Karim al Qasem, was extremely jealous of Egyptian President Nasser, and saw a chance to settle a score by arresting Clovis.

He was taken straight to Qasem, who sat him down and asked whether he still thought Nasser was more popular in the Arab world than Qasem. Clovis looked around at his captors, then conceded that he no longer felt as strongly about Nasser's leadership abilities as he once had. Qasem then forced Maksoud to accompany him to a housing project where he made a speech to the gathered assembly. Again Maksoud had to listen. He was then taken to a hotel and placed under armed guard, until evening, that is, when a couple of cabinet ministers—holdovers from the previous regime who were friends of his—knocked on the door of his hotel room. They told Maksoud that everything had been arranged with his guards, and that they were taking him to a dinner being held in his honor at which there would be no fewer than eight cabinet ministers in attendance. Maksoud went with them, gave the after dinner speech, and was returned to his hotel room and again placed under guard. The next morning he was taken by the same taxi to the airport and put on a plane for Beirut, but not before he was made to pay for the taxi, which included all the time that it had waited since his arrest the day before.

Clovis was living in Beirut at the time of my first visit there in 1973, and he accompanied me to my parents' village. A car caravan of local residents formed some three or four villages before we got to Kfeir, and by the time we arrived there, more than fifty cars were in the caravan.

Just before reaching Kfeir we drove into the small village of Mimas, where the mayor and Mimas villagers met us. Their welcoming ceremony was held at the edge of the village, where they had strung a large canvas sign above the road that read, in Arabic, "Welcome Senator Sheikh James Abu-rizk," and in English, "Fantome Jets Made in USA." To make their point a bit stronger, the sign was strung across the road just next to a bomb crater, which I was told had been made by an Israeli Phantom jet. I discovered from the villagers that Israel routinely bombed the village, presumably aiming at PLO guerrillas who were based nearby.

With Clovis accompanying me as both guide and interpreter, we drove further, stopping our car about a half mile from Kfeir and walking the rest of the way. Literally thousands of people from neighboring villages as well as from Kfeir jammed into the streets to show their welcome. Kfeir's mayor, Elias Abu Jamra, sent two women dressed in black to the edge of the village to greet me and to sing the traditional welcoming song. Because they had no idea what I looked like, and because Clovis and I were walking arm in arm, they stopped directly in front of Clovis, looked straight at him and began singing the welcome to him. A sheepish smile covered his face, and with his right hand he made a sort of under-the-counter gesture pointing toward me. The two women stopped their song in mid-chorus, did a ninety-degree turn directly toward me, and began singing again from the top.

Later, when the Antiochian Orthodox Bishop, who had traveled from Zahle, a couple of hours north of Kfeir, held mass in my honor, Clovis, a Maronite Catholic, assisted him by singing the Orthodox liturgy totally from memory.

It seemed that the entire village marched with me when we went to the house where my mother grew up, and where she raised my older sister, Helen, and brother Chick. She had lived, during her years alone, with the two children in a tiny room in one part of her parents' house. Amazingly, it still had a dirt floor, and when I bent down to pick up a small piece of paper, Clovis, always the PR agent, turned to the assembled crowd, which included journalists, and shouted dramatically in Arabic, "He touched the floor of his mother's house."

I was still reeling from the reception beside the bomb crater in Mimas when Mayor Abu Jamra rose to make his welcoming speech, which, when translated, went something like this:

> We welcome you to your village of Kfeir. This village has sent many of its sons and daughters to the United States. In fact, they have gone to live in all parts of America. They have done so because we here have always thought of America as the haven for oppressed people, as a country with a democracy where everybody has a chance. But since America has been giving Israel airplanes and bombs to bomb us here, we now think of America as the oppressor.

The unfortunate villagers of Mimas and Kfeir, as well as those who lived in hundreds of villages in the south of Lebanon, had been caught squarely in the middle of Israel's geopolitical calculations. In 1970, after the PLO and King Hussein ended their bloody fighting, the PLO was expelled to Lebanon, where it set up bases in the south from which they could conduct raids into Israel. Beginning that year, Israel carried out a "scorched earth" policy of relentless and indiscriminate bombing of Lebanese villages, the objective of which was to force Lebanon to expel the Palestinians. What happened instead was that villagers in most of Israel's target area became refugees, moving to Beirut to live in shantytowns. The majority of the refugees were Shia Moslems, who, when some 500,000 of them ultimately flooded Beirut, upset the political balance. Their numbers threatened the political privileges of the Maronite Christians, eventually setting off the Lebanese civil war in 1975. Israel armed, financed, and trained the Phalangist militia that lashed out at the Palestinians and the leftist political coalition, beginning a war that has never ended.

The country now called Lebanon was for ages a part of Syria. Most of the Middle East was under Ottoman Turkish domination for some four hundred years before World War I. After the collapse of the Ottoman Empire in 1918, the Middle East was divided between Britain and France, with Syria (including what later became Lebanon) going to France, and Palestine, Iraq, and what is now Jordan going to England. Few people who have been to Lebanon before the 1975 civil war have been untouched by the beauty of the country and the charm of its people. Beirut's beaches exist less than two hours from ski resorts in the mountains, and from the lush Bekaa Valley in central Lebanon. Part of Lebanon is European in spirit, mostly French, which gives, or gave westerners a feeling of familiarity, buttressed by the part which is Arabic in body as well as in spirit, and which accounts for its warmth and hospitality.

Lebanon is a country of great anomalies. It was carved out of Syria in 1943 by the French as a haven for the Maronite Catholics, who had lived in one part of Lebanon for centuries. The area that the French designated as Lebanon also contained Moslems as well as other Christian sects. The governmental structure, based on an unwritten pact, requires a Maronite Christian to be president, a Sunni Moslem to be prime minister, with other religions assigned to increasingly minor posts on down the line. This agreement was made after the first and only census in the 1930s when it was thought that a majority were Maronite Christians. But despite the fact that Moslems are now in the majority, the government has refused to take another census, understanding that its results would provide reasons to change the power structure. Ostensibly, this structure was meant to establish power sharing. In reality, the president held all the power, including that of handing out most jobs in the ministries and throughout the government. Although a great many factors contributed to the civil war, the tremendous imbalance in power was perhaps the most significant one.

Now raging for more than fourteen years, the war has changed everything. Even the indomitable spirit of the Lebanese has been worn down by the senseless kidnapings, the bloody killings, the constant danger for everyone. The Lebanese economy, which held up even during the worst years of internal fighting, finally gave out after the Israeli invasion and subsequent occupation. The Israelis delivered the economic *coup de gras* when they began dumping tons of their own goods on the Lebanese market, causing the Lebanese pound to fall for the first time.

Certainly the Lebanese civil war has been one of the most bloody civil wars, if not the most bizarre. Ghassan Tueni, the publisher of *An Nahar*, an independent Beirut newspaper, told me of an amusing incident in the early part of the civil war. He was in his editorial office in Beirut when the Phalangist militia (sometimes called the "Christian" militia) began lobbing artillery shells that exploded very near the newspaper's building. The Phalangists were unhappy, he said, with an editorial in *An Nahar* critical of them. When the shelling stopped, the telephone rang in the editorial offices. The Phalangist artillery commander was on the line, asking how close they had come. The editor who answered the phone began swearing at the commander, calling him a bloody fool, that he was blind and unable to hit anything. Immediately after he hung up, the shelling began anew, this time coming closer, hitting the building next door to the newspaper. Again, the phone rang. It was the artillery commander again asking how his aim was. But before the editor could answer, Tueni tore the phone from his hand and, feigning panic, shouted, "We can't talk. We're all bleeding and dying. You've killed us." The ruse worked. As soon as the phone connection was broken, everyone watched as the Phalangists, now certain they were on target, destroyed the building next door.

Although the American press played the Lebanese civil war as a Christian-Moslem struggle, it was more a war of the haves against the have-nots. In general, the Phalangist party received the bulk of its support from the Maronite Christians, and the leftist parties received the bulk of their support from Moslems, Druze, and Antiochian Orthodox Christians. The PLO came in on the side of the Left, partly because they were part of the have-nots, and partly because the right-wing Phalangists saw the Palestinians in Lebanon as a group tipping the political balance against them, threatening the privileges that they had built up for themselves since Lebanon's independence. Because Israel's leaders saw anarchy in Lebanon to their advantage, they armed, financed, and supported the Phalangist militia.

I had a brief acquaintance with the Gemayel family, the leaders of the Phalangist political party, headed by Sheikh Pierre Gemayel. Sheikh Pierre, the family's leader, visited the 1936 Olympics in Berlin and was impressed by the discipline of the Nazis, inspiring him to found the Lebanese Phalange party shortly afterward. His party members adopted most of the outward accoutrements of Hitler's Nazis, including a stiff-armed salute. I didn't meet his son Bashir until 1975, when he asked to see me in my Senate office. By then he had taken over the military wing of the Phalangist party, and was riding high in Lebanon, funded by the Israelis and killing as many Palestinians and leftist Lebanese as he could. As *Washington Post* journalist Jonathan Randal once wrote, "He murdered his way to the top." During his visit to my office, Bashir and I talked about many things, but the meeting ended abruptly when I bluntly asked why he had allied himself with Israel against other Arabs. Before stomping out, Bashir exploded with anger, telling me that he would ally himself with the devil, if necessary, to insure the survival of the Phalangists.

It was not too long afterward that I began getting reports of vicious attacks on me by Phalangist radio in Beirut. The verbal assault never bothered me, but I did become worried when I learned that I was at the top of Bashir's hit list, along with my friend, Washington lawyer Richard Shadyac. Shadyac was even in more danger, because he is a Maronite who didn't agree with Bashir, which made him a traitor in Bashir's eyes. I was simply an enemy.

Bashir was killed by a bomb a few days after his election as president of Lebanon in 1982, although it could hardly be called an election. It was held after the Israeli invasion of Lebanon. Ringing the Parliament building in Beirut with tanks, the Israelis rigged the voting in a way that would have made Mayor Daley proud. Members of Parliament were threatened with death if they voted the wrong way, so, quite naturally, they voted the way the Israeli Army wanted—for Bashir.

Lebanon is in worse political shape today than it has ever been. The right-wing Phalangists have denied the Parliament a quorum needed to vote on a new president. Both the Phalangists and the left-wing parties have installed a president of their own, one a Christian and one a Moslem. Until someone strong enough comes along to take the guns away from the multitude of militias, I'm fearful that Lebanon's march toward total disintegration will proceed with deadly certainty. The country will dissolve into something resembling the Swiss system of cantons, each independent, but none strong enough to maintain an independent economy. Because the "confessional" system—holding office based on religious affiliation—is one of the major causes of the internal fighting, it will have to be discarded before Lebanon can be put back together again. The militias that now rule various territories in Lebanon are really nothing more than gangs, sustaining themselves from a combination of armed robbery, drug dealing, and financial aid from outside powers. Only the people of Lebanon are opposed to the system, but they are the ones who are helpless to change it.

Few foreign leaders seem to be interested in Lebanon's dilemma. The French, perhaps for reasons of nostalgia, have tried a time or two to help the Maronites, which has served only to anger the rest of the population. Each time the United States has interfered unilaterally, the result has been disastrous. For example, Reagan's totally ignorant 1983 intervention culminated in the detonation of the U.S. Marine barracks in Beirut, killing 265 marines. In a fit of temper following that disaster, Reagan ordered the indiscriminate shelling of the villages surrounding Beirut, which succeeded only in making even more enemies for the United States.

* * *

I returned from my first trip to Lebanon in 1973 to learn that my mother was seriously ill in the hospital in Winner. She had lived for another twenty-two years after the death of my father. Stricken by guilt that he had died first, she made a yearly pilgrimage to his grave in Gregory, almost one hundred miles east of Mission. Her reaction was always the same. Standing at the headstone, she would look up at the sky to ask God why she could not have been taken with him.

As she grew older and her arteries clogged, she began to lose her memory and her ability to comprehend events around her. When I was campaigning for the Senate in 1972, I stopped in to visit her at her home in Mission. By then her mental faculties were leaving her, and, seemingly in response to the heavy television advertising my campaign was running at the time, she said, "I hope you get the job you're trying to get, Jimmy. You need to work."

I went to see her in the hospital shortly after my return from Lebanon, just before her death in September 1973. She had always said that she didn't want to go back to the old country because her only memories were memories of suffering. I desperately wanted to tell her about her village, about the dirt floor in her house, and about the people who still remembered her, but by then she was beyond understanding. As I spoke, she looked at the wall for a long time, staring blankly, then she looked up at me and said, "Charlie, where are the boys?" I was unable to hold back my tears. The strength that had carried her and her family through the hardest of hard times, both in Lebanon and in South Dakota, was finally giving way. She died a few days later, her mind no longer able to function and her body no longer able to withstand the assault of old age.

10

The Crazy Horse Cafe

I was sitting in my mother's hospital room, trying to talk to her, knowing that I was perhaps saying goodbye for the last time, when one of the members of the American Indian movement (AIM) burst into the room, asking me for help. A few days before, Vernon Bellecourt, an AIM leader, had been shot by one of his colleagues in a dispute out near the Rosebud Agency, some fifty miles west of Winner. Bellecourt had been brought to the Winner Hospital for treatment and was recuperating from the trauma of his wound. Winner has always had more than its share of anti-Indian racists, most of whom were out in force that night, threatening to kill Bellecourt. The Indian who had come to me for help told me that several heavily armed white men were waiting outside the hospital in their pickups, harassing Bellecourt's bodyguards and delivering death threats. He was genuinely frightened.

When I asked why he did not call the Winner police, he told me that he had, but that they, apparently pleased that someone was going to rub out Bellecourt, had ignored his plea for help. I phoned the police chief, whom I knew, and told him that it was imperative

199

that he give Bellecourt some protection, preferably by dispersing the vigilantes. I eventually convinced him to do so, and a couple of officers came to the hospital to assure me that the matter was being handled.

* * *

American Indians have undergone a long period of brutalization, most of it resulting from the white invasion of this continent five centuries ago. As every American knows, Indians have been ignored, tricked, massacred, experimented with—whatever it took to move them off their land so that it could be confiscated by whites. The dominant white race sought not only to overpower the Indians militarily, but to finish them off as a race, either through subjugation and killing or through colonization and assimilation. If Indians could not be wiped out physically, as the settlers and the army wanted, then they could be assimilated into white society, as last century's "reformers" wanted. Either way, the "Indian problem" would be solved.

Although Indians resisted being driven onto reserves in the last century, a hundred years of life on the reservations have made them almost entirely dependent on reservation society for their survival. Their principal enemies today are the federal government, which mistreats them and mismanages their resources, and anti-Indian whites who still covet the little land remaining to them.

Most Sioux Indians live in South Dakota, which is where the government established their reservations. The Sioux, at one time Woodlands Indians centered around the lakes region of northern Minnesota and Wisconsin, were driven westward into South Dakota, Nebraska, Montana and Wyoming in the eighteenth century by other tribes who themselves were pushed westward after whites settled on the East Coast. Upon arrival in the Great Plains, the Sioux discovered horses, which had drifted northward following the sixteeth century influx of Spanish explorers to the Southwest. It was not long before the Sioux became master horsemen, dramatically changing the way that they had previously hunted and gathered food. From Woodlands Indians, who rarely traveled and who hunted small game on foot, they became nomads, hunting American bison and moving great distances with the seasons. They also became fierce warriors, which allowed them to dominate the territory they claimed as their hunting grounds.

The U.S. Army experienced the ferocity of the Sioux when it tried to drive them off their land in order to make room for white settlers in the nineteenth century. First came the immigrants who traveled to the West Coast through Sioux territory. The settlers trashed the prairies, killed the game along their trail, and in general disrupted the Sioux way of life. Then the railroads came, followed by white buffalo hunters who depleted the Indians' food supply by killing millions of buffalo only for their hides. When the Indians resisted with violence, the army retaliated, and the conflict escalated into an ongoing Indian-white war.

In 1868, when the army found that it could not defeat the Sioux war leader Red Cloud, they made a treaty with him at Ft. Laramie, Wyoming, in which they agreed to leave the Sioux unmolested in an area that stretched from west of the Missouri River in South Dakota into eastern Wyoming.

The 1868 treaty held until 1874, when General George Armstrong Custer led an expedition into the Black Hills of South Dakota—unquestionably Sioux lands—and discovered gold. After that, the army was unable to keep white gold seekers out of the Black Hills. Instead of enforcing the treaty against the whites, President Ulysses S. Grant tried to convince the Indians that a new treaty was necessary. When the Sioux refused to negotiate a new agreement, Grant had them declared as "hostiles," and ordered the army to round them up and to drive them onto reservations. Grant's actions culminated, two years later, in the battle that is called today the "Custer Massacre." Although the Indians emerged as the victors, they began to disperse, fearing the massive retaliation from the army that they were certain would ensue. Most were eventually captured and forced onto reservations.

The Sioux were among the last tribes to be defeated by the U.S. Army, and offered perhaps the strongest resistance to total white domination during the last century. But by 1890 they had been totally destroyed. The government had taken their hunting grounds and their weapons away from them, had herded them onto reservations, and had forced them to live on meager handouts—rations that were often withheld if it suited the whim of the Indian agents.

The last gasp of Indian resistance to occupation by whites took place in 1890 at Wounded Knee Creek in southwestern South Dakota. In reaction to the misery that occupation had visited on the Plains Indian tribes, a Pauite Indian from Nevada, named Wovoka, developed a new religion, called the "Ghost Dance" religion. Wovoka, who had been raised by a religious white family, combined the teachings of his father, who was a Pauite holy man, with the teachings of Jesus, which he learned from his adoptive parents. He counseled the Indians who sought his guidance to work willingly for the whites, to farm, and to send their children to school. Meanwhile, by performing the Ghost Dance, he said, they would ultimately restore the dominance of the red man, bring back the buffalo, and make the white man disappear. His vision attracted the once-free Indians, now living in unbearable conditions under the total control of the government and its often capricious Indian agents.

Like many of the Plains tribes, the Sioux sent a delegation to Nevada to learn the tenets of the new religion, so that they could teach them to the various Sioux tribes. When the Sioux delegates returned, however, they presented the Ghost Dance in a revised form. One of the delegates, Kicking Bear, introduced an element into the ritual that ultimately had serious repercussions for the tribe. He instructed the Sioux to wear a "Ghost Shirt," which he said would ward off the white man's bullets. When the army found out about the Ghost Dance, they set out to stop the practice. Especially fearful of Sitting Bull and his followers on the Standing Rock Reservation, the government ordered his arrest, during which he was shot and killed by an Indian policeman.

In December 1890, one of the Minneconjou leaders, Big Foot, left the Cheyenne River Reservation in northwestern South Dakota, leading his people southward to the Pine Ridge Reservation. He had decided to leave for two reasons—he was afraid of the army's aggressive behavior, and he had been asked to go to Pine Ridge to settle a dispute between some of the Oglala leaders. Concerned that he had gone off to join the Ghost Dance craze that had overtaken many of the South Dakota reservations, the army, specifically the Seventh Cavalry, set out to find him. They intercepted him in the Badlands of South Dakota, and began escorting him southward toward Pine Ridge. Camping overnight at Wounded Knee Creek, the troopers surrounded the Indians, their heavy guns placed on a rise and aimed at the Indian camp below them. The next morning the commander ordered the Indians disarmed. Resentful of the order, which would prevent them from gathering food, the Indians stonewalled the soldiers as they searched them for weapons. Somehow during the search, one of the weapons being confiscated discharged. Both sides panicked, and the soldiers responded by massacring one hundred and forty-six Indian men, women, and children. There were eyewitness accounts of mounted troopers running down and brutally killing fleeing women and children. The bodies were dumped into a mass grave dug on the hill where the army's Hotchkiss guns had been set up.

Wounded Knee has been called, alternately, the last Indian war, a massacre, and the last day of the Sioux Nation. Ever since, it has been, understandably, of great symbolic importance to Sioux Indians.

By the beginning of the twentieth century, the government and its agents had assumed total control over the lives of the Indians, dictating the kind of homes they would live in, the quantity and quality of their food, and the nature of their education. The government treated the Indians like children, then scoffed at them when they acted like children. The government created business training programs for Indians that were designed to fail, then complained because the Indians could not succeed in business. It offered courses in farming to Indians whose entire culture was based on hunting, and professed to be mystified when the Indians were unable to master farming on demand. The government kept Indians in abject poverty, then wrung its hands when alcoholism and suicide became rampant in Indian culture. The government prevented Indians from gaining equal access to social and cultural equality, then boasted that Indians were inferior to whites.

In 1934, Congress passed the Indian Reorganization Act, effectively and completely washing its hands of Indian affairs. It was a predictable response on the part of a political body. Indians have no votes to speak of, and there is no money to be extracted from the Indian reservations, so why should politicians spend time worrying about conditions there? The solution as far as Congress was concerned, was to hand over the "Indian problem" (which is really more a white problem) to the Bureau of Indian Affairs (BIA). This was done by providing blanket authorization to the BIA, which is no longer required, like other agencies, to return to Congress every year to ask for authorization of its programs. Instead, the BIA need only ask for money directly from the appropriations committees, which have no time to investigate whether programs are useful, successful, or just plain bad. Their decisions rest solely on how much money is available for Indian and other programs. Consequently, no one watches what the BIA bureaucracy does.

Sherwin Broadhead, who was at one time a BIA superintendent at the Colville Indian Agency in Washington State, and who later came to work on my staff as an Indian specialist, once testified to my committee that the BIA practiced "survival management."

Insuring the survival of its bureaucrats in their jobs was the only thing at which the BIA was expert, he said, leaving the Indians to pick on the bones that the bureaucracy left behind.

Someone once proposed that the Indian bureaucracy be abolished, and that all the money appropriated for Indians be sent directly to each Indian enrolled in a tribe now receiving benefits. The annual income per Indian would, of course, rise dramatically, and the domination of the Indians by the BIA would come to an end. As a senator, I played around with this concept a bit, and after asking the Indian Committee to provide me with some comparative figures on federal money allocated for Indians and the amount that they actually receive, I found the following. There are about 949,000 Indians in America. Roughly half live on Indian reservations, which means that the BIA serves about 475,000 Indians. The rest live in cities and are for the most part cut loose from Indian programs. The BIA's total appropriation for a fiscal year ranges from $800 million to $1 billion, which would amount to about $2,100 per Indian per year, *if the Indians were getting the money.* Adding the Indian Health Service's annual appropriation of $986,000,000 brings the per capita expenditure to nearly $4,200 a year. (It should be noted that the Indian Health Service spends its money considerably more efficiently than the BIA.) Now, compare that figure to the average annual income of Indians on South Dakota's reservations, which is approximately $875 *per Indian.* Of course, the income of Indians on other reservations varies somewhat from the South Dakota figure, but not much. As the statistics confirm, the bulk of the money intended for Indian reservations somehow doesn't make it to the reservations. I'm not so sure the suggestion of direct payments to Indians shouldn't be considered more seriously.

The BIA, as far as I am concerned, is a bureaucracy that has designed programs to insure that Indians will fail, in order to provide a rationale for the agency's continued existence. Unless one looks at it in these terms, it is impossible to explain some of the projects sponsored by the bureau. For example, near Mobridge, South Dakota, the BIA funded a tourist complex for the Standing Rock Sioux Tribe, consisting of a beautifully designed round motel. The project failed, primarily because it was placed so far from any highway that few tourists knew about it, and fewer still would drive off the beaten path to reach it.

As chairman of the Select Committee on Indian Affairs, I visited reservations around the country to see if the situation was different outside of my state, but I found only the same grinding poverty and hopelessness that existed in South Dakota Indian country. I once met with several representatives of Southern California rancherias—small ten-to-fifteen acre Indian reservations—asking for their views of conditions on their reservations. The meeting degenerated into a litany of complaints. One Indian protested at length about the failure of the Indian Health Service to bring in a power line to provide electricity for a water pump that had been installed two years earlier. The Indians had no means of bringing in the line themselves, and, of course, had no money to hire someone to do the job, which made them totally dependent on the Indian Health Service. After listening to similar complaints for a couple of hours, I asked why they hadn't asked their own California senators to handle what were obviously constituent problems. Their answer was about what I expected—that they couldn't get their senators' attention.

In addition to congressional apathy, I found very little sympathy for Indian concerns in successive administrations. For all his pretense as a liberal, Jimmy Carter did less for American Indians than Richard Nixon. Although Nixon did very little, he did sign an executive declaration that put him on record as favoring Indian self-determination.

Jimmy Carter hardly knew that Indians existed. Although, as chairman of the Indian Affairs Committee, I pushed hard for a full-blooded Indian to become assistant secretary for Indian affairs when Carter came into office in 1977, Interior Secretary Cecil Andrus instead appointed Forest Gerard, Washington Senator Henry "Scoop" Jackson's former staff member, who was the perfect part-Indian bureaucrat to appoint if you wanted nothing to happen in Indian affairs. And, nothing happened, despite Gerard's protestations during the Indian Committee's confirmation hearings that he would implement recommendations made by the American Indian Policy Review Commission. (The American Indian Policy Review Commission was created by Congress to do a major study of American Indian policy and to make recommendations for policy changes to the Congress.)

My entry into official Indian affairs coincided with the period of increasing Indian militancy. In January 1973, I had just been sworn in as a freshman senator, when I was appointed as chairman of the Indian Affairs Subcommittee of the Senate Interior Committee. Scoop Jackson, chairman of the Interior Committee, convinced me that he was doing me a favor by making the appointment. I strutted around for a while, boasting of the appointment to my friends and family, until I discovered that no one else wanted the job.

On February 28, not long after becoming the subcommittee chairman, my wife and I were having a birthday party for our son Paul, who was turning thirteen. To impress Paul's friends we held the party in the Senate Interior Committee's hearing room. It was evening, and one of my staff ran into the room to tell me that Wounded Knee had been taken over by the American Indian Movement (AIM), led by activists Russell Means and Dennis Banks. AIM had decided to take over a reservation in order to attract attention to Indian grievances. It chose Wounded Knee as the site for its confrontation with the government because of its historical significance. Russell Means is an Oglala Sioux who left the reservation in his youth and had lived in urban centers in his adult years. He was by far the most aggressive of the leadership, highly articulate, and, as it turned out, opportunistic. Dennis Banks, originally from Minnesota, is a quiet, soft-spoken Chippewa who is just the opposite of Means. Although both are articulate and intelligent, Banks is not given to loud pronouncements and all the bluff and bluster for which Means is famous.

After driving into Wounded Knee in a caravan, the AIM contingent had held a press conference at which they announced their takeover of the village. The U.S. Marshals Service already had a presence in Pine Ridge, and immediately moved in to surround Wounded Knee. After learning of the takeover, I went to my office, where I tried, unsuccessfully, to reach someone in Pine Ridge who could tell me what was happening. Then, using a Pine Ridge telephone book, I called the first number I found listed in Wounded Knee Village, which belonged to someone named Wilbur Riegert. It was an amazing coincidence. Riegert's house was being used by the Indians as their headquarters.

Russ Means, whom I had met years before, answered the phone. When I asked him what was happening, he told me that the Indians were holding eleven hostages. They would not be released, he said, until Henry Kissinger, Bill Fulbright, Ted Kennedy, and I came to Wounded Knee to listen to the Indians spell out their grievances. Our conversation was cordial until I heard Russ mumbling under his breath, "CBS is here." Suddenly his voice changed. He began shouting demands and conditions into the telephone. I told him that I would see what I could do about the negotiating team and would get back to him. That night as I watched the CBS evening news, Russ Means was prominently displayed in the story on

Wounded Knee, impressively shouting demands into the telephone at an unnamed caller.

I called him later to tell him that, with the exception of me, none of the people he had requested was willing to go to South Dakota. I told him that I would go, and that I would be accompanied by Carl Marcy of Fulbright's staff and Tom Sussman of Kennedy's staff. There would, however, be no one from the Administration.

"If Kissinger won't come, then I want John Ehrlichman," Means said.

"Russ, what have I ever done to you that you would force me to ride in the same airplane with Ehrlichman for three hours?" I responded.

Laughing, Means conceded my point. He decided to accept Marcy, Sussman, and me. I called George McGovern and convinced him to go with us. He had just gone through the presidential election process and was gearing up for his 1974 reelection race for the Senate. I thought that he could use some exposure on an issue that directly affected South Dakota and that he could help get the hostages released.

On the following day, reporters continued to call my Senate office trying to get information on the takeover. My staff suggested that I hold a press conference—an action that would not only answer the repetitive questions from the media, but which, they argued, would also get my name in print. Both reasons were persuasive.

Wounded Knee was big, big news. What appeared to be the entire national press corps gathered in the Interior Committee's hearing room for the press conference. It was my first national news conference, and I was nervous. Staring into the lenses of at least a dozen television cameras, I opened the conference with a statement about my intentions for the trip to Wounded Knee, then asked for questions. One of the first questions came from Hal Walker, who was then with CBS News.

"Senator," he said in his best radio voice, one that was booming in volume, pompous in quality, and exaggerated in somberness. "Do you intend to go to Wounded Knee and exchange yourself for those eleven hostages?"

Panic! I felt a klong coming on. How could I say "no" with all these people listening? What would people think of me if I admitted my fear?

"No, I do not." I said, knowing full well that this answer could mean the end of my Senate career.

Walker, smelling politician's blood, swooped in for the kill.

"Do you mean to tell us, Senator, that the life of one U.S. senator is worth more than the lives of eleven innocent hostages?" His voice boomed even louder.

I saw the wreckage of my life reflected in the lenses of the television cameras trained on me, recording, without mercy, my final humiliation.

I was desperate. "I don't look at it as the life of one U. S. senator," I croaked. I knew it was my own voice, but it seemed as though it was coming from someone else. "I view it as the life of one coward."

At first I vaguely heard the roar of laughter coming from the dozens of reporters clustered together. When the scene came into sharper focus, I realized that they were laughing, not at me, but at Hal Walker. For years afterward, reporters would come up to me to say that I had done a masterful job of handling what they thought was an insipid question.

We requisitioned a small air force jet early the next morning and flew to Ellsworth Air Force Base near Rapid City. From Ellsworth, the air force took us by helicopter to Pine Ridge where we were met by Joseph Trimbach, the FBI agent in charge of what was by then turning into a major confrontation. My agreement with Means was that as soon as we arrived in Wounded Knee the hostages would be released. Trimbach set out to inform the Indians of our arrival, and McGovern and I decided to wait in Pine Ridge Village—the headquarters for both the tribe and the Bureau of Indian Affairs, located some twelve miles southwest of Wounded Knee.

We set up camp in the Crazy Horse Cafe, the only eating establishment in town, and waited for nearly four hours for Trimbach to return. We passed the time by telling stories about the Senate to the reporters who had pulled up chairs to our table. At one point, the waitress took off her apron and went home to get her baby. "I want his picture taken with my senators," she announced proudly. When she returned, I held the baby while she took the photograph, which caused McGovern to tease me about being "that kind" of politician.

"I used to try to win votes based on my pretty face," I told him, "but when that failed I had to resort to holding and kissing babies."

Finally Trimbach returned to tell us that he could get no response from the AIM leadership. Tired of waiting, I said to McGovern, "Well, I know Russ Means. Let's you and I go directly to Wounded Knee and talk to him, George."

Wounded Knee Village was named after a small nearby creek,

which had been the site of a domestic quarrel in which an Indian supposedly was shot in the knee by his wife. To reach Wounded Knee, one must drive east of Pine Ridge Village on State Highway 18 for seven miles, then turn north for about seven more. By 1973, the village consisted of Clyde Gildersleeve's store and Indian museum, operated by his son-in-law, Jim Cyzinski, and a few houses spread throughout a valley along the creek, which was less a creek than a depression below a series of rolling hills. The entire village was dominated by a white wooden church built on the highest hill overlooking Wounded Knee. The church stood as a silent sentry over the mass grave into which the Indians massacred in 1890 had been dumped.

Immediately after the AIM takeover, the FBI and the U.S. Marshals Service established checkpoints on all roads leading in and out of Wounded Knee. Inside the government perimeter surrounding Wounded Knee was a no man's land, referred to by both sides as the "demilitarized zone." Inside the Indian perimeter were bunkers built and manned by AIM's warriors—mostly Vietnam veterans, some of them armed with Soviet assault rifles.

McGovern and I went into what I thought could very well be the valley of the shadow of death. At the government's checkpoint south of Wounded Knee we were transferred to a car driven by John Terronez, the Justice Department's community relations representative. (Years later, the head U.S. marshall, Wayne Colburn, told me that during the siege of Wounded Knee he used Community Relations Service employees to spy on AIM, because they had the confidence of the Indians and could move in and out of their perimeter at will.)

Just like actors in a western, we tied a white cloth to a tree branch and hung it out of the car window. With Terronez driving and McGovern and I in the back seat, we started the slow descent into the village of Wounded Knee. We left the government perimeter, drove through the demilitarized zone, then passed the first Indian checkpoint at the edge of their perimeter. It was not until then that my nerves began to shatter. Keep in mind that this was literally the second day of the Indians' occupation, and everyone was uncertain about everyone else. As McGovern, Terronez, and I progressed deeper into the Indian perimeter and closer to the village, we found ourselves staring directly into the barrels of an assortment of weapons—shotguns, rifles, automatic weapons—all aimed directly at our heads by the meanest-looking bunch of Indians I had ever seen. The tension inside the car increased in direct proportion to the number of rifle barrels aimed at us as our car crept deeper and deeper into Indian territory. Suddenly McGovern leaned over to me and said, "Jim, why did you have to be so fucking courageous?" McGovern had broken the tension with what I then thought was his all-time greatest one-liner, delivered with exquisite timing. It was enough to get us into the village without having an ulcer attack.

When we reached the village and told the hostages that they were free to go, we learned for the first time that all of them lived in Wounded Knee and had no interest in leaving.

The AIM leadership, Means and Banks, wanted us to set a time to hear the grievances of the traditional, full-blooded Oglalas. They were members of the group that had originally invited AIM to come into the reservation to confront the authorities—holy man Frank Fools Crow, his interpreter, Matthew King, Pedro Bissonnette, Sievert Young Bear, and others, known collectively as OSCRO, the Oglala Sioux Civil Rights Organization. We agreed to have a second meeting later in the day on a plateau within the demilitarized zone, then a third that evening inside Wounded Knee.

The afternoon meeting on the plateau could not exactly be described as a roaring success. Banks and Means wanted a tepee set up in which to conduct the "negotiations," but they could not find one. Meanwhile the cameras were churning. We were surrounded by the network camera crews and an assortment of newspaper journalists. We stood in a circle, and Russ Means opened the session by denouncing me for lying to him. I was stunned by the accusation, not yet used to his brand of showmanship. When I challenged him to name one time when I had lied to him, he would only respond dramatically, "Many times." Then a minute later he casually strolled around behind me, out of hearing of the reporters, and whispered in my ear, "Don't take what I said seriously."

The meeting eventually broke up and we went back into Pine Ridge. But in the evening we had a much more beneficial discussion. McGovern and I returned to Wounded Knee and joined the Indians at AIM headquarters in Wilbur Riegert's house. We stayed until midnight listening to the full-blooded, or traditional, Indians as they laid out their grievances. To me, their complaints were genuine. The tribe had been taken over by mixed-blooded Indians through elections that the traditional Indians neither understood nor wanted to participate in. The Sioux had historically chosen their leaders by consensus, according to the amount of respect that each leader commanded in his area of expertise—war-making, hunting, etc. To have the Bureau of Indian Affairs tell them they must emulate the white man's way of choosing leaders through elections was an affront. Consequently, they had, over the years, refused to take part in the elections held for tribal chairman and council members. They were now paying the price for standing on principle, because their wishes were being ignored by the younger oligarchy of mixed-blooded Indians who dominated the election process.

Their grievances had never been addressed by either the tribal leadership or the Bureau of Indian Affairs. What offended their sensibilities was the constant interference in their lives by the government and by the mixed-blooded oligarchy, with no concomitant benefit. Land ownership, for example, was an alien concept to them. Land was to be used by those in control of it, but it was not to be "owned" by anyone. The original sin regarding land ownership occurred in 1887, when the Congress passed the Dawes Allotment Act. The Act took the land out of tribal control and allotted each Indian adult 160 acres of land to be held in trust by the government. Because the land could not be sold, with the passing of each generation, ownership of the allotted quarter section had to be shared by all the heirs of the original allottee. As generations passed, an individual share of 1/256th of a quarter of land was not uncommon.

To make matters worse, because 160 acres of relatively unproductive land can only sustain a few head of cattle, the Bureau of Indian Affairs combined several quarters of land into a Range Management Unit, and then leased out the Unit to someone with a large herd—always a white or a mixed-blooded rancher. If an Indian landowner in the middle of the unit chose not to lease his land, his only recourse was to build a fence to prevent the lessee's cattle from eating his grass. Most Indian landowners could not afford to build a fence, and when the lessee's cattle ate their grass, their compensation was exactly what it would have been had they agreed to join the Range Management Unit in the first place—a pittance. The Allotment Act was intended to "civilize" the Indians and to get their land out of common, tribal ownership and into the hands of white men.

McGovern and I listened to all their grievances, and it was nearly midnight when we rose to leave. I said to Russell Means, "You know, Russ, this thing is going to have to end at some point. Why don't you end it now before someone gets hurt? You may have to face a kidnaping charge, but that would be better than a murder charge if someone gets shot."

Means had obviously been thinking about this, because he responded immediately. "You're right. We'll do it, but you have to tell the FBI that we want to know exactly who's going to be charged and with what crime, and how much bail will be set for each person. We need to give our lawyers this information so that they can be ready."

I agreed. I immediately passed Means's request on to Trimbach when we returned to the government checkpoint. McGovern, Marcy, Sussman, and I flew back to Ellsworth Air Force Base, where we spent the night, then to Washington the next morning, honestly believing that the matter had been resolved.

Of course, the confrontation did not end until some seventy days later, causing me to believe that the government did not want it to end. Someone in an official position obviously must have seen a political advantage in a publicized confrontation with a small band of militant Indians.

My feeling was reinforced years later when the AIM leadership trials were being conducted in St. Paul, Minnesota's federal court. William Clayton, the U.S. attorney for South Dakota, called to ask me to testify for the prosecution at the trials. I declined. He said that he would issue a subpoena, forcing me to do so. I told him that in that event I would tell the court what I had told Trimbach— that Means had wanted to end the siege the night I was there. Clayton said, "On second thought, I don't think we'll need your testimony."

On March 26, 1973, while the takeover and siege were still in progress, Senator Scoop Jackson called a secret session of the Senate Interior Committee to get the Administration to testify about what was happening at Wounded Knee. The first part of the hearing was taken up with wrangling between Jackson and the Republican members of the committee, each side trying to blame the opposing political party for the confrontation at Wounded Knee. The Republicans traced fault back to Lyndon Johnson's leniency after the urban riots—specifically the one in Washington, D.C. in 1968—to which Jackson responded that the confrontation was happening because Nixon was in the White House. Finally we got around to questioning the gathered officials from the Justice, Interior, and Postal Departments about events in Wounded Knee.

The Postal Department attended the hearings because, strangely enough, four postal service inspectors had received wide publicity after having been "captured" by the Indians inside Wounded Knee and, in a sense, publicly humiliated by them with the cooperation of the press.

Incredulous at the presence of postal inspectors in the middle of a highly-publicized political confrontation, I took the opportunity to ask Chief Postal Inspector William Carter what they had been doing at Wounded Knee in the first place.

"We wanted to make certain that the mails were moving," he said with a straight face.

Carter explained that the postal inspector in Rapid City had been instructed by his supervisor in St. Paul, Minnesota to maintain close contact with other federal authorities with respect to the Wounded Knee situation. The Postal Service was, he said, concerned with what was happening to mail delivery within the Wounded Knee area.

They had been told that the post office in Wounded Knee had been looted, giving rise to violations of federal laws. Their information, he testified, was that $100 in "postal cash" and $600 or $700 in stamps had been taken.

The postal inspectors had heard, on March 12, that the Indian roadblocks had been withdrawn, and so they decided to send a search team into Wounded Knee on March 13.

Carter's testimony is worth repeating here, "When they [the four postal inspectors] were about a quarter of a mile from Wounded Knee on the highway leading into town, they were stopped by . . . three individuals some distance from the car.

"One looked like a Caucasian, perhaps a marshal, a federal officer—he was wearing that type of jacket.

"But when they got closer to the group it became apparent that they were all Indians. Inspector Graham laid out his credentials and stated that the purpose of their visit was to inspect the post office at Wounded Knee.

"The Indians then suggested that they escort the four inspectors to Wounded Knee. The Indians were armed with rifles.

"They were joined by two more Indians. They were taken into town, and at that point the Indians asked, 'Are you fellows armed?' When the inspectors said they were, they were relieved of their revolvers, credential badges, and all their personal effects, credit cards, cash, and so forth.

"They were taken into a building and seated on a bench facing the wall. They were then tied up and given a lecture by one of the Indians about what was wrong with the United States."

I interrupted Carter at that point and asked if the Indians had complained about the Postal Service itself. Carter, a large, muscular, red-faced man with a delightful Irish brogue, never missed a lick.

"That was one area where we received no complaint."

The Indians had great fun with the postal inspectors that day. After untying them, the Indians escorted the inspectors out of Wounded Knee. As they were marched past the waiting press corps, the Indians told the inspectors to put their hands on top of their heads, and they complied. One photographer was not quite ready, so he asked the Indians to march them by again—a request that the Indians gleefully granted. The inspectors were then released, having received their allotted fifteen minutes of fame.

* * *

In America there are millions of examples of injustice, of the unfair treatment of people who have no power or no money. Treatment of Indian people in the United States provides us with a clear illustration of inequitable justice for the poor. The day after President Ford pardoned Richard Nixon in advance of any indictment or trial for the crimes that he committed while in office, I was taking my turn presiding over the Senate. It was September 9, 1974, when several senators were speaking on the Senate floor, discussing Nixon's pardon for the record. I was unable to contain myself after hearing a number of speakers rationalize the pardon as a good thing because it manifested a merciful quality in the new president. I asked someone to take my place for a brief time, got down from the presiding officer's chair, and sought recognition. What prompted my move was the fact that Nixon's pardon coincided with the prosecution of Sarah Bad Heart Bull. She was an Indian woman who had been convicted in South Dakota for taking part in a riot in Custer, South Dakota, in one of the actions which led up to the Wounded Knee takeover. Actually, the short talk I gave to the Senate is self-explanatory:

> . . . in February of 1973, a little over a year and a half ago, a group of Sioux Indians, just prior to the Wounded Knee takeover and occupation, went to the town of Custer, South Dakota, to engage in a protest against what they considered to be unfair treatment of an Indian who had been stabbed and killed by a non-Indian. The non-Indian had not been charged with any serious crime. During the course of the protest, the chamber of commerce building and a

part of the courthouse in Custer, South Dakota were burned. As a result of that action, a number of people were charged with rioting and with arson, and stemming from those charges, an Indian woman by the name of Sarah Bad Heart Bull was convicted, just this year, of taking part in the riot. She was sentenced to an indeterminate sentence of one to five years. Although Sarah has no husband and she has five children, she was given twenty-four hours by the judge to take care of her affairs before she went to prison. In addition to that, Sarah Bad Heart Bull was denied bond pending appeal of her case. Because Sarah has no friends in high places, no money, and no power, she is now in prison. I do not know whether her lawyer is being paid or whether he is working *pro bono*. With all of the explanations given for the pardon of Richard Nixon, and with the new definitions of the quality of mercy, I would hope that someone could define to Sarah Bad Heart Bull and her family the new definition of mercy, because I am unable to do so.

Like most pleas for justice, this one fell on deaf ears.

* * *

When I first came into the Senate, Scoop Jackson had assigned only one staff member—Forest Gerard—to the Indian subcommittee. Although I was the subcommittee's chairman, Gerard took his orders from Scoop, making the situation both uncomfortable and untenable. It appeared to me that Scoop was there to make certain, among other things, that Indians did not interfere with whites anywhere in the United States, and particularly in Washington, his home state. When I asked for more staff money, Scoop refused on the grounds that other subcommittee chairmen might also ask for money, although he did agree with me that Indian affairs needed a lot of work.

I solicited and received a large private contribution from a supporter in New York, which enabled me to hire Sherwin Broadhead as a special Indian staffer. I continued to press Scoop for more Indian staff, but to no avail. Bill Van Ness, the Interior Committee's chief counsel, suggested that I try to put together a special commission to study Indian problems in order to get more staff. According to Van Ness, the other committee members recognized that something more had to be done about American Indian policy and would not object to a special commission.

Van Ness came up with an ingenious idea, and we put together a plan that was eventually approved. We appropriated a few million dollars for a two-year study of Indian policy by a body called the

American Indian Policy Review Commission, with a mandate to come up with recommendations for both the Congress and the Administration. There were to be eleven commissioners, six congressional and five Indian. Because I had pushed the program through, I was named chairman. The early complaints about an Indian study commission controlled by whites ended when it was discovered that I voted with the Indians 100 percent of the time.

Lloyd Meeds, a congressman from Washington State, who had been a champion of Indian rights, was appointed vice-chairman. Meeds's sympathies were rapidly changing, however. He had just finished an extremely close race for his congressional seat and was feeling the heat from anti-Indian voters in his state, particularly those who were rebelling against the federal court's fishing decisions favoring the Indians. He eventually—I'm certain much to his own dismay—became the chief opponent of pro-Indian activities on the commission.

There had been previous studies of Indian policy, most notably the Merriam report issued decades earlier. But there had never been a study done by the Indians themselves, which was one of my principal objectives. I hired Ernie Stevens, a Wisconsin Oneida as staff director and Kirk Kickingbird, an Oklahoma Kiowa, as staff counsel, and instructed them to hire Indian staff members whenever possible. The upshot was that nearly all the staff members hired— some 150 or more—were Indians. Max Richtman, an American Jew, was the only exception. Max, a delightful young man of great competence, came to my staff from that of Congressman Sid Yates of Chicago. His parents had survived Hitler's death camps, and he had been born in a displaced person's camp in Europe shortly after his parents' liberation from a Nazi concentration camp. Max was the controller for the commission, handling the flow of money and related matters. He was made famous during a House Appropriations Committee hearing when he, Ernie Stevens, and Kirk Kickingbird all appeared before it to request money for the commission. One of the committee members, a Texas congressman, interrupted Kickingbird's statement to ask, "Kickingbird is an unusual name. What is its background?" Kirk explained it was a Kiowa name, not all that unusual in Oklahoma.

Then the congressman turned to Ernie Stevens, commenting that his name didn't sound at all Indian, to which Ernie responded, "I'm a Wisconsin Oneida. My people sided with the British during the French and Indian Wars, and were all given English names back then."

Looking at Max Richtman, the congressman asked simply, "From what tribe does the name 'Richtman' derive?" Sid Yates, who was chairing the committee hearings interrupted and said, "He's from one of the ten lost tribes of Israel, Congressman."

One of my objectives in bringing in Indians to do the work of rooting out Indian policy successes and failures was to build cadres of Indian leadership. Indians had rarely had an opportunity of this kind, and I wanted to make certain that they could take full advantage of it. The final commission report, written by the Indian staff members, came out with several hundred recommendations for change, to be implemented by the Administration and Congress. It goes without saying that the recommendations for the Administration were largely ignored. They included major changes in BIA operations that were proposed by a professional management consulting firm that had worked *pro bono* for the commission.

When Salt Lake City lawyer John Boyden, representing the leaders of the Hopi tribe, wanted to throw the Navajo off their land in the now famous Hopi-Navajo dispute, Scoop Jackson publicly supported the Navajo, but privately had his staff working against them in favor of Boyden's proposal.

The Hopis, part of the Pueblo people, are a wonderfully kind and gentle tribe of Southwest Indians. They were such a peaceful people that way back in their history they hired mercenaries—the Tewa people—to defend them from outside attack. The Tewas are much more aggressive in character, and over the years they were absorbed into the Hopi tribe by marriage.

In 1882, the government drew boundaries on a map, designating territory in what is now Arizona for the Hopi tribe. The territory outlined by the executive order landed squarely in the middle of land where the Navajo traditionally moved their livestock. The designated land, called the "1882 reservation," was then ceded by the government to the Hopis, although their ancestral grounds were elsewhere. The cession of land was ignored by both tribes until the 1970s, when the Boyden law firm and a Tewa chairman of the Hopi tribe decided to press their claim for the land. By then, the Navajos had pretty much settled in the area, a great many of them having made their permanent homes there, blissfully unaware that the government had given the land to another tribe. Arizona Senators Barry Goldwater and Paul Fannin introduced legislation that would move the Navajo off the land and turn it over to the Hopis. I have no idea what Fannin's motives were, but I was pretty certain that Barry Goldwater hated Peter McDonald, the controversial chairman of the Navajo tribe, driving him to support removal of the Navajo from the disputed area.

The dispute brought together a strange political mixture. Al Barkan, who was the political director and bagman for the AFL-CIO, had become friendly with Peter MacDonald. MacDonald had traditionally been a Republican, but welcomed Barkan's support, and in return allowed Barkan to organize and register voters for the Democratic party on the Navajo reservation. Barkan's support, of course, meant that all of the labor union lobbyists zeroed in on Scoop Jackson who was ordinarily attentive to union issues, as well as to other Democrats on the Interior Committee. Hence Scoop's public mouthing of support for the Navajo.

I saw the issue as another act of wrongdoing against innocent Indians. The traditional Hopi refused to run and to vote in tribal elections, giving the more aggressive Tewas almost free rein in conducting the tribe's affairs. Interestingly, the traditional Hopis sided with the Navajo, refusing to be a part of the effort to move them off the land. It was clearly a painful event for them. Historically, the land had never been used by the Hopi, whose original villages were built on top of sharply rising, steep mesas, offering fortress-like protection from their enemies. There were always rumors—never proven—that precious minerals had been uncovered on this land, which was the reason for the unusual interest in the Arizona desert by Boyden's law firm. The Navajo, now settled on the land, never suspected that they would be required to leave. Under the Goldwater-Fannin legislation, however, they would be forced out, creating a new class of refugees. I had seen enough of refugees in the Palestinian camps in the Middle East, compelling me to try to prevent the Navajo's ejection from their homes. Tragically, I was able only to slow down their eviction. But the difficulties of uprooting the Navajo have been demonstrated, because, to this day, only a few Navajo have been relocated, and at tremendous cost to the government as well as to the Navajo families involved.

In the 1950s, the Congress, led by none other than Scoop Jackson, began introducing termination legislation. Indian tribes recognized by the federal government have what is called a "trust" relationship with the government. This means that Indian-owned lands are held in trust by the government either for the tribe or for individual Indians. If a tribe is "terminated" by federal legislation, the trust relationship comes to an end, and the tribe and its members are thrown on the mercy of the white man's world. There are many people who believe that termination is a desirable policy, but it results in both human and economic disaster for the Indians, who are ill-prepared to enter a culture that is to this day totally alien to their way of life.

On another occasion when I proposed a reorganization of the Bureau of Indian Affairs, a plan designed to strip the BIA's area directors of their destructive power, the area directors began preaching to the tribes that termination would be the end result of my legislation. Frightened to death, the tribal leaders opposed the reorganization plan, which of course killed it. The area directors retained their power by controlling the allocation of funds intended for the tribes, giving more money to the tribes that submitted to their wishes.

The Indian Affairs Committee did manage to pass a couple of worthwhile bills, however. The Indian Freedom of Religion Act was one. Although it is a Congressional Resolution that has no force of law, it has given the Indians a platform from which to protest the trampling of their religious freedoms by the government. It was spurred by the disregard that some federal agencies had for Indian religious practices and the sanctity of their ancestral burial grounds.

I think that the Indian Child Welfare Act was perhaps the most far-reaching bill that we passed. Prior to the Act's passage, white welfare agencies were working their will on Indian families, much to the detriment of the Indians. Totally ignorant of Indian culture, white welfare workers in all parts of the United States took Indian children away from their mothers based on the standards of the white community. Thus, if an Indian mother was an alcoholic, her baby would be taken from her and given to a white family to raise. Ignored was the fact that this kind of removal was more damaging to the Indian child than its mother's disease. Transferral to white culture served to destroy the identity of Indian children, resulting later on in emotionally disturbed Indian adults. The Indian Child Welfare Act required that a tribal court must decide where a child belonged, taking the decision out of the hands of the white welfare agencies and white courts.

* * *

The question of "state jurisdiction" of Indians and Indian lands has been debated for years in South Dakota. In 1963, the state legislature passed a law that stripped the South Dakota Indians of federal and tribal jurisdiction and placed them under state jurisdiction. A coalition of church groups and supporters of Indian rights referred the law to the voters and overwhelmingly defeated it. In 1974, in response to the Indians' increased militancy, the question of putting the Indians under state jurisdiction once again came alive. Major catalysts for the drive were the Wounded Knee take-over and the inflammatory public statements of Russell Means. The so-called "state jurisdiction" move would subject Indians on the reservations to state court jurisdiction, rather than their own tribal court jurisdiction, and it would put all of the Indian trust lands on the state and county tax rolls. Hardly anyone, if they were honest about it, would dispute that this would result in a great many Indian people losing their lands to tax auctions within a very few years.

Tensions between Indians and whites were increasing, and the situation was growing ugly. I decided that my contribution to peace and tranquility would be to hold a series of gigantic sensitivity sessions—I called them simply public meetings—around the state in areas containing the greatest number of hostile whites. The first one was held in the high school auditorium in Sisseton, in the northeast corner of South Dakota.

Sisseton was in an unusual position. Although all other Indian reservations in South Dakota were under joint federal and tribal jurisdiction, by some sort of erosive process, Sisseton's reservation had been under state jurisdiction for several decades. A recent court decision had returned the reservation, including the town of Sisseton, to Indian jurisdiction. For the first time in history, the white residents of Sisseton found themselves subject to the rules of the tribal police force. This was almost too much for some of the whites, who had been accustomed to mistreating Indians all of their lives.

The first controversial incident occurred when a gas station owner, whom I will call Hans, refused to sell gas to a carload of Indian men whose hair was braided, the symbol of Indian militancy. He leveled his rifle at them and ordered them off his premises. In a move that surprised everyone, they called the Indian police, who arrested Hans—an act that drove him to the edge, pushing him even further in favor of state jurisdiction.

The Sisseton meeting was attended by about five hundred white people. Because the Sisseton-Wahpeton tribe was content with the status quo—they now controlled law enforcement on the reserva-tion—it boycotted the meeting. The result was that only twenty-five or so Indians attended—Indians who were sort of double outcasts, that is, on the outs with both the tribe and the white community. They sat in the auditorium's highest bleacher seats, huddled together away from everyone else.

Hans was the first person on his feet when the meeting started, charging at high speed to the audience microphone. For a while, he tried attacking me for changing the federal Indian education regulations. In the middle of his tirade, I mentioned something about Indian lands. Hans interrupted me and shouted, "Why don't you tell me where the Indians get the right to any of these lands?"

"Well, we could start with the 1868 treaty between the Sioux and the U.S. Government," I began. But Hans, now white-lipped with frustration, interrupted again.

"Why don't we go back further than 1868. Why don't we send 'em back where they came from," his angry voice reverberating throughout the auditorium.

I was stricken nearly speechless with disbelief at what he had said. "And where would that be, Hans?" I asked, finally.

"Send 'em back across the Bering Strait. That's where they came from. All they're doing is having kids, and being on unemployment and welfare anyway." As soon as he had shot this volley he started back toward his seat.

In high dudgeon, I began lecturing him on the evils of racism when I was interrupted by a young Indian woman, in her mid-twenties, who had charged down from her bleacher seat to grab the microphone. As she began speaking in a measured, almost poetic cadence, she pointed her finger directly at Hans.

"Youuu want to know whyyy we have kids . . . and whyyy we're on welfaaarrre. I'llll tell you why." Then she swept her right hand, index finger pointed, grandly around the auditorium.

"It's because you white men . . . are screwing us Indian women . . . and we're having your kids . . . and you're not supporting them. That's why we're on welfare." Then came her thunderbolt, causing, I suspect, more than one family disruption that day.

"I could name eight or nine of you right here in this auditorium," she again swept her index finger over the audience, "who refuse to support the kids you've fathered." There was noticeable discomfort among some of the white males.

Of the three television crews in the auditorium, not one had their cameras running at the time, missing an incident, the film of which I would have gladly paid a year's salary for.

As we were leaving the auditorium at the end of the meeting, I was walking out with the Indian contingent, and the young woman who had put Hans in his place walked over and said to me, "Thanks a lot, hey. Us Indians need to stick together."

"But I'm not an Indian," I told her. "I'm Lebanese." She looked at me in genuine shock, then turned to the other Indians who were keeping pace and shouted, "Hey, he's Lebanese. No wonder they're selling us out."

The jurisdiction meeting in Rapid City, while not as graphic, was nearly as interesting. Fully one thousand people attended, about half of them cowboys and the other half Indians. Although the sensitivity part of the session was beneficial, the highlight was the oration by Sylvester Black Crow, who drove 120 miles from his home on the Pine Ridge Reservation to attend. "Celo," as he was called, asked one of my staff to write a statement for him to read to the audience. Before he got to the microphone, he handed in the statement, "for the record," he said, and proceeded to tell the story of how he had made the deputy sheriff of Washabaugh County stop pasturing his cattle on Celo's land without paying him.

Apparently, the deputy had been dropping off his cattle there for years to eat Celo's grass free of charge, and Celo had not been able to do anything about it. In 1971, when my oldest son, Charlie, moved in with Celo and his family, Charlie urged Celo to complain to Al Trimble, the Indian agent at Pine Ridge. Charlie and Celo also refused to allow the deputy to pick up the cattle after they had eaten Celo's grass and the deputy had come to retrieve them. Although the deputy called the FBI and accused Celo and Charlie of stealing his cattle, Trimble stepped in and straightened out the matter.

Celo's version of the story, which he told on the day of the meeting, had even the most hostile cowboys in the audience laughing. He related, in his best Sioux accent, what he had told the deputy when he came to get his cattle, "Why deputy, I don' know why you treatin' me so good, to give me this cattle as a present. I tell you, I'm gon' do something nice for you to pay you back. I'm gon' have a BIG feast right here on my lan', and I'm gon' have it in your honor. We gon' kill all this beef you give me and we gon' invite all my neighbors and all my friends to your party. How you like that, deputy?"

"When I say that to the deputy," Celo went on, "he ask me, 'How much do I owe you for grazing fees?' "

* * *

Following the 1973 Wounded Knee takeover, I held hearings to try to determine its causes, using as a vehicle the Indian Affairs Subcommittee of the Senate Interior Committee. Hearings were held in Pine Ridge, eliciting testimony from tribal chairman Richard Wilson, and in Kyle, where the dissident AIM members held forth. There were, of course, no buildings remaining in Wounded Knee, because they all had been destroyed at the end of the takeover.

During the hearings in Kyle, as AIM leader Russell Means was testifying about his conflict with tribal chairman Richard Wilson, I interrupted him to admonish him against Indian factionalism. "If there's one thing that I will prevent as long as I have the power, it's Indians fighting against Indians. You have enough external enemies to fight with . . ." I began to say. But Means interrupted me in turn.

"Why can't we fight?" he asked, angry that I would dare suggest peaceful coexistence. "The blacks get to fight amongst themselves. Most other groups get to fight. Even the whites do it. Why do you single out the Indians?"

Russell Means was eventually convicted of rioting and sentenced to serve time in the South Dakota State Penitentiary. When he became eligible for work release—a program that allows inmates to work in a civilian occupation during the day, while returning to prison at night—no one in Sioux Falls, where the prison was located, would hire him. He was so politically controversial that businessmen capable of putting him to work refused to do so. Rejection would, of course, keep him behind bars for the remainder of his sentence. Because he couldn't find an employer, I hired him to work in my Senate field office in Sioux Falls. I braced myself for the storm of criticism that was certain to follow my announcement that I had hired him, at the minimum wage, then $3.15 an hour.

Amazingly, only one critical phone call came into the field office, a male voice—anonymous—who said, "This world is going to hell in a handbasket, and Abourezk is helping it along by paying those outrageously high wages to Russell Means."

11

My Trip to
the "Evil Empire"
and Other
Unforgettable
Junkets

For years I had tried desperately to get included on a trip to China. Travel to China started with Nixon's trip in 1972, but I was repeatedly omitted from every list presented to the Chinese by the State Department. I wasn't certain why I was rejected, although I suspected that my name could never get past the great China list-maker, Henry Kissinger. But rejected I was, that is, until January 1978, not long after I had filibustered the natural gas bill. When folks around the Senate found out, the hard way, that I could bollix up the works simply by manipulating the Senate rules, I was accorded a new respect. Well, maybe the words "fear" and "hatred" would more aptly describe their reaction. In any event, I was finally included on the 1978 list of American politicians going to China.

It has been an American article of faith for as long as I can remember that congressional trips, usually called "junkets," are an unnecessary waste of taxpayers' money. It's fair to say that congressional visits to the Caribbean, for example, deserve such criticism. However, if congressional trips abroad were designed to strip away the scales of ignorance from the eyes of our policy-makers, we would actually save both money and lives in the long run. For instance, if every member of Congress who served since 1945 had been required to travel to the Soviet Union, China, and Vietnam to learn about their cultures and their political thought, the taxpayers would have been spared untold billions of dollars in arms purchases, to say nothing of the lives that have been lost, wasted, and ruined in pursuit of that elusive policy objective called "containment of Communism." Had they traveled in order to deepen their understanding of the world, our leaders might have learned that the Russians are more afraid of war than we are; that Ho Chi Minh actually had wanted to be an ally of the United States, that is, before we began propping up regimes in South Vietnam in an effort to destroy him and his popular revolution; and that we might have achieved détente with the People's Republic of China long before we tried to match it, soldier for soldier, in Korea. Too late to save the money and lives we lost, we are now enjoying the relative calm of détente with those nations who were once our bitterest enemies. The Soviet Union, not long ago Ronald Reagan's "evil empire," is now a country that allows free elections and political criticism, much to the chagrin of cold warriors such as Jeanne Kirkpatrick and others of her ilk who feel deprived of a target for their intemperate hatred. When I saw Reagan hugging Gorbachev on television, I thought, "Why couldn't American and Russian leaders have done that years earlier?"

And in spite of our outrage at what the leadership of China did to their student demonstrators in 1989, an understanding of China's foreign policy objectives earlier in their revolution would have saved countless lives in the two wars that we fought ostensibly to contain China and Chinese Communism—in Korea and in Vietnam. We've learned that China, while a threat to its own people, is not a threat to the United States. Nor is Vietnam. I remember when we were being told by our government and an assortment of war hawks that Vietnam was a tool of the Chinese Communists—the first "domino" that the Chinese would topple in their effort to dominate Southeast Asia. Amazingly, Vietnam is today an enemy of China.

Clearly it has been our ignorance of the people of these countries that has propelled America into the awful self-destruction that we have called "maintaining national security." And in my view, properly focused congressional travel could have done a great deal to erase that ignorance. It is imperative, I think, that members of

Congress become familiar with official and unofficial thinking in the hot spots of the world, those places where we tend to want to spend both blood and treasure, such as the Middle East, Latin America, and the Eastern bloc nations. Once they do, perhaps we will be able to rid ourselves of the awful pain that comes with our xenophobia. Some people, however, will never be changed by travel. Henry Kissinger traveled all over the world, but his mission was not to understand, but to stamp out indigenous liberation movements. Should he ever come to public office again, Congress would be wise to restrict his travel solely from his home to his office and back again.

One of my first committee assignments in the Senate was to serve as a member of the Senate Space Committee. In the summer of 1973, I was offered the chance to attend an aeronautical symposium in Moscow, which turned out to be a gigantic sales session put on by U.S. aircraft and avionics companies. Because I was from an agricultural state, I requested that I also be allowed to visit an agricultural area in Russia, and so I was scheduled to visit a state-owned farm in Krasnodar, in Southern Russia, with a stop in Leningrad later.

With my son Paul, I boarded a plane chartered by a national aeronautical association, which was full of their members. We arrived in Moscow on Saturday, staying only long enough to eat lunch in one of the city's downtown hotels and to pick up the American Embassy's agricultural attaché, Tom Huth. The three of us flew to Krasnodar, arriving that evening. We were to visit the state-owned farm on Sunday and return to Moscow on Monday morning for the beginning of the show.

In this age of openness and reform in the Soviet Union, it is a bit difficult to recall how closed Soviet society was before Gorbachev came to power. In 1973, there was neither openness nor reform, and those who visited the Soviet Union were in for what can best be described as a "different" experience. We were met at the Krasnodar airport by the Intourist guide assigned to us, who announced three conditions for our visit. First, Mr. Huth would not be allowed to visit the farm; second, rather than return to Moscow on Monday morning, we would be required to take a flight back at midnight on Sunday; and third, Mr. Huth would be lodged in a separate hotel across town.

It required very little insight to understand that Tom Huth was being isolated, as well as the reason why. The Soviets did not want him trying to estimate the size of the Russian wheat harvest, either on the farm or from the airplane on Monday morning. This was a time when Russia was buying a lot of wheat from us, and it stood to reason that if our government knew the size of their harvest, it would be able to jack up the price accordingly. Whereas the Russians' isolation of Tom Huth made sense from their point of view, I did not want to lose Huth because he was good company. So I protested, but our guide insisted that the matter was out of her hands. I would have to take it up with the Intourist manager, whose office, it turned out, was in the same hotel at which Paul and I were staying.

Sunday morning I asked our guide to accompany me as an interpreter when I went to see the Intourist manager, a large, beefy-looking bureaucrat. I made my protest both official and vehement. Instead of responding to my protest, he reached down, opened a desk drawer, and pulled out a bottle of Armenian cognac and two glasses. He poured each of us a drink, lifted his glass, and offered a toast to the continuing friendship of the peoples of the Soviet Union and the peoples of the United States.

I joined in the toast, downing the cognac in one swallow. I knew trouble was coming, because the cognac was smooth and it tasted good. He refilled the glasses. I repeated my argument that Huth should be allowed to visit the farm and that we should be allowed to leave on Monday morning. Impossible, the Intourist manager said, again raising his glass, this time offering a toast to the continuing friendship between the farmers of the Soviet Union and the farmers of the United States of America. This was Sunday morning, mind you, a time when coffee was the strongest thing I was ordinarily able to swallow. But I was determined to continue pressing my case. I downed the second glass in one gulp.

He filled the glasses again, so I decided that protocol required that I offer a toast. I said, "Here's to the continuing friendship between the peoples of the state of South Dakota and the peoples of your province."

We continued, sitting face to face across his desk, alternately offering toasts to the peoples of virtually every political subdivision we could think of and debating the fate of Tom Huth. I remember finishing off the first bottle of cognac with a toast to the continuing friendship between the peoples of the Fourth Ward, First Precinct, of Pennington County, South Dakota and the workers on the Tallinen state-owned farm in the Krasnodar region of Southern Russia.

My mind was full of clever thoughts brought on by the cognac.

We were working on the second bottle when I stood up and said, "I am willing to sacrifice Tom Huth with respect to the farm visit, but I will not sell him out as far as the flight to Moscow is concerned." The Intourist manager lurched to his feet, obviously impressed by my hollow-legged capacity for Armenian cognac, and announced that he would now give serious consideration to my request. He would, he said, give me his decision upon my return from the farm.

Before I could clear the cobwebs from my brain, Paul and I were loaded into a car and driven out of Krasnodar to the Tallinen farm, while Tom Huth remained confined to his hotel room. It was pure luck that the farm managers decided that we should tour the farm before going into the conference room to meet with the leadership, giving me time to recover from my drinking bout with the Intourist manager, because as soon as I entered the conference room I learned that I was in for more toasting. I was introduced to the farm's manager, assistant manager, chief agronomist, and political commissar, the latter a short, balding man whose first act was to pour a glass of Russian vodka for everyone seated around the table.

By now, I had the toast routine down pat. Once again we began on a global scale and worked our way down to the precinct level. In between toasts we argued politics. The commissar began by denouncing the famous "Jackson Amendment," Senator Scoop Jackson's offering that would deny favored nation status to the Soviet Union if more Jewish emigration were not allowed. I told him that I was also opposed to the Jackson Amendment on the grounds that more Jewish immigrants going to occupied Palestine served only to displace Palestinians from their homes, creating even more refugees. He ignored what I said and renewed his attack on the amendment.

Surprisingly, I had enough of my wits left to counterattack. I asked how he could remain silent while the Kremlin mounted pictures of Richard Nixon all over Russia. Nineteen seventy two was the year of détente, and virtually every shop window that I had seen in Russia in the twenty-four hours that I had been there sported a large, poster-sized photograph of a smiling Richard Nixon. I then surprised the farm managers with the news about the Watergate scandal, a story that in August 1973 had not yet reached the Soviet Union. Sneering, I told the group that Nixon had been wiretapping his enemies, but the commissar asked, "What's wrong with that?" He insisted that Nixon had done the Soviet Union a great service by restoring dialogue between the two nations.

Finally, as the vodka was running low, he offered a compromise. He would agree that my dispute with Nixon was a domestic problem if I would agree that Jewish emigration was an internal matter for the Soviet Union. I accepted his offer.

Apparently my ability to hold my own with the Intourist manager had left a deep impression on him. By the time we returned to the hotel on Sunday afternoon, he had left word that we were booked on the Monday morning flight back to Moscow, and that he personally would be at the airport to make certain everything went smoothly. For good measure, he left a gift for me, a long-playing record album of a Prokofiev concerto. The lesson in all this was that we should never send a teetotaler to negotiate with the Russians.

* * *

I took my first trip to Cuba in 1975. It was illegal for Americans to travel to Cuba before 1977, but Senators Jacob Javits of New York and Claiborne Pell of Rhode Island had gone there as early as 1975. Senator George McGovern went in the spring of 1975. Not to be outdone by these senior members, I decided, in August 1975, to see for myself what was happening there. Accompanying me were my wife, Mary, my daughter, Nikki, and three or four of my Senate staff. I also asked Saul Landau to join us.

We were met at the Havana airport late at night by a large delegation from the Cuban government—a representative from the Foreign Ministry, one from Fidel Castro's office, assorted interpreters, and, to my astonishment, four bodyguards assigned to protect me. I didn't feel at all unsafe there, and I said so, but the Cubans explained to me that they were apprehensive that the CIA might try to kill me, then lay the blame on them. By then, a number of disclosures had been made public about CIA attempts on Fidel's life. Mindful of this, I stopped complaining about the presence of the bodyguards.

When I descended the airplane's ramp, I was carrying my own luggage, and the welcoming party, apparently thinking that I was a porter, walked right by me, in search of the senator. When they were told, that *El Senadore* was the fellow with all the luggage just then heading for the terminal, in perfect unison they about-faced and caught up with me.

By the time the entire party—both mine and theirs—arrived at the Atlantico Hotel for the welcoming meal, it was 11 P.M. When we were seated in the dining room, someone asked, "What would you like to eat, Senadore?"

"I would like, if you have it, some fresh papaya." I said.

I thought I was being polite, and could not imagine why the bodyguards began squirming. To my embarrassment, I learned the next day that in at least two provinces in Cuba—Havana and Pinar del Rio—the word "papaya" is slang for a female sexual organ. But that night I was ignorant, so I continued on my disastrous course.

"I've waited a long time to eat some papaya," I added, digging my grave deeper.

"In fact," I went on, "I could eat papaya twenty-four hours a day, I like it so much." The bodyguards, not trained in diplomacy as was the rest of the delegation, nearly climbed out of their ill-fitting suits. Everyone else was looking at the ceiling. The next day I was politely asked to refer to "*frutta bomba*" should I ever want papaya again in Cuba.

There were no more gaffes, at least not on that trip. But it was highly interesting. In those days I smoked cigars. Lots of them. By the end of a fairly long day I would have burned up fifteen or twenty of them. When I reached Cuba, with its wonderful Havana cigars, I thought that I had died and gone to heaven. I requested a tour of a cigar factory and I was taken to the La Corona factory in downtown Havana.

We walked through the various cigar-rolling areas where both men and women were artfully making the product that sells nowadays for $8 or $10 each in London and other world markets. (They are still banned in the United States, however, under the Trading with the Enemy Act, which not only punishes Cuba for being uppity, but which, in fact, also punishes American cigar smokers.) At the end of the tour, I was told that it was the custom to introduce honored guests from the stage at one end of the long production room where dozens of cigar workers, both men and women, worked at hand-rolling tables. Before the revolution, it was explained to me, the workers used to chip in and hire someone to read to them from the same stage so that their workday would go easier. After the revolution the government took over the reading chores.

My introduction from the stage went approximately like this:

"This is a *Senadore* from North America. Even though he is a *Senadore* from North America, he is a friend of the Cuban people. (smattering of applause) And I also wish to say that he is a personal friend of Yasir Arafat." (Thunderous ovation, including a great deal of pounding on the cigar-rolling tables.)

On the last day of our visit, Fidel Castro paid a call at the Santa Maria del Mar beach house where we were staying. After some initial palaver, he invited me to join him in the open jeep that he was driving. With our bodyguards following close behind, we drove and talked for about four and a half hours, touring new housing projects, a new cheese factory, and ending up at his farm somewhere outside Havana, where Fidel secluded himself whenever he wanted to escape the crush of people.

We talked about the Middle East, about American Indians, about Cuban-American relations, about the Soviet Union, about cross-breeding Holstein dairy cattle so that they would produce more milk in Cuba's hot weather, and about everything else that came to mind. I learned that Fidel himself had set up the cattle breeding program in 1959 (no one else knew how), when production of milk and other food was an urgent priority after liberation. I even met the all-time champion milk producer, a Brahma-Holstein cross-breed cow of highly complicated genealogy.

Fidel's stories about the numerous assassination attempts made against him by the CIA were enlightening, as was the news that U.S. warplanes were still continually overflying Cuba, "keeping us awake at night," as Fidel put it. He said that he didn't care if they spied on the island, but he wished that they wouldn't do it while people were sleeping.

He asked what the military strategy of the American Indian Movement was at Wounded Knee in 1973, and he roared with laughter when I told him that they had simply called a press conference to announce the takeover, that their hostages were not really hostages, but people who lived in Wounded Knee, and that the takeover was accomplished by driving into the village in a car caravan.

I told Fidel that before making the trip to Cuba I had talked to the State Department desk officer for Cuba about what might be done to start moving Cuban-American relations toward normalization. The State Department's official position, as articulated by the desk officer, was that the United States had done everything that it could do and that the next move was up to Castro. I asked for his response, and I began to understand why several American presidents had never succeeded in outsmarting Fidel Castro.

He cocked his head, thought for a few seconds, and said, "I could remove the blockade that I have around the United States."

We rode back from the farm in a Russian limousine, and just as we were saying our goodbyes at the beach house, I told Fidel that he was currently being accused by some American politicians of having had a hand in the assassination of John F. Kennedy. This got his attention. He postponed his departure and sat back down to spend another hour and a half explaining his position on Kennedy. He ticked off several reasons why he did not kill, nor could not have killed, JFK. What was particularly convincing was the vehemence of his statement about not wanting to commit suicide. "If we had had even the slightest thing to do with it," he said, "the United States would have blown Cuba off the face of the earth. I would not do that either to myself or to Cuba."

I had always heard that Fidel had not become a Communist until after he was chased out of the United States in 1959, shortly after he took over Cuba. I can still recall seeing him back then on television answering a reporter's question about the Eisenhower Administration's rejection of his request for financial aid. He was saying, in halting English, that he was being forced to turn to the Soviet Union for help. So at a dinner during my stay hosted by Carlos Rafael Rodriguez, who had himself been a long-time member of the Communist party, I asked Rodriguez when Fidel had actually decided to become a Communist. He placed it at about the same time, shortly after his being booted out of the United States by the Eisenhower Administration, although Rodriguez was not convinced that the U.S. decision was the determining factor.

We were taken on a tour of the Picadura Valley farm managed by Fidel's brother, Ramon. With great pride Ramon took us to a housing project for retired farm workers. We visited one of the homes, a small place now bursting at the seams with all of the American guests and as many of the retirees as could squeeze in to watch the show. Even more proud than Ramon was the beaming old farmer whose house had been chosen to show off to us.

"This housing project is called Vietnam Victory," Ramon Castro said, "because it was opened on the day that the war in Vietnam ended." Upon hearing this, I couldn't resist telling them a story. In April 1975, I introduced in the Senate Democratic Caucus a resolution declaring the Democrats' opposition to the $800 million that President Ford had requested for the Thieu regime in Vietnam. Because we were in the majority then, a favorable caucus vote would have insured its passage on the Senate floor. After heavy debate, the resolution passed. The next step would have been to report it out to the full Senate for a vote, but the publicity about its passage as a caucus resolution resulted in Thieu's almost immediate order for his troops to withdraw. The Thieu government collapsed just a few days later and the Vietnam War finally came to an end.

As soon as the interpreter had translated my story into Spanish, the old man who lived in the house threw his arms around me, kissed me on the cheek, and said, "Thank you for giving us this housing project."

It was a bit dangerous to go to Cuba back then. Some of the Cuban exile community in Miami was still so hostile toward Fidel Castro that I thought it prudent not to land our chartered planes at the Miami airport. So on this first trip to Cuba I called the commander of Homestead Air Force Base in Florida to ask permission to land there both on the trip going down and on the return, particularly for customs and immigration inspection. "It's for security reasons," I told the commander, an air force colonel. He was happy to accommodate me, but it turned out that he misinterpreted the reason for my request. I was worried about sabotage of my airplane, whereas the commander thought that I was on a secret mission for President Ford. He met the plane on the return trip and, as we walked to the operations office, he looked around to see if we were alone, winked at me, and asked, "How are the negotiations going?"

"Just fine," I said, winking back.

After I returned home and word had gotten around that I had followed George McGovern's visit to Cuba by just a few months, John Culver confronted me in the Democratic cloakroom. "Just what is it with South Dakota?" he demanded to know. "Most senators have to go to Israel to grease their reelection. Why is it that South Dakota's politicians have to go to Cuba?"

In 1977, I suggested to the State Department that the United States try to normalize relations with Cuba by having some sort of sports exchange. I told Philip Habib, who was then serving as under secretary of state, that I was willing to organize a basketball team from South Dakota to go play in Cuba. Habib first consulted with the White House, then gave me the green light to proceed with the exchange.

I asked both the University of South Dakota in Vermillion and South Dakota State College in Brookings, the agricultural school, to put together a team of ten players. I chartered a DC-9 from Southern Airways and filled it with members of the basketball team, college officials, some of my South Dakota constituents, and journalists from South Dakota, Washington, and New York. We flew nonstop from Washington to Havana.

In Cuba, we were lodged at the Marazul Hotel in Santa Maria Del Mar, which is where the Cuban Sports Ministry held its welcoming banquet. Before the dinner ended and the speeches began, Bob Shrum, who was then on George McGovern's staff, came up to me and whispered in my ear, "I'll bet you don't have the guts to open your speech with something about the Bay of Pigs."

I liked the idea. It seemed to me to have great shock value, so I decided to do it. When my turn came to respond to the welcoming toast by the minister of sports, I opened by saying, "This is the largest group of Americans to gather in Cuba since the Bay of Pigs invasion." The Cubans in Cuba thought it was funny, but when my comment was reported in U.S. newspapers, it generated a great deal of nasty mail from Cubans in Miami.

I did not see Fidel again until 1983, when my second wife, Margaret, and I were invited to attend the thirtieth anniversary of Fidel's attack on the Moncada Barracks in Santiago de Cuba, which the Cubans mark as the actual beginning of their revolution.

We ran into Fidel at the Havana Airport, and in the course of his flattering me by telling me how much younger I looked than I did eight years ago, I said, "It's all because of my new, young wife," pointing toward Margaret, who was then thirty-six and looked even younger. Proving once again his great charm, he spun around to look her over, then said to me, "Don't change wives again."

In 1977, a large delegation from the Minnesota Chamber of Commerce chartered a plane and went to Cuba for what was called an exploratory visit. The trip took place after the basketball exchange, at a time when it appeared that Cuban-American relations might return to normal. Upon his arrival in Washington, Bower Hawthorne, the Chamber's executive director, phoned to tell me that Fidel had sent gifts for Hubert Humphrey, Fritz Mondale, George McGovern, and me. "What are they?" I asked Hawthorne.

"He's sent each of you a jug of twenty year-old Cuban rum and a carved cigar humidor filled with one hundred Cohiba cigars. If you can get the others together in one place, I'll bring the gifts and make the presentation," Hawthorne told me.

I couldn't wait. I personally called Humphrey and McGovern, who both agreed to the meeting, but when I called Vice-President Mondale to tell him about the gifts, he was hesitant. "Jesus, Jim," he said, "I can't accept a gift from Castro . . . not at this time. We're just going into delicate negotiations with the Cubans over opening our respective Interest Sections and renewing relations in general."

Then before I could respond, he asked, "Are they those long, sweet cigars that you give me sometimes?"

"That's them," I said.

There was a long silence on Mondale's end of the line, then he sighed and said, "I guess I could resign from the vice-presidency."

* * *

I guess it was because I had played such a major part in the passage of the Panama Canal Treaty that I was invited to accompany President Carter to Panama to watch him and President Torrijos sign the treaty. As I was fond of saying, Jimmy and Rosalyn and Mary and I went down to give away the Panama Canal to Omar and Mrs. Torrijos.

Everyone who was invited, meaning every senator who voted for the treaty, gathered at Andrews Air Force Base outside Washington for the trip down to Panama. Carter and his favorite members of Congress and other hangers-on were to ride in Air Force One, and the rest of us would ride in either Air Force Two or Vice-President Mondale's DC-9. When New York Senator Daniel Patrick Moynihan arrived at Andrews and learned that he would not be traveling on Air Force One with the president, but on Air Force Two with "the rabble," he refused to go. He stomped out of the waiting room and returned to his Senate office, missing a great trip.

We toured the Panama Canal, saw how a canal lock worked, and had a great meal at the grand banquet, which was like no grand banquet I had ever attended. The banquet table was arranged in the shape of a U, with Carter and Torrijos seated in the center, or bottom, of the U, and the rest of us distributed around its sides. What was strange and different about this very formal banquet was the presence of dozens of guests, both American and Panamanian, who stood immediately behind the seated dinner guests, kibitzing. They were given no food because, as I soon learned, they had been invited only to be present for the festivities after the meal. An American woman standing behind me leaned over my shoulder to admire the appetizer course that had just been served, saying, "My, that looks good."

"Do you want it?" I asked, with what I thought was just enough sarcasm to drive her away from my food.

"Yes," she said, totally unembarrassed. I handed the plate to her over my shoulder. She ate the appetizer, then handed back the empty plate.

After the giving-the-canal-away ceremonies, I had a scare at the Panama airport just as we were about to embark for the United States. While waiting to board the plane for the return flight, I decided to run to the airport shop to load up on Cuban cigars, leaving behind all of my cameras in the airport's VIP lounge. Just as I was buying the cigars, the White House staff man in charge of Air Force Two came in shouting at me to get on board the plane.

I calmly told him that I had to go to the VIP lounge to get my cameras. He said, as though he meant it, that the plane was going to take off whether or not I was on it. I told him that they goddam well better not leave me behind, and that there was no way I was going to leave two expensive Nikon cameras and several lenses in the VIP lounge of the Panama airport. He told me that I was out of luck, that Torrijos had already said goodbye to Carter and had gone back into the VIP lounge, and that I would never get past the security guards. I told him that the entire Panamanian army wasn't going to stop me from getting my cameras. I entrusted the cigars to one of my friends, then explained my problem to the Panamanian security man at the door of the VIP lounge. He nonchalantly waved me into the lounge.

President Omar Torrijos, supreme dictator of Panama, the predecessor of General Manuel Noriega, was sitting in the chair exactly next to where I had parked my camera bags. He was talking to several men gathered around him.

I tiptoed over to the chair, in much the same way the Pink Panther does in those great cartoons, and bent over to pick up the camera bags. At the exact moment I was at eye level with Torrijos, he stopped talking and turned to look at me. We were literally eyeball to eyeball, our faces not more than a few inches apart.

The Panamanian ambassador to the United States, Gabriel Lewis, who was standing in the circle of men talking to Torrijos, told him in Spanish that, "This is Senator Abourezk, from South Dakota, the one who held back his vote on the treaty until the last minute."

Torrijos leaped to his feet, shouting in English, "So you're the one who has caused me all the trouble—who almost gave me a heart attack—who caused me to lose sleep every night!"

I saw the end coming. Carter was gone. His arrogant staff man would no doubt be delighted to have me either imprisoned or rubbed out by the Panamanians. There was no one left to save me. But as abruptly as he began his tirade, Torrijos broke out in a huge grin and said, "I have to have my picture taken with you. Please stand here with me so that I can always remember you."

After his photographer finished snapping us, I handed him one of my cameras, saying that, of course, I wanted to always remember the president as well, and would he kindly stand with me so that I could have my picture taken with him.

* * *

I had heard of NATO Parliamentarians' meetings, but I never knew what they were until 1977, when I was invited to attend a session. I went to Paris with the rest of the boys, senators and house members alike, on an Air Force 707. The meetings turned out to be a waste of time. I attended sessions of the Political Committee to which I had been assigned, but they were both boring and useless. However, just to show the flag and to justify the junket, I decided to try one more meeting of the Political Committee. Bored at the meeting with the endless wrangling over insignificant points, and tired of doodling, I drafted in longhand a resolution calling for the committee's condemnation of Israel's illegal settlements in the occupied territories of Palestine.

The meeting suddenly was no longer boring. Not only were Senator Jacob Javits of New York and Congressman Phil Burton of San Francisco on their feet denouncing the resolution, but some unidentified person, I think an Israeli political operative, was buzzing around the room like a bee in heat, furiously whispering instructions to several delegates on how to oppose it.

After Javits and Burton finished excoriating both me and the resolution, the delegate from France rose to his feet and said, "I cannot support this resolution. It is too one-sided, because it only condemns the colonies that *Israel* has established in Arab territories."

"Well," I said, trying to be as serious as he was, "To be more fair, I am willing to accept an amendment by the delegate from France that would also condemn any colonies established by Arabs in Israeli territories." The French delegate knew there were no Arab colonies on Israeli soil, but he had absolutely no sense of humor. My resolution, of course, failed to pass.

* * *

Following separate junkets in 1975, Tom Eagleton and I agreed to meet in Damascus, Syria. Our plan was to visit there, then go on to England where our wives would meet us for a week's vacation. When we went to the U.S. Embassy in Damascus to visit Ambassador Richard Murphy we found there the *Newsweek* correspondent, Arnaud de Borchgrave. De Borchgrave, whose current job is editor of the Moonie newspaper, *The Washington Times*, was then, according to his own account, the world's greatest living foreign correspondent. He was also a world class name-dropper, spewing out famous names faster than a seagull drops guano.

Washington Times reporters tell of the time someone confronted De Borchgrave with the charge that he dropped too many names. "You know," De Borchgrave is supposed to have replied, "the Queen Mother said the very same thing to me just the other day."

As we entered the embassy's reception room, De Borchgrave was in the middle of telling Ambassador Murphy: "If Anwar [Sadat] had listened to me he wouldn't be in the trouble he is in today. Yitzhak [Rabin], however, did follow my advice and came out much better," he continued. It was more than we could take, so after a few minutes we slipped out of the room to make our escape.

Eagleton then decided that he wanted to visit the Jewish quarter of Damascus. He wanted to be able to report to his Jewish constituents that he had checked on Syria's treatment of its Jewish citizens. That year, the Israeli lobby had made a big issue of the alleged mistreatment of Syrian Jews—until CBS television punctured their balloon. Mike Wallace of "Sixty Minutes" ran three separate programs showing that Syrian Jews were being treated exactly the same as Syrian Arabs.

I decided to join Eagleton, because I wanted to see what all the fuss was about. The Jewish quarter was supposed to be in the old section of Damascus. We wandered around the narrow streets, marveling at the ancient architecture of the world's oldest city and feeling as if we had gone through a time warp into the last century. The original wall that protected the city thousands of years ago was still partially intact. The streets were bustling with people in various kinds of dress. The smell of cooking, of spices, of bodies was everywhere.

We never did find the Jewish quarter, but as we stood in the middle of one of the ancient streets, trying to decide which direction to take, a small, grizzled Arab man came out of a walled courtyard. He wore a Turkish fez, a remnant of the 400-year Ottoman occupation of Syria that ended in 1918. As he emerged from the gate his eyes widened in recognition. Both Eagleton and I assumed that he would acknowledge my notoriety as the first, and at that time, the only U. S. senator of Arab descent. But he surprised both of us. "You are Senator Eagleton, aren't you?" the old man asked.

After Eagleton finished roaring with laughter, he was kind enough to introduce me to the old man. And, although I attributed the old man's recognition of him to his brief run for the vice-presidency in 1972, he has never let me forget what he calls his fame and notoriety in the Arab world.

* * *

I first met PLO Chairman Yasir Arafat in Beirut in 1973. According to the instructions I received from his handlers, I was to wait for a telephone call in my room at Beirut's Phoenicia Hotel. When the call came, I was instructed to drive to a certain street corner in Beirut where I would be picked up by a PLO car and driver. I did as I was told. Not long after I was dropped off by my own driver, a small Volkswagen bug pulled up, and the PLO driver asked me to get in. Although I was unfamiliar with Beirut, I could tell that we were taking an extremely circuitous route to wherever our destination might be. After winding through a great many narrow streets, we finally disembarked in a high-rise apartment area.

On the balconies of the two apartments flanking the PLO head-quarters stood hundreds of Palestinian guerrillas with automatic weapons slung over their shoulders. I was escorted into the building, literally pushing a submachine gun aside in order to get into the elevator. I was led to a fourth-floor apartment where Arafat was waiting, along with other members of the PLO Executive Council.

For me it was an impressive event. Our serious political discussion, however, was interrupted by a loud burst of automatic weapons fire just outside the window.

Leaping out of my chair, I asked, "What's that?"

The interpreter told me that it was probably a wedding party. Then a few minutes later the telephone rang. Arafat answered, and began shouting excitedly in Arabic. The interpreter turned to me and said that Israeli helicopters were reportedly circling the area, looking for Arafat in an effort to assassinate him. The story was credible, because not too many months earlier Israeli terrorists had landed on the tourist beaches of Beirut at night, climbed into cars rented locally by Israeli agents, and assassinated four Palestinian leaders. That meeting with Arafat and all the peripheral activities surrounding it remained sharply engraved in my memory.

Later that year I arranged for Senator Adlai Stevenson, who was traveling to the Middle East, to meet with Arafat. When Stevenson returned to Washington, I asked him about his trip, and particularly about his meeting with the chairman.

"Fascinating," he said. "It was kind of a James Bond arrangement where I had to switch cars and move all over Beirut to find Arafat's headquarters. I was finally taken to an apartment building complex full of armed Palestinians. During my meeting with Arafat there was a lot of gunfire outside of the window. It was explained to me that it was a wedding party. Not long after that Arafat got a telephone report that Israeli helicopters were circling the area looking for him."

12

Starting Over

I went into law practice in Washington, D.C. shortly after I left the Senate early in January 1979. That month I was sitting in my office waiting for my first client to walk in when the phone rang. A male voice with a foreign accent came on the line, identifying himself as an Iranian in charge of the students who had been protesting the shah each day in front of the Iranian Embassy on Massachusetts Avenue. He told me that he intended to lead a delegation to the embassy, where they would present the shah's ambassador, Ardeshir Zahedi, with a statement from the revolutionary forces. Naturally, the protests at the embassy had brought out the Washington police, and the caller said that they wanted me to be present as an observer, fearing police abuse. I told him that, as an attorney, it would not be proper for me to act as an observer, but that if trouble developed they should call me.

Later that afternoon I was called again, this time by a different person who also did not give his name. He informed me that the police were arresting the protesters by the dozen. Two lawyers from my office and I went immediately to the embassy and found

243

the police making mass arrests of the protesters. Hundreds more were sitting on the sidewalk continuing their silent protest while waiting to be arrested.

I negotiated with police department attorneys, who eventually agreed to allow the protest to continue, but only if the sidewalks were kept clear. We then began to bail out the sixty-odd Iranians who had been arrested. I went home, leaving most of the work to the younger lawyers who had accompanied me. Then, at about two o'clock in the morning, I was awakened and asked to go to the police station to write a check for the students' collective bail, because the police would not accept a check from any of the Iranians or from my legal staff. I paid the bill, and thought no more about the incident.

A few weeks later, after the shah had fled Iran and Khomeini was on his way to Teheran from Paris, I was called by Shahriar Rouhani, the son-in-law of Iran's new foreign minister, Ibrahim Yazde. Rouhani had been a divinity student at Yale, but now, after the revolution, he was running the Iranian Embassy. He asked me if I would like to represent the embassy. After lengthy bargaining over terms, we finally struck a deal, and my law firm began handling a few small accounts for the Iranians.

I regret not knowing a lot more about Iranian politics at the time; I had to learn what little I now know from the ground up over the years since the revolution. I had always opposed the kind of rule that the shah had visited upon his own people. His regime was touted by the Western press as one that had tried to "modernize" Iran. In reality, the shah had made a Faustian bargain with the U.S. government, all in the name of containment of Communism. In exchange for his alliance with the United States, he allowed Iran to become a base for the U.S. military establishment, spending a great deal of his country's oil wealth on American weapons. Much of Iran's capital found its way into the pockets of arms brokers and commission agents; the rest swelled the bank accounts of the shah's family and his cronies.

Most Americans did not know that everything that the U.S. government did during the shah's reign was seen as an attack on Iran, its religion, and its culture. Neither did we know that the shah's secret police, SAVAK, were operating torture chambers with U.S. government support. If we had known that the shah was busy turning Iran over to the U.S. government and brutally suppressing dissent, we would not have been so surprised, first at the 1979 revolution, then at the anger directed toward the United States by Iranian revolutionaries. We also would have understood how Ayatollah Khomeini was able to reverse the westernization of Iran and to reinforce his own popularity and power by denouncing "the great Satan," the United States.

On November 4, 1979, Iranian militants seized the U.S. Embassy in Teheran, held the occupants hostage, and demanded the return to Iran of the shah, who had taken refuge in the United States. On the same day a group of Iranians, supporters of Khomeini, took over the Statue of Liberty in New York's harbor. I was able to find a lawyer in New York to represent those who were subsequently arrested at the Statue of Liberty, but there seemed to be little that I could do for the American embassy personnel in Teheran.

A number of journalists contacted me for information. For the most part, they were interested in doing stories on what the shah had done with all the money that had disappeared from Iran during his reign. They all indicated a desire to go to Iran to cover the story, but they were having difficulty getting visas. Trying to think of something constructive to do, I finally decided to go to Iran, to take the journalists with me, and while there, to try to talk the Iranians into releasing the hostages. I invited Nick Horrock, then of the *The New York Times*, and Walter Pincus of *The Washington Post* to accompany me, scheduling my departure for Friday, November 23. Jed Duvall, who was then with CBS, called on the night of November 20, so I invited him to come along as well. I got agreement from all the reporters that they would not write about my attempts to release the hostages, because I felt that any press about the trip would be seen as grandstanding and would detract from the seriousness of the effort.

It occurred to me that Yasir Arafat was most likely on good terms with the Khomeini government and could help me get the hostages released, so my plan was to try to convince him to go with me. On Wednesday morning before my planned departure, I was told by Zuhdi Terzi, the PLO representative at the United Nations, that Arafat was in Tunis for the Arab summit meeting and that he would receive me if I could get there by Thursday. I moved up my departure to Wednesday night in order to catch up with Arafat.

In his place, Nick Horrock decided to send Ed Cowan, the *Times's* energy writer, and Jeff Gerth, their investigative reporter. Gerth was to meet us in Paris, and Pincus in Teheran. Cowan, Duvall, and I left for Tunis on Wednesday the 20th, arriving Thursday the 21st. We were met by an Arab League representative who delivered us to a hotel, but we heard nothing from Arafat. On

Friday morning, I went to the Arab League office where Secretary General Chidli Klibi informed me that Arafat had left for Beirut. I learned much later that Arafat had no desire to face me on the question of the hostages, because he had already tried with Khomeini and failed.

Gerth, Cowan, Duvall, and I landed in Teheran at 6 A.M. on Thursday, November 25. We were taken to the VIP lounge by a tight-lipped Iranian escort, and from there we took a taxi to the Intercontinental Hotel. I spent all day trying to contact several people in the government, without much success. Finally I got a message instructing me to go to the Revolutionary Council at seven o'clock that evening for a meeting with Abol Hassan Bani Sadr, who was then Iran's foreign minister.

When I learned that Bani Sadr spoke only French and Farsi, but no English, I asked CBS's interpreter, Azam Mofid, to accompany me. When we arrived at seven, Bani Sadr was still meeting with the Revolutionary Council, at that time the only governing body in Iran. At 8:45 P.M., he finally came out, and we met for a little over an hour. I told him that I thought there was a great danger of military confrontation with the United States. After describing the hysteria being drummed up by the American media, I suggested that he allow an independent observer inside the embassy compound each day in order to assure the American public that no harm was coming to the hostages. I also told him that the U.S. government had announced its willingness to participate in an international tribunal on Iran simultaneous with the release of the hostages, but he was not interested in the proposal.

On Monday afternoon, the 26th, I was asked to go to the Foreign Ministry to meet Bani Sadr again. I suggested that we try to work out a deal for release of the hostages and I proposed a three-step process. First, I would ask the U.S. Senate to announce hearings on Iran's grievances against the United States to be held by an ad hoc Senate committee. Second, Iran would release the hostages, and third, the hearings would be held. "The fourth step—give us the shah," Bani Sadr quickly added. I told him that Carter would never agree to his extradition and that he should forget about this condition.

He agreed to take my proposal to the Revolutionary Council if I would try to sell my end of it to the Senate. I then called Senate Majority Leader Robert Byrd and told him about my discussion with Bani Sadr. I suggested that he talk with some of the Senate graybeards to see if there was support for hearings, and I said that I would consult with him after returning to Washington.

Idaho Congressman George Hansen, who was also in Teheran seeking the release of the hostages, called me from his hotel in Teheran to tell me that Wisconsin Congressman Henry Reuss had announced hearings on Iran, and that Bani Sadr had responded positively to the news. Hansen was highly visible both in Teheran and on American television as a conciliatory force. I later heard on BBC Radio President Carter's vehement reaction against the proposed hearings. In fact, Carter and his flacks were stirring up public opinion against both the Reuss hearings and Hansen's efforts in much the same way that Khomeini was whipping up Iranian sentiment in support of holding the hostages. I thought that the way Carter's people were savaging Hansen was unfortunate, especially for the hostages, because Hansen was having a positive effect on Iranian public opinion. But as I later learned, what was in the hostages' interest was not necessarily in Jimmy Carter's.

On one of the days that I spent waiting for appointments in Teheran I received a telephone call from a woman who informed me that Mr. Abolghassem Sadegh, who was the director of foreign press for the Ministry of National Guidance, was on his way to the hotel to see me.

I gulped, not knowing the purpose of his visit. Among the thoughts that ran through my mind, foremost was that he had found some reason to deport me. As I waited for him to show up, my imagination conjured up a worse scenario. I envisioned one of the younger revolutionaries coming through the door, accusing me of counterrevolution, or of collusion with the CIA, which was a favorite charge during those early days, and hauling me off to an Iranian torture chamber.

By the time I heard the knock at my door, I was in a state of panic.

"Senator Abourezk?" Sadegh asked, as he came into the room.

"Yes," I said in a hoarse voice.

"I spent two years in the VISTA program on the Pine Ridge Indian Reservation in South Dakota, and I have come to tell you that I think the way you handle yourself in relation to the Indians is fantastic. You're much better than Karl Mundt used to be."

Greatly relieved, I invited him to sit down and talk with me about the good old days in South Dakota.

While in Teheran, I tried to elicit the views of as many Iranians as possible. One of the Foreign Ministry's experts on America, Daroush Boyander, discounted any military action by the United States against the Iranian oil fields because of the threat of disruption of the world economy. He also believed that Carter neither would, nor could, do anything to Iran as long as the hostages were not harmed.

He also told me that when the radicals took over the American embassy, they found in the basement a CIA operation that had been counterfeiting Iranian currency and forging Iranian passports since the revolution. Not surprisingly, the Iranians saw the counterfeiting operation as a direct threat to the stability of their new government. Allowed to print enough phony money, the CIA could have ruined Iran's economy before too long. Although the discovery was widely publicized in Iran and in Europe, it was never reported in the United States.

Late on the night of the 27th, I visited Sadegh Gotbzadegh, who was then minister of radio and television. I asked him how he saw the hostage matter ending, and he said that as long as there was no escalation of rhetoric on the part of the United States and no overt military movements, the matter would end quietly in a couple of weeks or so. He told Elaine Sciolino, the *Newsweek* correspondent who sat in on the meeting, that all the radical students had been taken out of the American embassy compound by what he called the "Committee of Decision," and had been replaced with people who would make certain that no harm came to the hostages.

I told Gotbzadegh that I believed Carter would try to prevent any congressional hearings on the shah's relationship to the United States, because he would fear being seen as weak and as having caved in to pressure.

"I certainly will not tell Khomeini that tomorrow," he said.

I added that I believed that both Carter and Khomeini were playing the same game of international chicken. Gotbzadegh nodded his head in agreement.

I learned from Gotbzadegh that evening that the Revolutionary Council had organized the demonstrations in front of the American embassy—the ones that had provided a field day for the U.S. television networks—both to prevent any effort to free the hostages and to generate political support. He reiterated his opinion that the hostages would soon be set free unharmed, and speculated that Carter would become a hero and get reelected. He said that the Iranians, by and large, preferred to see Carter as president.

I returned to Washington the next day, and phoned Senator

Byrd, who reported that he had discussed the hearings with some of the senior senators, both Democratic and Republican. According to Byrd, they thought that it would be best to follow the leadership of the president. I asked him if he had talked with anyone in the Carter Administration about it. He said that he had talked to Warren Christopher, the under secretary of state, and that Christopher was of the same opinion.

"Bob," I said, "I would have thought that Carter would approve this idea under the table, no matter how tough he might want to sound publicly." When Byrd began talking to me in condescending terms, as if he were humoring an angry constituent, I saw the handwriting on the wall and rang off. Neither I, nor anyone else, knew whether my idea of trading hearings for hostages would have worked, but I thought that it was worth a try, which is more than Carter thought at the time.

I will forever be convinced that, at least in the early stages of the hostage crisis, Carter's polls showed him picking up support against Ted Kennedy, who had started out in his primary race ahead of Carter, and that, consequently, he did not want the hostages released—just yet. The hostage crisis had served to rally public opinion around Carter, and Kennedy's lead was beginning to slip. In the rarefied atmosphere of the White House, cynicism about such matters is not the exception, it is the rule, no matter who is president. If the public had understood this, they would have better understood Carter's actions during the hostage crisis.

To make matters worse for Kennedy, during a television interview he brought down on his head the entire Carter election machine by severely criticizing the shah. By the time Carter and his flacks were done with him, Kennedy's slippage in the polls was accelerating at an extremely fast clip.

In December 1979, I was approached by Jan Kalicke who was then Senator Ted Kennedy's foreign policy staff expert. Kalicke brought with him to my Connecticut Avenue apartment Ted Sorenson, who was once Jack Kennedy's top aide, and former Senator John Culver of Iowa, a close friend of Kennedy's. They discussed the effect of Kennedy's criticism of the shah, then asked if I would be willing to go to Teheran to ask the Iranians to release any number of hostages to Kennedy. If the strategy succeeded, they said, it would restore Kennedy as a credible candidate. I supported Kennedy for the nomination, so it took little convincing for me to agree to their request. However, I laid out two conditions for them: The purpose of my trip had to be totally confidential and the

Kennedy campaign had to pay for my ticket, because I could not afford to pay for it myself.

Looking back on the incident, if I had known that Khomeini had intended to use the hostages to bring his own people, the hardliners, into power, I would not have made the trip. But I then thought, wrongly as it turned out, that the Iranians might listen to a plea. I advised Kennedy's people of the strong possibility that I would fail, but added that I thought it was worth a shot. Anxious to try anything that might turn the election in their favor, they dismissed the prospect of failure.

So I again went to Teheran to meet with Sadegh Gotbzadegh, who was by then foreign minister. Although I was not aware of it at the time, he was totally powerless to act. He put me off in very polite ways, saying that he needed to consider it, to discuss it, and would see what could be done. He said he thought that Kennedy deserved better treatment than he had received and genuinely wanted to help. However, I returned home empty-handed, holding on to the dim hope that he might call after my return with good news of a hostage release. Nothing happened.

To prove once again that no good deed goes unpunished, nearly five years later, a reporter for the *Baltimore Jewish Times*, Arthur Magida, called and said that he would like to write a profile of me for his newspaper. I asked him to give me one good reason why I should talk to someone from a paper that would very likely do a hatchet job on me. His response was that he believed that American Jews would eventually have to deal with Arab Americans. He thought that I was misunderstood in the Jewish community, that I was seen as an anti-Israeli monster, and that he wanted to present me in a different light. I eventually agreed to the interview.

When his article appeared, I was stunned to see a reference to my trip to Teheran on Kennedy's behalf, although his version of it was unrecognizable. He quoted an unnamed Kennedy staffer as saying that I had approached Kennedy with an offer to get some hostages released to him, that I wanted "lots of money" to do the job, and that Kennedy had refused my offer. I called up Magida and asked him who his source was, telling him that what he had written was an outrageous lie and that I intended to sue both the newspaper and his source for libel. He refused to divulge the name of his source, but I have always been convinced that the false story was given to Magida by Tom Dine, who was on Kennedy's staff at the time I went to Teheran, and who had since become Executive Director of AIPAC, the Israeli lobby's lead organization.

I told Magida to call Jan Kalicke for verification that his version of the story was a lie, and I was unnerved when for several days Kalicke refused to return Magida's calls. When he finally did, he informed Magida that the report was a hoax.

* * *

In September 1980, I was called by Gotbzadegh's Paris attorneys who, in desperation, were seeking my help on a matter of great importance to him. A French newspaper had published a photograph of a check made out to Gotbzadegh for one million dollars. The signature was illegible, but typed on the bottom of the check was the statement, "FOR THE RELEASE OF THE U.S. HOSTAGES." I needed no further explanation. In the paranoid atmosphere of Teheran, a simple rumor was sufficient to convict a government official of treason. Someone wanted to see Gotbzadegh dead.

The check was drawn on the Army National Bank of Fort Leavenworth, Kansas. I called the president of the bank, Everett Covington, and after explaining the problem, he told me that the check could not possibly be genuine. First of all, he said that there were no accounts in the bank that held a million dollars. Second, the check itself was obviously an old one, because it did not contain the coded account numbers that were added in 1972. Covington speculated that, because the Iranian Army under the shah used to send officers to Fort Leavenworth for training, the check was probably one left over from that time. He suggested that Gotbzadegh try to cash the check, which, he said, would prove that it was bogus. He agreed to sign an affidavit swearing to the attempted fraud, and I agreed to send him a copy of the check.

I called a Fort Leavenworth lawyer, John Tillotson, and, after explaining the situation to him, he said that he would draft the affidavit and get it signed by Covington. Tillotson called me sometime later with the disturbing news that Covington had refused to sign the affidavit. After being contacted by a number of news outlets, including *The Washington Post*, Covington decided to hold a press conference. The timing could not have been worse, because he talked to the press *after* promising to sign the affidavit but *before* Tillotson could get his signature on it. What stopped him was a question asked by one of the reporters during the press conference: "You surely aren't going to sign an affidavit to help the foreign minister of a country that's holding our hostages, are you?"

It's a bit difficult to capture how vitriolic the national mood was toward Iran during that time, but vitriolic it was. Covington's patriotism was being tested on camera for all the world to see. "Absolutely not." Covington responded firmly, painting himself into a corner as far as the affidavit was concerned.

When I called him to ask why he had broken his promise, he explained that if he were subpoenaed to testify, he would say that the check was a phony, but he was not about to do anything voluntarily to help Gotbzadegh.

Fortunately, attorney Tillotson was remarkably resourceful. He located the just-retired, former president of the bank, securing his signature on a sworn statement that said the same things Covington would have said prior to the press conference. Gotbzadegh was able to use the statement to survive the attempt on his life.

Sadegh Gotbzadegh, who sat next to Ayatollah Khomeini when he flew from Paris to Teheran after the shah went into exile, became Iran's foreign minister in 1979. But in September 1982, he was executed by the Revolutionary Government of Iran on charges of treason. I knew Gotbzadegh as a decent, gentle human being. He was a revolutionary, but to my knowledge he never committed an act of violence. In the circumstances in which Iranians found themselves under the shah, I am certain that most Americans would have been revolutionaries as well. Gotbzadegh was opposed to holding the American hostages, which is why, I'm convinced, he was removed from power and killed by the hardliners.

* * *

The Arab image—either as a high-rolling, spendthrift, woman-exploiting sheikh in flowing white robes, or as a bearded, evil looking barbaric terrorist—for years filled America's airwaves, its newspapers, its movie and television screens. There was no let-up. Thus when the Arab world embargoed oil shipments to the United States in protest over American support of Israel during the October 1973 war, politicians such as William Simon, then an official in the Nixon Administration, never missed an opportunity to lay it on thick and heavy about the "Arabs" and their "fourfold oil price increase," which, according to the standard line at the time, was responsible for impoverishing America. There was no mention by him, or by others like him, that U.S. companies produced most of America's oil, and that they had also sent the price of crude soaring. We were then importing no more than 6 percent of our oil from the Arab oil exporting countries. But making Arabs—all Arabs—the scapegoat for our economic problems was too convenient for demagogic politicians, multinational oil companies, and, of course, the Israeli lobby. During the Arab oil embargo B'Nai B'rith ran full-page ads in *The New York Times* blaming Arabs for America's economic woes, complete with racist drawings of white-robed, oil-rich sheikhs.

By the end of the 1970s, it was clear that, in part, anti-Arab racism was driving American Middle East policy, the high water mark being the Abscam scandal, which broke into public view in February 1980. Abscam was an entrapment scheme, centered in Washington, DC, in which the FBI dressed an Italian-American agent in the flowing white robes of a gulf Arab, who succeeded in convincing a number of members of Congress that he was bona fide, and that he would deliver cash to them if they would perform certain favors for him. Each bribery session was recorded on video and played back in the ensuing criminal trials of the congressmen in question. In the case of New Jersey Senator Pete Williams, who kept refusing the money offered, the prosecutor repeatedly sent the FBI back to him with new incentives in order to get the evidence they needed to put him on trial.

After the scandal broke in the press, FBI Director William Webster was asked why the agent had been dressed as an Arab. He responded that it was necessary to choose some ethnic group that the public would believe was capable of bribing congressmen. And yet, no Arab or Arab-American had ever been even accused of bribing an American politician. There had been, of course, lots of publicity about Koreans, Wasps, Jews, and members of other ethnic groups convicted of bribery, but not about Arabs. Why Webster, ordinarily a respected public servant, felt it was necessary to use *any* ethnic group is a mystery, but his choice was solid evidence of the bottoming out of the image of Arabs in the United States.

A reporter from *The Washington Post* called me on the day the Abscam story broke, in February 1980, asking me what I thought of the word, "Arabscam."

"What do you think of the word 'Jewscam?'" I replied.

"It sounds horrible," she said.

"You have my answer," I told her.

Use of a phony Arab figure in Abscam was the direct result of the seven-year escalation, following the oil embargo, of anti-Arab racism that was projected by the media and cheered on by the Israeli lobby. It was clear to me that unless something was done about it, the outcome would be disastrous generally for Americans and specifically for every Arab American.

In 1974, I had suggested to the leadership of the National Association of Arab Americans (NAAA) that it form a subcommittee on
discrimination, but they had shown no interest. However, in 1980,
with Abscam on everyone's mind, it seemed to me to be the perfect
time to try to organize people against anti-Arab racism. I called a
meeting of several Arab-American leaders who were coming to
Washington for a convention of the NAAA, and presented to them
the idea of establishing a separate organization to combat racism
against people of Arab descent. There was no hesitation. Agreement
was enthusiastic, and the American-Arab Anti-Discrimination
Committee, or ADC, was born.

At the time I founded ADC, I was doing well in my law practice,
so I made a vow to myself never to accept a salary from ADC. It's
a promise I've been able to keep, although I never anticipated how
much of a financial sacrifice I would have to make over the years.
My work as a volunteer, however, has made more credible my call
to others to join and support the movement. In order to build ADC,
I spent several years dragging myself from city to city throughout
the United States, haranguing audiences about the dangers of racism of any kind, the folly of remaining unorganized while the Israeli
lobby was politically hammering away at people of Arab descent,
and asking for their membership in the new grass-roots organization that I was forming. My efforts were successful. Membership
surged during the invasion of Lebanon, spurred by anger at the
Israeli onslaught, but it continued to rise even after that. ADC has
since blossomed into the largest and most politically aggressive
American-Arab organization in the United States. It has brought
together Arab Americans as well as non-Arab activists from virtually every part of America, making the Arab-American community
aware of the political benefits of organization for the first time. I
now chair ADC's board of directors, and raise most its money.
Abdeen Jabara, a lawyer from Detroit, who gave up his law practice
and a comfortable income to help keep the movement going, directs
the organization on a daily basis. Since ADC's founding, a number
of other Arab-American organizations have sprung up, adding
numbers and strength to the overall movement.

Arab-American political activism has not been without its risks,
however. Some ADC activists have become social and political
pariahs, as well as targets of violence. In 1985, what the FBI
publicly described as a "Jewish extremist group" attached a bomb
to the door of ADC's office in Santa Ana, California, which killed
Alex Odeh, ADC's West Coast organizer. Before that, the same

extremist group attempted to bomb ADC's Boston office, placing a pipe bomb in the doorway. That bomb was discovered before it exploded, but not before it succeeded in seriously injuring two Boston policeman who were attempting to dismantle it.

The FBI's chief suspects for the Odeh killing are affiliated with the Jewish Defense League, and, according to an internal FBI document leaked to journalist Robert I. Friedman, they are hiding out in Kiryat Arba, a right-wing Jewish settlement on the West Bank, protected from extradition by the Israeli government.

I was notified in 1987 by the FBI that, during the course of investigating Odeh's assassination, they had uncovered a plot on my life by the same Jewish extremist group.

Politicians, under pressure from the Israeli lobby, also have taken part in attempts to stigmatize and to isolate the Arab-American community. I had a souring experience with Joe Kennedy, Bobby's son, that demonstrates how it's done. When I first met Joe Kennedy in 1979, he asked me to help him buy crude oil from the Arab oil-exporting countries. Joe had set up an energy company that would provide inexpensive heating oil to low-income people in Massachusetts. I thought that it was a worthwhile cause, something that should be done everywhere in the country, so I agreed to try to help him. I also liked Joe. With his big smile and friendly Kennedy banter, he had the makings of a great Irish politician.

I introduced him to a Saudi Arabian acquaintance who traded in oil and lived in Washington, asking that Joe be presented to Zaki Yamani, the Saudi oil minister. I never knew what came of that introduction, whether or not Kennedy received any oil from Saudi Arabia. Then in January 1986, I was pleasantly surprised to learn that Joe intended to run for the U.S. House of Representatives, hoping to replace Tip O'Neill. The news came to me when Joe's campaign sent me a contribution request. I was a little short on money just then, but I scrounged up a $100 contribution and sent it to him.

About four months after I sent in the contribution, I received a call from Steve Rothstein, Joe's campaign manager. I was certain that he was calling to give me the good news that Joe was running ahead of his opponents, but instead, he informed me that he was returning my contribution.

When he told me, I was stunned. "Why?" I asked.

"Because we're not accepting any PAC money in the campaign," Rothstein answered.

"But I'm not a PAC. That's my own money, money I couldn't even afford to send."

"Well," Rothstein went on, "We just don't want to get involved in the Middle East this way."

I couldn't believe what I was hearing. "I'm not asking you to get involved in the Middle East in any way," I told him, my anger rising. "I made the contribution because I like Joe Kennedy. Hell, I wanted to see him run for president someday. But you tell Joe Kennedy for me that he can send the money back, and I'll be damned if I'll ever help him again with anything." I slammed the phone down.

That was on a Friday. I stewed over Rothstein's call all weekend, and by Monday morning I had decided what I would do. I wrote Joe a letter in which I recounted the admiration that I had for his uncle Jack, whom I supported in 1960; for his father, Bobby, for whom I was a delegate in 1968; and for his uncle Ted, who had asked me to go to Iran in 1980—at considerable risk to myself— to try to get the American hostages released. I supported these Kennedys, I wrote, because they were courageous men, which was a great deal more than I could say for Joe.

Then I called a press conference in Washington for Tuesday. The letter to Joe was part of the handout that I had prepared for the press. All day Monday Joe tried to call me, I'm certain only because he had been notified about the press conference. I refused to take his calls until after I had held the conference, which was well attended, especially by the Boston media, who had now found another Kennedy to stick a needle into.

Ted Kennedy called me that evening, joking that if he'd known I had a hundred dollars, *he* would have asked for it. But his mission was to convince me that Joe knew nothing about the return of my contribution. I told Ted that I would take his word for it. Joe called the next day to tell me that he was sorry, that he didn't know about Rothstein returning the money, and that the "Arab cause had been advanced in Boston," as a result of the flap.

I found out later from one of Ted Kennedy's staff that Joe had called members of the Kennedy family a week before, telling them of his intention to return my contribution. I also learned that, all of them—Ted, Steve Smith, and others—had advised him against returning it. It was obvious that Joe's fear of the Israeli lobby had overridden the common sense that the more seasoned politicians in his family had tried to press on him.

Kennedy's insult was not the first delivered to someone of Arab descent, out of fear of retaliation from the Israeli lobby. In 1983, when Wilson Goode was running for mayor of Philadelphia he attended a fundraiser at the home of Naim Ayoub, a member of ADC's national board of directors. Naim raised a little less than $3,000 from his friends and gave it to Goode that night. The next day, Goode's opponent, speaking before a Jewish group, denounced Goode for taking "Arab money," prompting Goode, in a burst of great political courage, to publicly return the money to those who contributed it. He made one exception, however. Goode's staff called one of Naim's contributors, and when they learned that he was Jewish, he was told, to his outrage, that he was O.K. and that the Goode campaign would keep his money.

In 1984, Walter Mondale, during his presidential campaign, met with five wealthy Arab Americans in Chicago, after which each of them contributed one thousand dollars to his campaign. Mondale's Chicago area finance chairman, an American Jew, later returned the money, because the meeting had covered matters dealing with the PLO.

ADC demanded that both Goode and Mondale apologize for their affronts, but they refused. But to prove that no one is beyond redemption, however, Joe Kennedy appeared before the American-Arab Anti-Discrimination Committee's annual convention in 1989 and apologized for what he had done. I introduced him to the audience, and after his speech I remarked that of all the cowardly candidates who had insulted Arab Americans by returning their campaign money, he was the only one decent enough to admit that he had been wrong.

* * *

I went into the hostage-release business again in 1986, when I led a delegation of Arab-American leaders to Damascus, Syria, in an effort to obtain release of the American hostages being held in Lebanon. Syria was the only country that I thought could provide access to the Hezbollah, or Party of God, which was presumed to be holding them. I had circulated petitions to the ADC membership that asked the captors to exercise the compassion required by their Moslem religion by releasing the hostages to their families. Our group flew to Damascus, armed with the petitions, printed in both English and Arabic, and with thousands of signatures. We were full of hope that we would succeed.

In Damascus, we met with Foreign Minister Farouk Sharaa, Vice-President Abdul Halim Khaddam, and President Hafez al-

Asad. We appealed to Asad to set up a meeting between our group and Party of God leaders in Lebanon, He immediately offered to make the arrangements. But the next morning Vice-President Khaddam summoned us to his office to give us the news that the Party of God had turned us down. "We had Gazi Kanaan, our man in Lebanon, make the request. He argued with the Hezbollah for more than three hours, but they kept rejecting the request, finally saying that they refused to meet with you because you're nothing more than a bunch of Americans."

As we were digesting the bad news, Khaddam sighed and said, "You know, we've had more trouble with the Party of God than with anyone else in our history. If ever I am able to communicate with God," he continued, "I will ask him never again to organize a political party. He should leave that to us down here."

Our hostage mission failed, of course. At the time we had no idea that Ollie North and Ronald Reagan were just then delivering weapons to Iran—and lying to the nation about it—in the hope of achieving the same end. Had we known that missiles, not signatures, were needed to free the hostages, we could have saved the price of our airline tickets.

13

Easy Come, Easy Go

Leaving the Senate voluntarily is becoming more and more common nowadays, but it was unusual enough in the 1970s that several people who had been interested in running for the Senate came to talk to me to find out if it would be worthwhile. I encouraged each one to run for one term, telling them that the education was worth the price of admission, but cautioned them that if they fell in love with themselves and with the job, it would most likely not be good for them, the Senate, or the country.

My announcement that I would voluntarily step down at the end of only one term in the Senate created only a minor sensation back then, a tiny blip on Washington's political radar screen. Barbara Walters and Roger Mudd, among other media stars, felt the need to conduct farewell interviews with me. Phil Jones of CBS filmed the farewell party that my staff threw, featuring a thousand or so of my friends. And Dick Shadyac and Danny Thomas threw an even bigger one at the Washington Hilton, with the proceeds going to St. Jude's Hospital.

I had been designated by the establishment as a "maverick," an outsider. But I have always thought that those who are defined as "the mainstream," or "the establishment," are the real outsiders. They are the ones who are ultimately destructive to our society. Using money and power, they have been able to worm their way to the center of our institutions, labeling those with whom they disagree as "mavericks." They impose their own narrow definitions of what is socially and politically acceptable and what is not. Those Americans who can see and understand the difference between major and minor crimes, and who seek to point out that the government—wittingly—spends its time and resources focusing public attention on misdemeanors while the felonies remain unattended, are targeted by the power elite as "mavericks," "kooks," and "flakes." Such shifting of the public's attention away from bread and toward the circus is as old as history itself. Dissenters from the popular view have been called, at different times in history, "religious heretics," by the Catholic Church, "witches," by the Massachusetts establishment, and "Communists," by the Republican Party, when it wanted so desperately to return to power after World War II.

Not long after I left the Senate to return to civilian life, I attended a backyard party hosted by *Washington Post* reporter Walter Pincus and his wife. Kay Graham, who owns the *Post*, walked over to me during the party and hissed, "Are you representing a lot of rich Arabs now?" I don't think that it ever occurred to Mrs. Graham to ask any other lawyer if he were representing a lot of rich Jews or rich Republicans. But she, like most members of the power elite saw me as an intruder, as someone who had crashed, in Mark Twain's words, the giant barbecue being held by those who run the country. People who are proper and decent don't speak out on behalf of Palestinians or against the Israeli government. They don't hold the oil companies' feet to the fire, or spend their time trying to help Indians and other disadvantaged groups. They don't, from Mrs. Graham's point of view, sign statements of protest on behalf of *The Washington Post's* unions.

I learned in Congress that merely making proposals to the establishment to improve life for the weak and vulnerable is not enough. As my friend Louie Freiberg used to say, "You can't beat 'em with a love-in." The militant American Indian Movement learned this, a fact that drove them to increasingly violent confrontations in order to focus public attention on their views. The Palestinians learned the same lesson when they tried persuasion and diplomacy to prevent the Zionist movement from taking their land to make an

Israeli state. While Israel was telling the world that the Palestinian problem was solved, the Palestinians were being driven to desperate acts of violence, having had all other avenues closed to them. The same was true for people who felt the oil industry was having its own way, unhindered, with the public's money. In short, those people on the cutting edge of issues learn, as I did, that at times political confrontation is the only way to make one's demands heard. The 1977 natural gas deregulation legislation would have passed without a whimper had Howard Metzenbaum and I not chosen to filibuster it. While we failed to prevent the industry from picking the public's pocket, at least we demonstrated precisely who was doing it.

The nature of the Congress has changed since I stepped down in 1979. There were more politicians then who were willing to try to slow the rush of the greedy and the power hungry. But no longer. I was both saddened and angered during the Reagan years as I watched Reagan and his clique undertake a massive transfer of wealth from the lower to the upper classes. Reagan set up America for future class warfare, making greed once again highly fashionable, while at the same time creating a new class of desperate and homeless people. There was nary a protest from Congress as the numbers of homeless people grew while the massive corporate takeovers and leveraged buyouts increased the profits of the rich.

A majority of Congress passively went along as Reagan, Stockman, and company set out to put an end to public interest in favor of private interests. They cut taxes for the wealthy, pushing the country into deep debt and punishing the poverty-stricken. Their purpose was to finance a military spending spree and to put the squeeze on social programs, which were unable to compete with "national security" for money from the budget. We have yet to experience the full negative consequences of this squeeze, but when we do, we will be looking around for someone to blame. Just as Lyndon Johnson was no longer around when the social and financial bill for the Vietnam War came due, neither will Reagan and his cohorts have to take responsibility for what they did to the economy.

It has been an era of cheap, meaningless, military victories—à la Grenada—and of economic chaos. Through it all, the Congress, with a few brave exceptions, has stayed above, or as the case may be, below the fray, hoping only for reelection, and the public be damned. We are told that over 95 percent of incumbent members of the House of Representatives are reelected every two years, sufficient evidence that incumbents tend to avoid controversy. That means, of course, that rarely will members of congress try to do something to alter the internally crumbling status quo. Congress has yet to face the major issues of racial and economic justice, the lack of which may yet tear this country apart. It is easier for Congress to denounce the Supreme Court's flag-burning decision than it is for them to take steps to redress the injustices suffered by people of color and the poor.

We saw only a few congressional mavericks challenge the Reagan ethos that "greed is good." After George Bush became president, the Senate chewed over such exotic issues as John Tower's supposed drinking problem. It ignored his coziness with the defense industry, just as it had earlier ignored the fact that former Secretary of Defense Caspar Weinberger, who drank very little, almost sent the country into bankruptcy buying unnecessary weapons.

Similarly, the media, despite all its protestations to the contrary, generally have been afraid to take on the real issues, choosing instead to follow the easier route of writing about politicians' drinking and sexual habits and an occasional juicy corruption scandal. Ronald Reagan and his band of pirates became respectable because the press declared their respectability. Dissenters were not squelched; they were simply ignored. Without press coverage, they didn't exist, in political terms at least. When Reagan destroyed the low-income housing program, dramatically increasing the number of homeless families and individuals, it took Mitch Snyder's act of fasting on the steps of the Capitol to get press attention and to force the government to set up temporary shelters for the homeless. The press reported on the sit-in, but continued to ignore the need to discuss renewal of the low-income housing program. And despite the mounting disgrace of private campaign financing, very little has been said in the press about public financing.

When the Palestinian uprising exploded in the press in December 1987, Americans were shocked to learn that Israeli soldiers were actually beating and shooting unarmed Palestinian protesters. The shock came, not because the uprising was anything new, but because we Americans knew little about what Israel had been doing for the past twenty-one years in the occupied territories. Israel's brutality and humiliation of the Palestinians and Lebanese have been ongoing since 1967, but on a lower scale prior to the uprising. With the exception of Tom Brokaw's 1987 documentary on NBC on the twentieth anniversary of the occupation, the mainstream press had refused to talk about Israeli violence. The press, the public, and the politicians chose to look the other way, to believe what the government of Israel and its American supporters were saying. We were told that, by and large, the Palestinians were happy with the occupation. Amazingly, Israel's more daring propagandists still try to peddle the story that it's not the occupation, but the inherent "barbarism" of the Palestinians that is the root of the uprising in the West Bank and the Gaza Strip.

The explosion in December 1987 was on so massive a scale, however, that even the docile American press could no longer ignore the realities of the occupation. We saw, before long, the evils of arrogance on the part of the Israeli government. Not yet aware that things were changing in America, that the press was no longer automatically making excuses for Israel, Israeli Defense Minister Yitzak Rabin announced that Israel would be "humane" in its treatment of the Palestinian protesters. They would, he said, be beaten instead of shot. We were then treated to the image on television of several Israeli soldiers holding a Palestinian boy while one soldier systematically broke his limbs with a huge rock. Yet another Palestinian was tied to the front of an Israeli army jeep, serving as a human shield against stone-throwing protesters, a sight reminiscent of World War II when Nazi soldiers tied Jews to the front of railroad trains to prevent partisans from blowing up the tracks. America, or most of it, recoiled in horror.

The uprising could have been avoided—the suffering could have been ended—had the press reported fairly and accurately forty years earlier. Israel continued taking Arab lands and brutalizing Arabs, because they were rewarded with favorable press coverage and more money from the Congress after each act of aggression. Israel became a part of the American establishment's cause. Despite all our knowledge now of how Israel has been treating the Palestinians and Lebanese under their control, there is still a tendency on the part of the American media to protect Israel as much as it can.

"Will a Palestinian state be viable? Can it survive on its own?" is one of the media's favorite questions to Palestinians. Either the questioners are shameless propagandists, or they are just plain thoughtless. Did anyone ask whether Israel would be viable before the Zionist movement was encouraged to destabilize the entire Middle East with its land grab? Would Israel be viable without massive transfers of American money to its economy? It is this double standard on the part of opinion leaders that becomes so frustrating.

But that is the story of those who represent the American power establishment, comfortable with their own condition, making more money than they need or can ever hope to spend, enjoying a modicum of power, at the expense, of course, of other, less fortunate people both here and abroad.

Henry Kissinger, whose entire life has been devoted to seeking power, understood all too well how to advance his own ambitions. He knew better than to act as an intruder. He strove to join, to become a part of the establishment, to avoid maverickism, although I sometimes think that he was temperamentally suited to it. Knowing exactly where the levers of power were and how they should be pulled led him straight to a retainership with the Rockefeller family, where he prospered, and where the Rockefellers could boast the possession of an in-house intellectual. From that point onward his future was assured.

Kissinger spent a great deal of his time in government on what is fondly known as the Georgetown cocktail circuit, stroking the giants of American journalism, charming them both with his wit and the aura of power that he had learned to flaunt over the years. He thus was able to build a teflon shield, to borrow a phrase from Congresswoman Pat Schroeder, that kept the sky from crashing down on him as he knifed, shot, and bombed his way through Central America, the Middle East, and Southeast Asia. Very little of the victims' blood clung to him, but it splattered all over the people of Third World countries that refused to bend to his wishes.

Amazingly, Kissinger has maintained an exalted reputation. Equally astonishing is Richard Nixon's comeback of sorts in the media. He frequently consulted with President Reagan during his terms in office, and is occasionally heartily cheered by high school students and others who boast either short or nonexistent memories. His refusal to consider his disgrace a disgrace is one of the more interesting phenomena of our times.

Whatever the outcome, I have never regretted challenging the establishment. I have looked upon it as a responsibility that I could not avoid. I wanted to be satisfied at the end of my life that I had done something to advance our civilization, that I had not just ridden out my time by taking advantage of the weakness or vulnerability of others.

* * *

I was divorced from Mary, my wife of twenty-nine years, in 1981. We were unable to live together anymore. She has since moved to Auburn, Nebraska, her birthplace. I hope that she has found a way to escape what was for her the torment of political life, a life she neither wanted nor could ever adjust to.

Margaret Bethea and I were married in 1982. When we met, Margaret had been involved in politics for some time. She came to Washington as the administrative assistant to South Carolina Congressman Ken Holland. In 1978, she returned to South Carolina to manage Dick Riley's successful campaign for governor. At the time we were married, she was raising by herself a wonderful daughter from her first marriage, four-year-old Chesley. As evidence that I'm unable to take too much of a good thing, Margaret and I separated and divorced after six years of marriage. As my old friend Pits Jaros is fond of saying, "Them women are too good for you, Jim."

Writing an autobiography does strange things to one's mind. As a result I spend long hours now thinking about my parents, my brothers, Chick and Tom, and my sisters, Helen and Virginia. My thoughts are at times filled with happiness, and at times with unremitting sadness, wishing I could bring back the too few hours and days that we were able to spend together before our lives were interrupted by the coming of age and leaving home, by wars and by other tragedies that are part of the human struggle.

Running in reverse the reel of my life has brought forth more nostalgia than I care to confront, and perhaps more than I've allowed myself to feel in all my adult years. But looking back, I've come to realize how fortunate I've been. In the words of Robert Duvall, "It's been one hell of a party."

* * *

I never got to finish telling about the rest of my conversation with Mark Raskin. At one point, as he was alternately pleading with me to stay in the Senate and demanding that I not step down, he asked, "How can you give up all that? The Senate seat, the status, the prestige, the committee assignments, the perquisites?"

Harking back to what a gambler friend of mine once said, I told him, "Mark, easy come, easy go."

Acknowledgments

My thanks go to those who reviewed the original manuscript, correcting my memory and sharpening my ideas. They are Harlan Severson, Charlie Abourezk, Marcus Raskin, and Don Neff. Further thanks are due to my assistant, Linda Donnelly, who devotedly worked long hours at the word processor. And special thanks go to Shirley Cloyes, director of Lawrence Hill Books, who taught me how much I still have to learn about writing.

Index